One Football, No Nets

Justin Walley

BENNION KEARNY

Published by Bennion Kearny Limited, 6 Woodside, Churnet View Road, Oakamoor, ST10 3AE

www.BennionKearny.com

Photo Credits. All rights reserved. All photos courtesy of Justin Walley unless otherwise referenced. [13] Courtesy of Thandazani Photography & the Matabeleland Football Confederacy. [19] Courtesy of Dominic Stevenson. [20] Courtesy of Matt Perrella. [21, 23, 33, 34, 35] Courtesy of Chris Hansen & CONIFA. [22] Courtesy of John Mottram. [25] Courtesy of Chris Piper. [26, 37] Courtesy of CNN Inside Africa. [29] Courtesy of Marc Mosull. [36] Courtesy of Liam Potter. [38] Courtesy of Nqo Nkomisto [39] Courtesy of Matt Perrella. [40] Courtesy of Chris Dolman. [44] Courtesy of Kolizeum. [48] Courtesy of Julia Novikova.

Author Note: Opinions in this book are my own, and mine alone.

DEDICATION

I am grateful for so many things in my life, in particular, the wonderful friendships I have.

I want to say a big thank you to everyone who supported me and the Matabeleland Football Confederacy project! As well as the tens of thousands that were raised for an unknown team in a forgotten corner of Africa, there was also the emotional support and goodwill, and the lovely positive vibes and encouraging words from friends, old and new. It wasn't just a handful of us that made the Matabeleland fairy-tale, it was an army of kind-hearted people! You have all positively impacted the lives of others!

Tragically, some friends leave us far too early.

In 1997, my friend Andrew Steven passed in his twenties, burning so bright one moment and gone the next. One of the most genuine and positive individuals I've ever known, there was always fun and laughter when Andy was around. Away from home for the first time in my life, at university, Andy was one of the few – one of the first – who made me genuinely start to think outside of the box; to question and dream more. To laugh more, in fact. To defy conformity and be silly in a serious world. With his tragic passing came the desire to do more, see more, have more fun. The realisation that life is too short and we should try to treat each day as a gift. The memory of Andy's early passing has always stayed with me.

Riga United Football Club has helped forge friendships with people from all over the world. Kareem Gouglou was part of the Riga United family for many years. We called him the Moroccan Magician. One of the most exciting and remarkable amateur footballers most of us have ever seen, Kareem could do things when he played that seemed frankly impossible to the rest of us. If football is the beautiful game, then it is Kareem who truly enabled it to be called such.

But it was his qualities as a human being that marked him out even more than his phenomenal abilities with a football: kind, charming, sincere; Kareem was truly a classy gentleman who touched the lives of all lucky enough to spend time with him.

I heard the news that Kareem had passed away the same morning that I signed the contract to write this book. Not even forty, his passing broke hearts all around the world.

I wish to dedicate this book to Andrew Steven and Kareem Gouglou. Two wonderful young men who inspired me and touched my life. Neither of you brilliant lads will ever be forgotten!

Justin

TABLE OF CONTENTS

PART 1

1: If you want to make God laugh, tell him your plans

January 15, 2017 | Saint Jovan Bigorski Monastery, Macedonia

God, this is surreal. And God is certainly playing his part.

I glance around at the dozen lads crammed in tightly together with me. Most of them look like they have done time. The majority have certainly had or are living hard lives. This is incredibly intimidating.

And, at the same time, it is definitely one of the best things I have ever done.

Just over my shoulder, an Orthodox monk, impossibly long beard specked with grey, fully dressed in black robes, begins chanting prayers from a Bible that looks like it started its life centuries ago. It is mostly unintelligible to me aside from regular mentions of *Slava Bogu* (Glory to God). The devotions abruptly finish and we all jump to our feet, twelve tiny clouds of icy breath shooting across each of the four benches. We each cross ourselves before hurriedly collapsing to our seats where, heads all bowed in complete silence, we begin eating the vegetable soup, slightly stale doorstep brown bread, refreshing yoghurt and rectangular lumps of unpleasantly salty white cheese. The only noises are the slurps of soup consumption, the sound of spoons clanging on metal bowls and the coughs from winter colds.

I have wanted to do this for years. Cut myself off from the rest of the world through physical and mental isolation; residing briefly among those who have chosen this path indefinitely. I feel overwhelmed by the sense of mystique, tradition, a reminder of the centuries gone by, of the majesty of simple things and the everything of those mountains, forests, lakes, snow and ice that surround us here. I feel like a different person inside this monastery.

Occasionally, I feel brave enough to glance up for a moment or two to take in the scene. One or two of the other lads do the same, and mostly they focus their brief glances on me. Everyone here is Macedonian as far as I can gather. I suppose some might be Serbs. You don't tend to get many foreigners staying in Orthodox monasteries 1,400 metres up in the Mavrovo National Park on the Albanian-Macedonian border with its wild, where-in-the-world vibe. Certainly not in mid-January when it's minus 15 outside and minus something inside this medieval looking refectory.

I don't communicate with the other lads. One of the reasons for being here is to live in silence and contemplation. On my second day here though, I have concluded, either wrongly or rightly, that many of the 20- and 30-something young men are indeed ex-criminals and lads doing a kind of penance. Frankly speaking, some of these lads could be hiding out. Certainly many of them, and I don't mean this disrespectfully, could earn good money in Hollywood playing the parts of extras in mafia films, especially the lad with the gold jacket and perfectly manicured beard. Like I said, I am intimidated but I am not scared. It is apparent to me that this place represents redemption for many of these young men. Despite the hardships, I can recognise, even in the space of a couple of days that, eyes sparkling, they are growing as human beings. It is apparent that some of the lads respect me for turning up here; an English bloke walking in during a heavy snowstorm with a small backpack, asking in broken Russian for a roof over his head. Sergey, who welcomed me here, says he's been here for two and a half years and *stays for the peace in a world where respect and love largely no longer exist.*

It is so cold inside my monastic cell, with its single bed, pile of thick brown blankets, and two small icons on the otherwise bare whitewashed walls, that I can barely find the adjectives to describe it. I sleep in all of my clothes with my winter jacket zipped up, and its hood pulled up over my woolly hat. It is miserable. It is a torment. It is wonderful. It focuses the mind. The views of the majestic mountains and the ancient-looking citadel are mind-blowingly beautiful. I spend minutes on end with my face pushed up against the cold window glass, just taking it in.

At 5am, the banging of a wooden Semantron summons us all to gather for prayers. Snow and ice crunch noisily underfoot in the pitch darkness, bells chime. Large, slow-motion snowflakes land on my nose and remind me just how cold and how alive I feel. We enter a chapel where monks chant and candles flicker – their reflections flashing off icons – snow tumbling down now past the window.

The harsh realities of this place also affirm just how good my life is away from this religious Colditz. It acts like a prison for the mind.

There is nowhere to run. There is very little to distract yourself with in here.

How the hell have I ended up here, and why you might ask?

Back in September, I decided it was time for me to walk away from the football club I was running in Latvia. Riga United Football Club had completely taken over my life and was affecting my health to such a degree that I ended up in hospital a year earlier. At the point when I called it a day, I was the Club Secretary, Marketing Manager, Social Media Manager, Ladies Head Coach, and a youth academy coach. I was also serving my fifth consecutive term on the club's board and was responsible (on a daily basis) for the constant stress of paying all the club's bills. I found myself cycling home, so tired I could barely peddle, from a friend's house at midnight on a Sunday having worked through our accounts. The parents of academy kids were calling me at 7am on a Saturday to ask whether training was on. It wasn't unusual to be sat in a minibus returning from a 10-hour 500-kilometre round trip with my ladies' team. In winter, I got home at 11pm on a Monday from training, soaked and frozen. Much of what I and others did was voluntary. I was totally exhausted.

And I had been doing this from 2012 when myself and a handful of club regulars decided to take the club to a higher level. In 2013, Riga United joined the Latvian National League. We founded Riga United Academy. I began coaching in the international schools, and I did my level two coaching badge in England.

In just a couple of years, the club boasted two men's teams, two ladies' teams, eight kids' teams, and thousands of followers on social media. We appeared in British football magazines, broke the Latvian women's football attendance record, were televised live on national television, had a documentary film made about us, hosted NEC Nijmegen, created a board, held AGMs, and had our kits sponsored by the same clothes brand as Aston Villa.

There comes a point when an individual can become too big and influential within an organisation. It's as if you are the club. Clearly, this is neither sustainable nor a healthy state of affairs. I needed to move on from the club and the club needed to move on from me.

My girlfriend, Katya, and I left Latvia and went backpacking around the Indian Ocean for three months. For far too long, I had been guilty of putting the football club ahead of her. Now was our time. We shared an incredible adventure in such weird and wonderful places as Madagascar, Réunion, and Sri Lanka. Of course, I missed friends, players, and supporters. But I certainly didn't miss the coaching, management and 24-7 responsibility towards the 200 footballers, young and old, at the football club. The sense of relief of being unchained from its multiple burdens was overwhelming. For the first time in several years, I felt free again. I started to feel healthier too.

One of the reasons for the Indian Ocean backpacking was for Katya and me to decide what came next. We had been together for four years. Fleetingly, we even considered moving to Mauritius to start a new life. After all those mountains and beaches and the world in all its beauty, I concluded it was time for me to move on from football and do something different with my life. After much soul-searching, I realised the thing I most wanted to do was to work in elephant conservation! So, when we returned to Europe, just in time for Christmas with my family, it was agreed that I would find a job working with elephants, most likely on the Indian subcontinent; Katya would finish her Uni course, and then later in 2018 we would begin a new life, somewhere… with no football involved.

If you want to make God laugh, tell him your plans.

It is a month later, and it is fair to say that things haven't gone to plan. I can't get a sniff of a job in elephant conservation. Most organisations want me to cough up thousands of pounds for the honour of working 'voluntarily' and I just don't have the funds. I'm gutted to be honest. I was convinced that this was going to be my next vocation in life. I had an entire development plan in my head for an elephant rehab centre in Sri Lanka which I visited back in November. I was almost certain they'd offer me a job, and I would return there this year to aid the dire plight of the elephants. The Sri Lankans didn't even bother replying to my emails.

With Katya back in Latvia finishing her Uni course, I look at a map of Europe and conclude I need to find a cheap bolthole to base myself for a few weeks. Somewhere allowing the correct state of mind to begin looking at Plans B and C. I spot a 17 quid one-way flight with Wizz Air to Lake Ohrid. Macedonia and Kosovo are two of the cheapest, good-value places in the world, never mind Europe. And they are each blessed with stunning scenery and rich culture.

Three days later, I am staring out of the window of my piping hot 15-quid 4-star hotel room at a snowstorm on Lake Ohrid, trying to decide what the hell I am going to do with the next chapter in my life. And another few days later and I am staring out at this far fiercer snowstorm, from the window of my Monastery of Saint Jovan Bigorski cell.

Life is short. Too short.

None of us know how long we have on this earth and we should live keeping that thought in mind. We should also remember that the majority of people on this planet have to struggle to get by, fighting poverty, disease and the unfairness of their lot.

All too often, we don't do the things we want to do in life because we are too concerned about what others think of us. And yet the truth is that nobody on this planet knows what they are doing.

We are scared of failure. But, surely, not being who you want to be, or not doing what you want to do, is failure. Ultimately, unless you try, you have failed anyway.

We also don't end up doing what we want to do because so many human beings live and work to acquire stuff; things. It is truly absurd if you think about it. We all have so much potential. We can all be something much greater than what we are. Achieve much more than we achieve. Live a great adventure.

I have failed so many times. My mate Kelvin calls me *Balboa* because of the number of times I have been face down on the canvas and managed to wobble back to my knees again to fight on. Whatever happens, the one thing I continue to be committed to is trying to do the things in life I dream of doing. I know a lot of people think this is bollocks. I haven't got a problem with that.

But, what do I know? Like I said, nobody knows what they are doing, least of all me.

Anyway, this is where this story starts. Trying to chase my dreams and do what I want to do.

I begin scribbling down notes on various bits of paper: random thoughts, affirmations, hopes, dreams – the things I am grateful for. Quite aside from dreams of exotic places, reminding myself of the importance of family and close friends, and the realisation that a monastic existence would mean no women in my life, I have concluded that I need to return to football. There is no escaping the fact that it is the area of life in which I believe I have the most to offer and where, I feel, I can make the biggest difference. I volunteered in Sierra Leone in 2013, and I would like to volunteer somewhere in Africa again. *Volunteer again*, goes on the list. I take the piece of paper in front of me and, as absurd as it sounds, also find myself scribbling down:

I want to be an international football manager.

January 31, 2017 | Geneva, Switzerland

Switzerland is a two-hour flight but a complete world away from Kosovo, Macedonia, and Bulgaria, where I just spent the past three weeks. Not only does everything cost about ten times more here but this beautiful, absurdly rich nation just feels soulless and unreal in comparison to the Balkans. One thing that is real though, it seems to me, is CONIFA.

I am attending the Confederation of Independent Football Associations' AGM. A few months ago, I had never heard of CONIFA but selling some old match-worn shirts on behalf of Riga United to a German shirt collector called Jens Jockel, who just happened to be a member of the CONIFA Executive Committee, I became aware of the organisation, and here I am. I very nearly changed my mind at the last moment to avoid the stupid cost of being in Switzerland.

This is fascinating. Among CONIFA's members are the likes of Kurdistan, Abkhazia, and Tibet. I love how surreal the whole thing is. I love how the organisation allows anyone and everyone to play competitive international football, regardless of where on the planet they come from and how right or wrong others perceive their existence to be. I love how friendly and open it is. I am hooked and have decided to join the organisation.

During the AGM, I get chatting to representatives of several weird and wonderful FAs. When I mention that I have a background as a football coach, some even suggest that – maybe – I could work for them one day. I collect business cards from far-flung, exotic federations, and immediately my mind lights up with the possibilities. *I want to be an international football manager.*

February 27, 2017 | Leicestershire, England

Things happen in life, but you are not always entirely sure quite how they happened. It is almost as if you are subconsciously piloting the ship. I have just completed a training course at Millwall FC and become a coach for Tackle Africa, a fantastic organisation that teaches HIV education & prevention through football. I applied for the course after reading about their work on the SportDev website while I was soul searching in Macedonia. At some point, I will travel out to Cameroon or Uganda or elsewhere, to volunteer for the organisation. In the past few days, I have also become the Africa Director of CONIFA, a hell of a personal honour. Amusingly, most people assume it comes with a huge salary when in fact it is a voluntary role.

I say I am not sure how this has all happened but leaving Latvia, travelling around the Indian Ocean, and ending up in a sub-zero monastery with a load of black-robed monks and lads in Adidas tracksuits in Macedonia is what led me here. The next step in my evolving plan is to volunteer with Tackle Africa in April, 'work' for CONIFA at the Euros in North Cyprus in June, then do my UEFA B in Latvia in August. Beyond this, in 2019, I believe I will be able to start looking at options in international football management in weird and wonderful places.

June 4, 2017 | North Cyprus

I am in sunny North Cyprus rooming in the same hotel as the likes of South Ossetia and the Isle of Man football teams. It is a working holiday in an all-inclusive five-star hotel, paid for by the hosts, with lots of football matches and travel involved. It is a lot of fun and, in many senses, reminds me of how football used to be before it became fat and bloated and obsessed by its own fame.

I am delighted to be here and I am committed to writing a full report about this tournament for CONIFA to help it plan better for next summer's World Football Cup, which will likely be held in London. Sadly, though, the other parts of my grand plan have fallen apart. Tackle Africa cannot send me out to Africa before at least October, and the Latvian Football Federation have thrown a curve ball at me saying I can no longer do the UEFA B with them in August due to rule changes. It will be 2020 before I can hope to start coaching an international team.

The English FA are no help at all. They won't even let me join a B course without me coaching a team in England. The Leicestershire FA have turned me down. Again. To be honest, I am very tempted to quit coaching. I certainly can't go back to Riga United now. That wouldn't make any sense. If I had known this was going to happen, I could have spent the summer with Katya and her family in southern Russia instead of returning to Latvia to twiddle my thumbs. All of my plans are up in the air. Yet again, I find myself face down in pursuit of the things I want to do.

June 20, 2017 | Riga, Latvia

One door closes, another one opens.

One of the lads who used to play for Riga United, Uldis, has asked me if I can help out his new club AFK Aliance, who play in the Latvian Second Division. I feel honoured that a club might approach me and ask such a thing. Almost out of the blue, at a time when I was seriously thinking of quitting football, I am the manager of a Latvian third-tier side.

July 1, 2017

I am really enjoying my time with AFK Aliance. They're a sound bunch of lads; what I call 'tight' as a group. They enjoy their football, but they also do it for all those positives that come out of being part of a football team collective. They are like brothers, and I like that. Although my involvement is not as committed as it could be, I feel that I am having some positive impact on them. And, to some extent, they have restored my faith in football. As well as this, I am also playing regularly in what will likely be my final full season as a player with Riga United Reserves. In other words, I am loving my football, especially after a fantastic CONIFA Euros in North Cyprus.

Through my early dealings with CONIFA, the realisation has sprung that I might be able to coach at a higher level with a non-FIFA team or perhaps work in the backroom staff of a FIFA women's national team in the developing world. I begin contacting the women's departments of some FAs in the Caribbean and forgotten corners of South America. I scour the map for obscure parts of Africa and Asia where my questionable services might be coveted. Today, I have also started talking to the foreign representative of a Pacific island nation's football team.

I want to be an international football manager.

July 30, 2017

"OK, so I can confirm that you and Tony are to be joint coaches of the national side."

The Skype call ends, and I am absolutely buzzing. Can it really be true? I am about to become the national team football manager of a Pacific state! Talk about dreams coming true. I felt that to take on the running of a small national team, there needed to be two of us working in the Pacific, and one month ago approached my friend Tony – a former English and Welsh semi-pro goalkeeper and someone I consider to be an excellent coach as well as a good, trustworthy friend. Tony is absolutely made up when I tell him.

I have been working on this for a month. There have been dozens of Skype calls to the bloke setting up the deal, countless emails, and lots of sitting on benches on warm July evenings in Riga parks with my mate Tony discussing the seemingly real-but-unreal possibility of the two of us becoming the joint national team head coaches of a country. Yes, a country!

Now, we are down to the nitty-gritty: the contract, when we go, where we live. I am the kind of person who doesn't care very much what people think of me. But, at this point, I am just exploding inside with the desire to tell everyone I am a national team head coach.

OK, so the bit I should mention is that the job is voluntary, flights to the Pacific might cost Tony and me two grand each… and, the two of us will be living in a rudimentary hut at the bottom of someone's garden. It's also a fairly isolated place, hours from anywhere else, and suffering from water shortages and the threat of ecological disaster. Small details.

July 31, 2017

Just to be sure that there have been no misunderstandings, I write to the federation chief, clarifying the official position of Tony and myself when it comes to the contract. I make clear that the title of Joint National Team Managers is important to us. We need those titles in exchange for two years of our lives, in order to grow our CVs, and develop our careers.

August 14, 2017

The chief is happy with the contract proposal I sent him some days ago. The word is to go ahead, book our flights, and just turn up. But I am not spending two grand and flying for thousands of miles without a contract in place.

Still, things are progressing and looking good.

Tony, though, has been offered a lucrative role working at one of the international schools in Riga. Naturally, it has made him wobble a bit given that he currently has no income and the Pacific will set us both back thousands. If we can get that contract signed off in the next week though, I think he will still join me.

August 25, 2017

There's an email from the chief.

Finally, I hope, this is the contract signed by the football federation. I open the email, and my eyes cannot believe what they are reading. I want to be physically sick.

We are not to be offered the manager role; Tony and I would be assistants only. I re-read the email to make sure I am not hallucinating.

I absolutely cannot believe it.

After 25 days with a simple two-page contract – and the belief that there were just small details to iron out before we signed on the dotted line – everything has changed. The chief has waited 39 days from when we discussed being joint national team coaches, and almost four weeks from when the contract proposal was originally discussed. Now, to rub salt into the wounds, I am also being asked whether I have any coaching material or plans I could send over. I close the email in disbelief. What a piece of work this guy is!

There is nothing I can do.

Yesterday, I was the head coach of a nation's football team. Today, the dream is dead.

2: A risk worth taking?

My overwhelming emotion is one of anger. I want to get on the first available flight, find the federation chief, and slowly strangle him to death with my bare hands.

I have wasted months of my life on this, turned down job offers, and called notice on my apartment. It has caused so much strain in my relationship with Katya. Where do I go from here? I can't imagine how I would feel now if Tony hadn't been able to take the job at the international school. If he had turned them down and waited for the signed contract, he'd now be left with nothing.

Days are passing by. I feel very very down. What the hell am I going to do?

Paul Watson and Sascha Düerkop are absolute diamonds. Paul is CONIFA's Commercial Director, Sascha is CONIFA General Secretary. Not only do they both work themselves silly for CONIFA but they are super empathetic to the needs of others. They have had to put up with me sending them long 'woe is me' emails these past few days. They are both sympathetic and say they want to help me find a coaching role somewhere else, within CONIFA or elsewhere.

Paul says he would be very happy to send me out to Micronesia. Paul went out there in 2007 hoping to fulfill the dream of playing international football by joining one of the world's worst teams. But when he and his mate, Matt, reached the Pacific, they discovered there was no national team and instead of playing international football, set about creating a national team (of sorts) for the Micronesian island of Pohnpei.

Fast forward ten years, and if I follow in his footsteps, there would be no salary but I would be living in paradise. And, in terms of development, it would be an amazing opportunity to continue Paul's fantastic work there. Aside from Pohnpei, there are also potential options in Samoan club football and perhaps even with a CONIFA member in Asia Pacific. It is all exciting stuff. Suddenly, hope has returned.

Pretty much on the same day that Paul pushes these fantastic opportunities my way, Sascha contacts me and tells me that Matabeleland are looking for a coach. Mata who? I say jokingly.

I do actually know who Matabeleland are, thanks to my role with CONIFA. They are a three-province region in western Zimbabwe, and it was Sascha who travelled there earlier in the year to visit the Matabeleland Football Confederacy and subsequently helped bring them into the CONIFA family as the organisation's newest member.

With summer rapidly turning into a miserable, wet autumn in Latvia, I have been googling images of Micronesia for two solid days. If I could, I would get on a flight there right now. After losing out on the Pacific island national team job, this is an amazing plan B. I can't believe my fortune really. But there is certainly no harm in speaking to Matabeleland before I make a final decision.

Emails and Facebook messages to the Matabeleland people follow. Then a long Skype call. It is all very positive. I like their vision. There is the incredible once-in-a-lifetime opportunity here to potentially take a team to a World Cup. OK, it is the CONIFA World Football Cup, but the mere mention of it makes my heart beat faster.

Yes, they aren't a national team, but I would be an international football manager, pitting my wits against stateless nations and countries. As well as that, Matabeleland is an underdeveloped region of Zimbabwe. Working out there could help transform a whole community. I could help empower people as I believe I did when I worked in Sierra Leone. It is a role that ticks many many boxes for me in terms of what I am about as a football coach.

September 4, 2017 | Jurmala, Latvia

I have decided I want to take on the Pohnpei development role until Christmas and then fly home for a couple of weeks before joining Matabeleland early next year. Paul is good with it. He helps finance the Pohnpei team by selling colourful replica shirts and he reckons (through this) he can find the money to cover my flights to Micronesia. The MFC say they are willing to consider the idea of me joining them in January. Suddenly, after one of the lowest lows I can remember in a long time, I am absolutely buzzing with a situation pregnant with possibilities.

I spend a morning alone in beautiful Jurmala, strolling through the pine trees of the Dzintari forest park and then along the almost deserted beach; summer now gone and autumn rolling in. In my heart of hearts, I realise my plan isn't feasible. It is unfair to the Zimbabwe lads. They are totally committed to getting to London next summer and are already working 24-7 in their preparations. They need someone who is fully committed. In all honesty, I must go to Zimbabwe now or not at all. Micronesia represents paradise while Bulawayo strikes me as being a rather grim

Zimbabwean version of Johannesburg. I would much rather live in the Pacific, but the southern African role is a significantly bigger challenge as a coach, particularly with the CONIFA World Football Cup as the ultimate target.

After my recent disappointments, I am understandably fearful of losing out again. Matabeleland say they are about to speak to other coaches. One British coach was already supposed to have joined them a few months ago but changed his mind, late on, when he realised they had no package to offer him. I ask Busani, the President of the Matabeleland FC, to give me a couple of days to decide before he opens it up to other coaches. He agrees.

Poor Katya. She thought we might move to Russia for a while. Then, for weeks, she thought I was leaving for the Pacific. Then, she thought I was staying with her. Now, I take her out for dinner at Burga and explain that I am close to moving to Zimbabwe. It will mean me being away for two stints of three months. She cries. She panics about being alone. She is scared when I tell her that I am a little bit fearful about the security situation in Zimbabwe. The fact that I am planning to leave her within a few days to set off makes it all feel very very real rather than some pipe dream. But Katya says I must go. The opportunity is just too good to miss. She is sad and scared, but she will wait for me to return at Christmas.

I change my mind three or four times each day. One minute I am on the plane to the Pacific Ocean, the next I am headed to southern Africa. Micronesia is safe and (relatively) straightforward. Zimbabwe is risky. It strikes me I might get arrested if I coach the Matabeleland team. Robert Mugabe's regime has been committing human rights abuses and atrocities for decades. I know very little about the country, but the thought of going there actually scares me despite, or because of, all my years of travelling.

There is a contract on the table from the MFC. I play around with it a bit and ask for some amendments. They grant most of the changes. I speak to the CONIFA Executive Committee and officially request that the organisation funds my return flights to Zimbabwe. CONIFA has almost no money to its name. But as the Africa Director of CONIFA, being based in southern Africa could be a big positive for the organisation. I could visit CONIFA member Barotseland in neighbouring Zambia as well as Addis Ababa in Ethiopia, where we hope to host a future CONIFA AGM. There is also the plan to hold CONIFA's first ever Africa Cup, possibly in southern Africa. The Exco unanimously agrees to my proposal. It is fantastic news. If they'd said no, I think I might have reverted to Micronesia.

I call Busani. He seems delighted when I tell him I am going to accept his offer and join Matabeleland as their manager. I must say he seems like a very sound lad. With the political situation as it is, in Zimbabwe, I suggest that I travel out to Matabeleland as the Africa Director of CONIFA and 'officially' work under that role until Christmas. We certainly won't be announcing anything about me joining Matabeleland until after I travel out there or, for all I know, I might get turned away at the border.

September 11, 2017

It is September 11th. I have the amended contract, signed by the MFC, in front of me. My heart pounding, I pen my signature at the bottom of the third page, literally run to the nearby print shop, scan it and email it to Busani in Bulawayo. My word, I can't believe it! I am an international football manager!

In the space of a few days, I have gone from being the manager of a Latvian third-tier team, to national team manager of a Pacific Island country, to manager of nobody, to manager of an obscure region of Zimbabwe. You couldn't make it up.

Originally, when this story was about Tony and myself being joint national team managers in the Pacific, we planned to spend weeks formulating coaching plans for the team, putting together a nutrition strategy, and going mad on social media to spread the word about the nation's football side. Not only did we want to travel fully prepared in a football sense but we also wanted to create huge awareness of what we were doing so that the British press embraced our efforts and broadcast our story to the world. That way, we felt, we could immediately kickstart fundraising for the team.

With only a couple of weeks before I fly out to Africa, I have barely got time for anything, let alone compiling coaching plans. The sensitivity of Matabeleland and Zimbabwe also means that I cannot start creating awareness of the team, the region, nor my involvement. To get to London next year, Matabeleland will need to raise vast amounts of money, and in order to do that, we should start fundraising now. But we can't.

September 27, 2017 | Riga, Latvia - East Midlands, England

The AFK Aliance lads give me a great send-off, taking me out and getting me stupidly drunk as a way of thanking me for my efforts with them. With

Tony now staying in Latvia and working at the international school instead of beginning a life of international football management, I suggest they bring him in to work with them next season.

The few people I tell where I am going, and what I am doing, seem to collectively think I am completely mad. One or two think I will be deported and back in Europe within a couple of weeks.

Leaving Katya is a shocker. Our relationship has been under strain for months. As a Russian national, we rely on her having Schengen visas to live in Europe and hers finishes next Spring. It will be practically impossible to get another one immediately. My pursuit of doing (then not doing) the UEFA B in Latvia and coaching football internationally has put a huge added pressure on the relationship. And now, I must leave her for almost three months, only seeing her again the day before Christmas Eve. There are lots of tears. I feel sick inside doing it. And as my flight takes off from Riga, bound for the East Midlands, I seriously question the whole endeavour I am setting out on. This is stupid and dangerous and, at this point in time, I am regretting my decision to get involved in this whole hare-brained project.

Why am I actually doing this? Yes, I wrote down that I wanted to be an international football manager on a piece of paper and then set out to see if such a thing were possible. But the why of all this runs much deeper into my very being…

I fell in love with football when I was about six. That was when I first started playing the game for St. Albert's Football Team and began watching football on the TV, fascinated and enthralled by Brian Clough's 1978 title winning Nottingham Forest, and standing with my Grandfather, Jack, on the terraces at Northampton Town's County Ground. A 40-year love affair with the game began that has led to me still playing competitively until this very day.

I used to kick a ball in the street, in the backyard, or up the park with my mates practically every evening that I wasn't playing or training with a school team or local park side. I followed Northampton Town with my Grandfather until I was old enough to drive, at which point I began to travel home and away supporting them. My very decent school team won the county cup, and I began playing men's Sunday League at 16. At Bournemouth University, I became player-manager of the second team and at around that time I began following England home and away, beginning with the Euros in Sweden in 1992. I briefly moved to Holland to try to make it as a semi-professional player. I worked on a project for the Football Supporters Association at USA '94, was the Assistant Director for the city of Nottingham for Euro '96, and did my first coaching badge the same year with the English FA. Around 1996, a career in coaching and football management or even football marketing and development seemed to be on the cards. But despite my best efforts, somehow it just didn't happen. And when it didn't happen, I felt annoyed and frustrated and promised myself I would do something far more worthwhile by setting off to see the world in 1997. I love football, but travel is my greatest passion.

I remained in love with the beautiful game, but my priority changed to travel, partying, and chasing beautiful girls. There are worse things, to be fair. I did some bits of football journalism but it was only really a whole 15 years later, with the abrupt break up of a six-year relationship in 2011 and my decision to return to Latvia to try to take Riga United Football Club forward, that football became all-consuming in my life again. Since 2013, I have played over 50 senior games in the Latvian third tier, volunteered in Sierra Leone, and coached kids from 4 years old to 18, as well as men's and women's teams.

I tell you all this because, packing my rucksack in Leicestershire, about to leave for Heathrow Airport, it might now be more understandable how and why I took on such a job: the unpaid coach of a football team in an impoverished region of Zimbabwe, in a country in danger of collapse.

3: Dragon's Den

Thursday, October 5, 2017 | 18:34 Heathrow Airport Terminal 2

I am halfway down a pint of Seafarers at Heathrow Airport, surrounded by dozens of Swedish and German suits in a plastic pub, waiting to fly to Africa and begin my career – long or short – as an international football manager. It begins with a flight tonight to Addis Ababa where I've got one meeting on behalf of CONIFA, and a week of backpacking in Ethiopia, before I head to southern Africa to begin the World Cup adventure.

The suits are all necking six quid pints of lager, all self-congratulating themselves about today's money wars out there in the field; notching up their victories at others' expense. This scene only adds to the sense that what I am about to undertake seems anything but real.

England kick off against Slovenia, in a World Cup qualifier, just up the road in an hour. I used to follow England home and away. Twenty years man and boy. But the disappointments and frustrations finally ground me down. Now, I could hardly care less about watching them on ITV. And why sit on an overpriced plastic seat with the 90,000 at Wembley, when I can be the one in the dugout next summer trying to outthink Tibet and Panjab as Matabeleland win the World Football Cup!? It is a big, big, huge impossible dream but so was becoming an international manager in the first place!

Friday, October 6, 2017 | Addis Ababa, Ethiopia

Our flight touches down in Addis at around 6am. There is a nip in the air making this October morning in east Africa feel like a continuation of last night in London. 80 quid gets me a huge bundle of dirty 100 Birr notes. It takes barely five minutes to get a $50 visa-on-arrival stuck into my passport. Nobody is waiting to pick me up as arranged. These things happen. This is Africa.

Friday, October 13, 2017

I am about to fly six hours from Ethiopia to South Africa and meet the Matabeleland Football Confederacy. I guess you could say that today is my first proper day as an international football manager.

Yesterday, I started reading the latest online newspaper articles I could find about Zimbabwe. I purposely avoided travel updates on the Foreign

& Commonwealth Office website, and in the press, until the very last minute. Sometimes it is better to avoid creating anxieties in your mind. It didn't make for pretty reading. I had absolutely no idea that unemployment in Zimbabwe is by far and away the highest on the planet at 90%. I mean how is that even possible? How does a country function? Next, I read, there is a currency crisis. Public sector workers are not being paid. There is talk of social unrest on the cards, of food shortages, and a return to hyperinflation. I wish I had read none of this, to be honest.

Ethiopia was absolute class. Nobody ever managed to colonise the country meaning that in today's globalised world, it is completely unlike anywhere else on earth, boasting unique food, religion, dress, 80 different ethnic groups, customs, alphabet, language... they even have their own time!

I explored the mystical rock churches of Lalibela, hiked the Arthur Conan Doyle-style Lost World of the Simiens, was blown away by the very special vibe of medieval Gondar, and almost got tricked into being mugged outside an Addis coffee shop. I really wish I could have had more time here, but I'm grateful for the fantastic week I have experienced.

At this point, I am not thinking too much about the possibility of failure in Bulawayo. Zimbabwe is such a massive unknown that it is not worth speculating too much. It is literally one step at a time: Get to South Africa - Meet the Matabeleland people - Travel to the border - Get into Zimbabwe - Avoid getting deported - And then all that football stuff.

It is absurd really but, as I set off on this adventure, part of me is super excited, but I also cannot wait to get home to see my family and be back with Katya. In day-to-day life, I don't tend to think much beyond tomorrow. But, right now, I am thinking about Zimbabwe immigration, the safety of where I live, press conferences, training at the crack of dawn, friendly matches, and much more.

We take off from Addis. All is green below. I hope and pray to be back here on December 11, on my way home, safe and healthy, having made a positive difference.

10:35. Well, what about that! I just saw magnificent Kilimanjaro out of the plane's back window, rising majestically above the clouds with snow on its peak. A South African lad I chat to laments never having climbed it. I have seen it now from a train and a plane window; at this moment, I regret not having tackled Africa's highest mountain.

Would Pep Guardiola drink three miniature bottles of red as he flew in to meet his new bosses at Man City?

South Africa.

Touchdown in South Africa. After Ethiopia, Joburg feels like a different world as I anxiously drift through arrivals, passport control, and baggage reclaim. Busani, Khanye (his first name is also Busani but to save confusion from day one, we have agreed to use his surname going forward), and two other gentlemen are waiting for me at a crowded arrivals hall. We all shake hands and embrace.

Squeezing into a tiny Fiat Panda, we set off through the surrounding suburbs. To me, urban South Africa looks rather like a downtrodden British inner city in the 1970s or 80s. Razor wire and an automatic front gate open up to a tatty motel in Kempton Park where I've got a double bed and kettle for company.

I am going to struggle with the handshakes. Not only do Busani and the boys shake hands more often than the European Hand Shaking Champions, the Latvians, but I have counted five different kinds of handshakes in the hour since I arrived. In turn, a couple of the lads are easy to understand but it is really difficult to work out what the hell Khanye is saying with his accent and quietly spoken manner. My first observation is they are very young, much younger than I imagined. That does concern me. Have they got any real clue what they are doing? They are friendly, though, and clearly very decent human beings.

Exhausted, I crawl into bed. My whole body is starting to shiver. And I mean badly. I put a massive thick smelly blanket on the bed but still it's intensifying. I feel super weak. My head is throbbing. My stomach also throbs.

When the lads return in late afternoon, I am in bits and have to cancel our evening meeting. This certainly isn't how I wanted or imagined this all beginning. I am so relieved to get back into bed. I Skype mum, who cries. Then gorgeous Katya, who also cries.

Saturday, October 14, 2017

Justin Walley, international football manager, wakes up in the middle of the night to discover he has messed himself and the bed. To add insult to injury, I've soiled my only pair of tracksuit bottoms, which I was wearing to fight the shivering spells. I feel like I could sleep for weeks. I have got full on diarrhoea; probably ten visits to the bogs during the night. My resting heart rate has spiked to 91 from 58 in the UK.

I am relieved when the lads show up five hours late as we pay a visit to Western Union to change money. I need to cash out 600 Rand for the guesthouse and 550 for the bus to Bulawayo. Before I came here, I am pretty certain Busani said they were covering my accommodation in South Africa. I assume this means they are short of money and I let it go.

On a more positive note, Busani says Matabeleland v Darfur will take place in Pretoria on December 10. He is talking about an attendance of five thousand plus. How mad would that be?

Sunday, October 15, 2017

Despite swallowing half a dozen Imodium tablets, the diarrhoea is still going through me like water. My entire supply of rehydration sachets for the trip is also exhausted. It feels like I imagined the whole international football manager thing.

I check out and sit in the garden admiring the colourful birds coming and going; the razor wire and electric fence hiding me away in a secluded bubble. Busani and the lads arrive and tell me we are staying another night as they have things they need to do in the city. My head is spinning as I check back into my room. I eat my first meal in two days and we have our first half serious chat about football matters, although we all agree there isn't much point discussing it too much, in case I don't make it over the border into Zimbabwe. I thought I would be in Zimbabwe tonight but, instead, I am in full-on diarrhoea mode, watching Dragon's Den in a 1970s style Johannesburg motel.

Monday, October 16, 2017

Johannesburg gives me the fear. We walk from the gated Kempton flat development where we have stored our bags for the day and past a load of emaciated junkies rolling around on a sofa on some open waste ground. We cross the main road where almost nobody slows down for pedestrians, no doubt fearing they could be violent assailants, then onwards to the newspaper-strewn main street of Kempton Park where shopkeepers hand over products for cash through thick metal bars and some petty criminals are playing that three cups and a pea game in the street. "Walk fast," Khanye tells me. "They pick off the slow ones and then it is often too late."

I wouldn't mind but the Matabele lads have taken me down some subterranean subway which rather resembles a crumbling 1997 eastern European train station. Haggard small-time traders are going about their business selling handkerchiefs and mobile phone cards. There is the odd huddle of criminal types. I am the only white in sight and everything of importance is on my person: my passport, documents, bank cards, and cash. I hope to God it isn't like this in Bulawayo. I couldn't stand the constant daily paranoia. The reason for this apparent madness is that we are en route to a mall to buy international bus tickets, change money, and have a fast food lunch.

Dipping my chips into the acidic ketchup, which rather fittingly has the appearance of theatrical blood rather than a condiment, we have a long chat about the situation. There is a genuine fear about me getting into Zimbabwe tonight. I will be entering as a tourist, although I do wonder who in their right mind would want to spend two months holidaying in Zimbabwe right now. I was imagining a press conference next week to announce my appointment but, with things as they currently are in the country, there will be no press conferences; not even any social media from me. I have taken the personal decision that it is best that I leave South Africa, enter Zimbabwe, and then fall off the radar for several weeks. I am fearful of upsetting the authorities and the possibility of being expelled or perhaps imprisoned. I am also considering the implications for these lads. Quite how it is possible to go relatively unnoticed in a city of one million with only a few thousand whites remains to be seen.

"One problem of announcing you are the manager of the team is that certain people, knowing you are British, will assume an MI5 or CIA plot using our project to try and cause problems for Mugabe."

I breathe a huge sigh of relief when we make it back to the flat, which feels like a safe house. I don't know why, but I imagine myself as an Irish fugitive hiding away with some black blokes in a dodgy corner of east London in the 1970s; like an episode of Guerilla.

Worryingly, the MFC are imagining British businesses will be queueing up to drop 20 grand to sponsor the team (for what I would class as a politically-sensitive project, with an unknown brand, that will only be in the UK for ten days). If the team get visas. With every passing hour that I am here, with the Matabeleland lads, I realise the odds of all of this succeeding appear to be in the hundreds to one. They have set themselves a crazily unrealistic target of raising $100,000! Imagine the chances of us raising that kind of money, me hiding away in Zimbabwe without issues, getting British visit visas for the whole team, and not getting closed down by Mugabe! I think there is more chance Leicester will be EPL champions for a second successive season.

Anyway, lying on the sofa at the safe house, I tell Busani: "In my humble opinion you need to concentrate on multiple fundraising ideas like organising sponsored football charity matches in the UK, US, and here. You could do fundraising dinners, get NGO grants, organise paid matches where ticket receipts are collected… then look at stuff like replica kits, individual player sponsorships. You can reduce your costs by partnering, begging, and asking anyone and everyone to help. But honestly, mate, don't hold your breath about bringing in huge sponsors. I couldn't even find five grand for my old football team and we had millionaires' kids playing for our academy."

This is exactly the kind of situation I wanted to avoid. With Khanye and the driver returning late, a load of us are crammed into a car, rattling so much it sounds like it might explode, swerving in and out of lanes, doing 140, as we desperately try to cover the 20 kilometres to the bus station in 50 minutes. I used to find shit like this funny, and exciting, back in the day but now I just see it as risking your life because people cannot arrive on time. I am shitting it (although the diarrhoea has subsided), fearing a crash, as we hurtle down what looks like the M6 to Joburg central.

Joburg's CBD is far dodgier than I remember it being during FIFA 2010 when it was crawling with police and security. The destitute sleep rough on filthy mattresses, gaggles of lads gather in the shadows, rubbish and newspaper blow down the street, punters pay for groceries and alcohol through gated shop fronts, blokes – old before their time – swig cheap alcohol from bottles. Junkies in fluorescent jackets, pretending to be car parking stewards, demand imaginary fees as we pull up outside Park Station. There are lads everywhere, some just sat in parked cars and vans, observing. If anyone wanted to fuck you here, there is nothing you could do. There is no security, no police. We elect to run the 100 unlit yards to the entrance and into the relative safety of the bus terminal.

4: 17 players in a pickup truck

Tuesday, October 17, 2017

The South African border is stupidly overcrowded. Rough lorry drivers intimidate travel-weary coach passengers as they push straight to the front of long, snaking passport queues. South Africa should be embarrassed by the utter shambles this border post is.

Zimbabwe is quite the opposite. The junior immigration officer is well-spoken and friendly. I had hoped to enter on a three-month visa, but the only options are a 30-day or the £55 double entry. I have already dropped 150 quid of my own money since I flew in.

The sun edges above the horizon as the young official sticks the visa in my passport, and a blind trio with white sticks sing gospel and tiptoe past us with a plastic collection cup. A slightly scary one-legged bloke with more front than Woolworths unsuccessfully attempts to annoy passengers into giving him cash. The blind choir, I am pleased to announce, are more successful in their quest.

For weeks I'd been imagining being taken into a back room and grilled like the Israelis once did to me for three hours as to *why I am here, what I do, who I know*, etc. Of all the border posts I have ever crossed, Zimbabwe proves to be one of the friendliest and most straightforward. From my experience, this always bodes well.

The Greyhound bus leaves the Beitbridge border post behind and sets off into a landscape of bushland. Even at this early hour, the temperature is rocketing. The main road, stretching to the horizon, is flanked by overgrown bush on either side. Truly it is a borderland.

A dozen men, women, and kids greet us as at a toilet stop at the first town we reach, selling single bananas and cold drinks from coolers. I drift into the shop and find the shelves sparsely stocked. Nothing has prices marked on it. It is noticeable that while South Africa is the land of plenty, when it comes to the products in its shops, something is clearly amiss this side of the border in this downtrodden town.

Huge boulders jut out of the landscape, the ground almost turning to desert in places. I slip in and out of sleep. And then, 14 hours after leaving dystopian Joburg, there is the sign by the roadside for my new home: Bulawayo.

We pass huge colonial mansions. Think *Gone with the Wind*. Some have impossibly green, watered lawns. They look completely unreal after the past few hours driving across the overgrown bush. The main road is almost bereft of traffic, and we quickly reach the wide avenues of city centre Bulawayo.

As we park up, it is hard to explain quite how mad I am finding the scene. It puts me in mind of Back to the Future when Michael J. Fox goes back to the 1950s. It looks rather like that but with blooming Jacaranda and Red Flamboyant trees adding an African touch. The taxi drivers are impeccably mannered, and many wear suits – some going threadbare – giving them the look of cartoon character butlers. There is none of that intimidating vibe of South Africa. And I literally mean none. Yes, there are lots of men hanging around, but there is no eyeballing. No gangs of delinquents.

We wait to unload all of our bags from the trailer and then carefully balance them, one by one, in the boot of our driver's rusting car, which shudders from the weight.

400 yards. That is how far we manage before we have to stop for repairs. I don't laugh aloud, concerned that the amiable gentleman might feel embarrassed. Clearly, the state of things here is the state of things; it's not his fault or anyone else's. However, moments later, there is a collective roar as the driver gets out a spanner and starts tightening the nuts and bolts on the front left tyre. Clearly, the Zimbabweans can laugh at adversity. I already feel at home, here, with these first interactions.

We turn down a street of bungalows with their own private fronts and arrive at the house of Auntie Ethel. Apparently, this will be my temporary home for the first two weeks in Zim until a place is sorted out for me. If I last two weeks in Zim.

I am more than happy with this. Firstly, and best of all, Ethel is clearly a legend. Secondly, the house is super clean, comfortable, and has electricity and water. It even has a backyard. My bedroom is large with a wardrobe, work table, double bed, and windows that look out onto that garden. Ethel gives me clean sheets. I unpack my backpack and place its items in the wardrobe.

Ethel looks after other people's kids during the day; a sort of glorified nanny granny. If you are wondering about her name - well her mother was a domestic servant to whites and the lady of the house took it upon herself to give/propose that her mother's daughter took the very English name.

We have coffee in the lounge and chat for an hour, while the three kids play, one of whom keeps touching my skin and giggling. It is a relief to be inside away from the relentless 35 degrees heat.

After a much-needed rest, I awaken late afternoon and rejoin Ethel about 5pm. The temperature is dropping and it is pleasant outside on the metal chair she pulls up for me. We have Mazoe orange squash, which I am told, is universally adored in Zimbabwe and highly sought after over the border in South Africa. Spring onions and unripe tomatoes grow out of old tyres. It is a joy to spot banana, avocado and guava trees. Ethel is lovely. Smart and old school. I already feel privileged to be under her wing and know she has come along at this point in my life to help guide me on my current path.

Some estimate that three million Zimbabweans now live in SA as well as half a million in the UK. 90 percent here are unemployed. Ethel stopped working because it was almost pointless. During the worst times, people spent more cash getting to and from work, and having lunch, than they actually earned.

You could speak to this lady for days. We discuss how and why the whites left, what came next, and hyperinflation. She shows me a bag of useless cash from back in the day. Some of the notes are in denominations of millions and billions. I can hardly believe my own eyes. I knew these things existed but having a 500 Billion Dollar note in my hand really is insane.

Lightbulb moment! What if we could sell these worthless pieces of history to help the MFC reach the World Football Cup?! I don't know, maybe: "Become a millionaire for two quid!" "A billionaire for a fiver!" I reckon loads of people would hand over cash for one of these. I know I would.

At the height of hyperinflation you couldn't buy anything with these notes. New, bigger notes were issued every few days, noughts added. People's savings were simply wiped out. The largest note ever issued was the 100 Trillion Dollar Zimbabwe note. That had 14 zeros. The inflation rate is said to have reached 516 quintillion, annually. Only remittances, mostly from South Africa, saved those who stayed behind rather than fleeing. The currency collapsed in February 2009 and eventually the government allowed FOREX to replace it. Ethel thought of burning these notes like most people did. But she kept a few bags to give to museums and for curators' collections. Perhaps, all these years later, a football team in Matabeleland can benefit from the misfortune of yesteryear and raise some of the funds it needs.

Busani and Khanye pop round and take me out in the pitch dark for 'a surprise'. Up by the petrol station, I am introduced to half of the football team who are out on a 10-kilometre run.

"Hello, gentlemen. It is a pleasure meeting you. I am really looking forward to watching you play tomorrow."

It is a lovely, special moment and I appreciate Busani and Khanye doing it. You could almost imagine the scene in a film. It's funny, shaking hands in the dark, meeting my new team but unable to see their faces. We all chuckle at the slight absurdity of it. They seem super friendly.

Wednesday, October 18, 2017

I wake at 4am, confused as to where I am, then curl back into a ball. By six, people are already scurrying around. Enjoying coffee, there is a refreshingly cool breeze. When I lived in Sierra Leone, the heat was relentless and there were never these respites. Again, we chat non-stop for two hours about the colonial education system, which taught blacks to believe that farming was for losers. Language exams were marked in London with only the cream of the crop from Ethel's disadvantaged community making it to Uni.

'Bruce the goalkeeper' picks me, and Ayanda (the new team doctor), up in the afternoon. Ayanda studied in Perm, Russia for six years. He tells me there were 100 blacks in a city of one million. We laugh at the irony of me now being one of a few hundred whites in a black city of a million plus.

The car pulls off at the turning behind the local rugby stadium. There's barely any grass on a pitch that would be considered totally unplayable in the 'developed' world. I seem to have got my wires crossed. I was under the illusion there would be a thousand people watching tonight's game when in fact the crowd is actually… three.

I am here to observe and take notes. The opposition's warm-up comprises of them all standing around in the penalty area, hands on hips, while wingers cross it in. Our boys do nothing. No stretches at all. I write that down in my notes and underline it three times. OK, to be fair, half of them have jogged a couple of miles to get here, having just finished work or school but, all the same.

I'll be honest; my heart sinks. Fantasy and reality have diverged. As we are representing the whole region of Matabeleland, I imagined a packed stadium tonight, something akin to a poor man's English National League ground. Instead, I appear to have come all this way to be an African Sunday League manager on unplayable pitches. Hinckley & District Sunday League, aged 16, was sexier than this.

The game starts with our team playing something resembling a 3-5-2 against a very youthful Zimbabwean Second League side. But, seriously, look at the technical quality of these lads! My word! Most teams I know that play at a decent level would be mis-controlling every third ball on this surface but somehow Matabeleland are controlling and moving the ball at speed with barely an error.

Our boys race into a 2-0 lead. We look capable of hitting our opponents for eight or nine. There are, however, lots of things that need working on and improving: we play a three with a sweeper who seems obsessed with risk-taking. The goalkeeper is tiny. Maybe five foot seven. He likes dribbling around with the ball. The team is very young. Only one player has any height. And at 2-0, we play like we have already won the game.

The opposition pull one back early in the second half. Saw that coming. A third goal for us comes from a goalkeeping error. This reminds me of women's football where the teams are decent but the goalkeepers are often way off the standard. I like the 11. The sweeper, 15, worries and impresses me. But I am on my back at the overall quality of both teams on the ball. Attacking transition good. Defensive transition almost non-existent. And one of my pet hates: we leave one defender back against two opposition players when we have corners.

At the end, I prefer to say nothing to the players and quietly slip back in the car. Once I have done this, I feel like a bit of a twat. As if I think I am Jose Mourinho or something. Busani pays the groundsman and we are off. Why did I do that?

Thursday, October 19, 2017

The Zimbabwe Herald reports that some parts of Zimbabwe experienced record-breaking temperatures yesterday. More serious news is that cash withdrawals are now rationed down to $14 per bank day. Many public sector workers are working 12-hour days but not getting paid. People are said to be hoarding cash at home. Some products have doubled in price in a week. Milk has gone from $1.18 to $1.45 since I arrived!

Busani and Khanye take me into town where we are visiting one of Bulawayo's handful of modern high rises. The reception resembles the 1970s or Russian hotels in those years immediately following the end of the USSR. *Life on Mars*. Everything from the uniformed guards in clothes from another era, the paper clipboard sign in, the old-school lift with huge fiddly buttons, the wood laminate floors. Indeed, everyone is scared of the lift in case it breaks down and traps them; all of it is nostalgic, taking me back to my childhood days.

Centenary Park and Central Park are alive with Jacaranda, Red Flamboyant, giant palms and other glorious trees. With the rainy season still two weeks away, the grass is burnt from the recent scorching temperatures and months without significant rain. Elegantly dressed ladies hide under the shade of a timeworn bandstand; couples share romantic walks. It has the feel of one of those wonderful botanical gardens in the tropics. Our driver kindly donates his 1930s style cloth cap to save my balding head from the searing heat.

Centenary Park reminds me of those classic parks you find today in the likes of Almaty, Yerevan, and Tashkent, their former glory still apparent. The original high-quality infrastructure is still holding in there, despite all those summers and rains, everything overgrown and unkempt. The realisation that Zimbabwe was quite unlike anywhere else in Africa strikes home. Ornate fountains stand unused, a kids' train track still perceivably visible, the exposed concrete of the former electric speedboat pond now cracking, statues disappearing into the undergrowth. Cecil Rhodes, the founder of this city, no longer has his statue in the centre of a prominent avenue but instead in a forgotten corner of this park; the creepers quite taken by one of the British Empire's finest and most bastardly.

"The colonial statues actually save us today. At a time when some try to rewrite history, this memory of the past enables us to remember the good and the bad that came before."

Yes, don't destroy your statues of Rhodes, Mao, Lenin. Don't erase history. Allow people to judge for themselves. Rhodes looks rather pathetic rotting away behind some overgrown bramble bushes. But I have no doubt he should still be here, because without Rhodes there would be no Bulawayo; there would have been no Rhodesia or Zimbabwe.

Money, money, money. Must be funny. I foolishly brought no US dollars to Zimbabwe despite Busani telling me on at least four occasions that I must. Foreign bank cards do not work in ATMs. I cannot get a cash advance at a bank. There is a shortage of FOREX, particularly the currency of choice: the dollar. Zimbabwe has Bond Dollar notes, officially worth 1:1 with the US dollar. So in shops, you can purchase with Bond, while on the Black Market, US dollars are worth much more as nobody trusts the Bond and it is not actually backed by the central bank. The South African Rand is also widely accepted.

I find a money changer and get in a car with her. We drive two blocks, park and begin negotiating a rate to change my Rand to Dollars. My best offer for 3000 Rand in South Africa was 218 while the going rate in Bulawayo is currently 225. *210,* she says. *I could give you regular custom,* I suggest. She agrees to 225. I count 3000. She counts 3000. She puts it in her wallet and, without giving me any cash in return, gets out and disappears off with the driver. Ten minutes later she returns with my 3000. "I don't have enough dollars. My contacts don't want to change at that rate. The Rand is going down."

We have driven around Bulawayo's grid system so many times and in so many different directions that I am now totally dizzied as to where leads where. Three huge chimney stacks serve as one marker. They once supplied all of Bulawayo's electricity supply. Parts of the city look a little how I imagine Memphis, with pavements shaded by roofed balconies; so many grand buildings. I suspect, one day, UNESCO might even protect the magnificent architecture of this place. They certainly should. With vision, honest money, and management, Bulawayo could be absolutely transformed: cafes and restaurants with outdoor tables and chairs on the broad sidewalks, the streets kept litter free, those wonderful parks revamped.

I spot a giant billboard: Zimbabwe v West Indies. 21 October. That is this weekend. I can't believe it. A Test Match in my first week in Bulawayo. I am made up.

Back in the centre of the city, as darkness falls, the supermarkets are a hive of activity. The lads do a $15 grocery shop for me in Pick n Pay. Despite the obvious inflation, you feel no sense of a full-blown crisis unfolding. People do have money and, certainly in Bulawayo, the shelves are fully stocked.

I enjoy rice and beans with my family and briefly Skype Katya; but with the bad connection she sounds like Stephen Hawking.

Friday, October 20, 2017

Google has noticed strange activity from my computer. A tad worrying.

The first rains have arrived, a great relief from the blazing sun, although I am absolutely bemused that the MFC is calling off our training because of a few spots. I'd love these boys to see some of the snowstorms I have coached through on harsh November afternoons.

Thunder and lightning roll in as I work on the Zimbabwean currency fundraising idea. Remarkable news today that the United Nations has named Robert Mugabe as their Goodwill Ambassador. What on earth?

Saturday, October 21, 2017

We were supposed to leave at 9 for an 11 o'clock away kick-off. When Busani arrives to pick me up, more than two hours late, I let him know I am feeling put out at sitting around twiddling my thumbs all morning. Busani looks properly annoyed. "Do you know what time I left the house this morning? Six!"

"Things are so problematic here at times. I had to leave at six to queue at the bank for three hours to try to get enough dollars for today's petrol, food for the lads, refs' fees. And after all that, I could only get a few dollars."

To be fair to Busani, he is just educating me in the realities of this place. I have got to learn to get beyond my European mindset and adapt. Clearly, I need to be more flexible with arrangements. Clearly, it wouldn't hurt Busani to tip me off when he's going to be a couple of hours late, though.

We meet the team in central Bulawayo. It is a cool 18 degrees today after those recent days of plus 35. By the time we have bought juice, loaves of bread, and visited two petrol stations (the first is out of fuel) to buy blended fuel for $1.37/litre, we are off.

Imagine this! There are three coaches, three match officials, one supporter and 19 players and we have got a grand total of two vehicles! *Bruce the Goalkeeper* is driving one car, with me accompanying him in the front, and Khanye and the match officials squashed in the back. Meanwhile, more than a dozen of the players are crammed into the back of a Toyota pickup, with a load more in the front. It is like that joke about the phone box or the mini. Two of them even have to stand as they do 60 along the pot-holed road out of town.

I count eight minutes before we hit the first roadblock. Practically every Zimbabwean you speak to complains about the police roadblocks and how they are used to extract money from the population every single day. They are the bane of ordinary Zimbabwean citizens' lives. 17 minutes, second roadblock. The further we travel from Bulawayo, the more everything around us seems to deteriorate. Suddenly, 1980s Bulawayo is replaced by subsistence farming and scattered collections of round houses set on dusty fields. There is nothing romantic about most of these places. This is the kind of genuine poverty that most in the Western world simply cannot imagine and few ever see.

The road started off like a UK A-road, then a single track, and now a pot-holed nothingness only navigable with a 4x4. We hit our fourth roadblock by the time we reach Turk Mine, almost 50 kilometres away. The main mine is fenced off, with a second scattering of buildings outside by the roadside consisting of a butchers, a three-shelf convenience shop, and a rough-looking dive bar. You'd think the mining company would at least fix the road out front. I speculate they are extracting tens of millions in profits from this place but clearly don't give a flying fuck about the people who work and live here. I've seen the same story repeated across the entire developing world.

We drive further along a steadily deteriorating dusty road, past a troop of aggressive monkeys, until we reach some half-dilapidated buildings on one side of the road. Two lone goal posts on a dust 'field' stand opposite.

And let me tell you about the *second-best* pitch in the area…

Not only is it a dirt pitch with absolutely no markings and no nets, but items littered all over it include: a (recently used) condom, hundreds and hundreds of bottle tops (some rusting), broken glass (absolutely everywhere), rocks, dozens of discarded Chibuku beer cartons, old shoes, discarded plastic, cow shit. Lots of cow shit.

The kick-off has been put back because many of the opposition lads are finishing their no-doubt-gruelling shift in the gold mine. The very thought humbles the hell out of me. Meanwhile, two lads try to mark out the pitch by dragging big wooden sticks across the dirt. Six of our orange and green mini police-cones signify where the corners and the halfway line are. That is after the green cones are first used as drinking vessels by our players.

We provide pre-match food but this basically consists of five slices of a white loaf each, which most of the lads squeeze and pinch together making it look like a single sandwich. Some of our boys drink orange squash while others drink Coca-Cola, which – you have guessed it – is cheaper than water. Before I came out to Zimbabwe, I was devising carefully planned meals three hours before kickoff. It seems like quite a silly suggestion now.

Opposition players begin appearing from various directions and change under the shade of a single tree by the distant corner flag. Our lads don't have one ounce of fat on their bodies between them. They look like they have spent half of their lives in the gym but I doubt if half of them have ever stepped inside a gym. In saying that, it is pretty apparent that they have limited upper body strength and clearly need to work on that if they are ever going to compete against the big European lads, at shoulder level.

There is a warm-up this time, from the coaches, but it is more of a little-bit-too-intense twisting and turning through the cones. At least it is something. As of next week, I will be trying to drastically improve the pre-match routine. An elderly gent wearing a trilby strolls over and gives me some banter. "I hear you are good."

"Yes, we are pretty decent, haha."

"You are going to lose two nil!" he says prodding me and chuckling to himself.

I take a foldup chair from Bruce's car. It is a very different game from the one I witnessed on Wednesday. These opposition boys are tougher (understandably) and press the ball well. There isn't much in the two teams. I am startled by how few individual errors there are on this Godforsaken surface. The opposition have forced us into playing balls long; loads of hit and hope. And it definitely doesn't suit us. For some bizarre reason, one of our centre-halves, Kiwa, makes a comical cartoon road runner-type noise every time he clears the ball. We should have two penalties as our centre-forward is bundled over in the box, rugby league style. But it is a man's game in this part of the world. Meanwhile, Bruce the Goalkeeper continues to give me the fear with his eccentricities, regularly spilling the ball or going on mazy dribbles outside his own unmarked penalty area.

0-0 at halftime. Khanye gives his half-time team talk in Ndebele and then asks me for my comments. Not knowing what he has just told them, I don't want to contradict him. But as he's said nothing to me, here goes: *Be more patient boys. Less hit and hope. Build play. Don't be so anxious. Don't let them dictate how we play.* Apparently, Khanye said almost the exact same thing.

The crowd has swelled to 200. One of our lads puts his foot through the ball and clears it as far as the main road. It hits a passing pick-up truck and knocks off its wing mirror. The vehicle comes to a screeching halt. A miner and a rough lad, grasping a beer bottle, jump out shouting angrily.

They march over and next they are on the pitch, remonstrating with, well, everyone. The lad with the bottle is properly drunk and is giving me a bit of a fear. He is huge, has vacant bloodshot eyes, and the look of a head case. He won't let it go and the game is delayed for a full ten minutes as he runs around threatening people, until he is finally hauled off by half a dozen lads.

The van drives off, leaving the head case behind, but I am fearful of the other lad returning with a carload of psycho mates. I am still relatively new in Zimbabwe and have no sense of whether these kinds of incidents have the potential to turn into something very nasty. When you picture international football management, you don't imagine this place. You don't imagine some random nutter, who jumped out of a van a few minutes earlier, running up and down the sideline, jeans below his underpants like a cheap rapper, barking out drunken instructions as he somehow believes he is now the opposition gaffer.

1-0 to us from an opportunist goal. Red card for them. 2-0 to us from a pinpoint right-wing cross from our diminutive number 18. Red card for one of our lads.

2-0 is a good result against a quality team. Good focus from our lads because at 0-0 they could have lost their belief and our opponents might have won this. On the final whistle, Busani decides we should play an additional 30 minutes "as we are here". I am not a fan of this kind of thing because, as a player, you lose your focus when a match is no longer a real match. I mention I am not in favour but he insists we play the extra period. Sure enough, our big centre-half, Praise, gets injured. This is the kind of well-intended but very amateur football management that needs to be changed if we are ever going to be ready for London.

I shake hands with all of our lads at the end, thank the opposition, and try to scout one of their central defenders, who looks like a class act to me. Absolutely everyone wants to take selfies with me, including some friendly dolled-up female fans in bright and colourful revealing dresses. Five of our lads approach me for individual feedback about their performances. I like that.

5.15 becomes 5.50 and I am becoming anxious. I hate being out in the African bush in the darkness. If you break down, it is a serious security issue. Potholes, animals on the road, drunk drivers (it is Saturday) ... you just don't want to be driving in the dark in rural Africa.

The lads are out of the cars trying to negotiate black market petrol from the adjacent cowboy town. Apparently, we don't have enough fuel to get home. Surely to God, they must have bought enough fuel for a return journey when we were back in Bulawayo?

Home. It is fantastic to be back within the bosom of Bulawayo. The city is a world away from the poverty-stricken rural areas. I like the way the MFC dismisses the lads, taking them to a quiet section of city centre street where they are debriefed by Khanye, Busani and myself, before telling them they can then go home. A touch of class.

Litter is blowing everywhere as we drop one of the teenage lads at a darkened corner of the city for his minibus home. The remnants of the busy Saturday market are here, there, and everywhere: rotting tomatoes, discarded cabbage leaves, newspapers and plastic bags swirling in the wind.

5: Wooden airplane machine gun

Sunday, October 22, 2017

What a glorious reverse sweep for four runs. This is the life. A cool breeze blowing through the grandstand as Zimbabwe take on the West Indies on the second day of the two five-day tests. The West Indies were all out for 219 yesterday, and I am in here just after 10 to enjoy the Zimbabwean innings.

By noon the early morning attendance of 50 has increased by a factor of ten. It has cost me $2 for a VIP grandstand seat. Some lovely batting from Masakadza (42) and Ervine this morning; it is now 98/3. I guess it is around 28 degrees but in this stand, it feels perfect.

Busani dropped me off as he is coaching five of our lads who are playing Fourth Division football on Sunday mornings for match practice. I am certainly not a fan of lads playing two days in a row or indeed of them playing at a much lower standard. In my forties, I have played five seasons myself in the Latvian third-tier, so I am dubious about the positives of these boys playing fifth-tier football. Busani asked me to join him today when we were at *The Lounge* last night, but I stuck to my guns about coming down here this morning. I am still settling in and today's chilled Sunday certainly helps.

I managed to reach my mum on Skype this morning. How is it possible she is 70 today?! She still seems and looks so young. I am very sad to not be spending the day with her. One of the sacrifices I have made for Matabeleland is missing my own mother's 70th birthday. Next year, I intend to take her away to somewhere suitably exotic such as South America, to make up for me being here now instead of with her.

I awoke to the soothing sound of female gospel singing this morning as the ladies went about their housework. I think that was at about six. It sounded wonderful, almost as if today is Christmas. In many ways it is. The day the person who gave me life was born. Ethel's daughter is a little sweetheart. I almost cried this morning when Busani told me I am leaving Ethel's in two days' time. I pleaded with him to let me stay longer in my home from home.

The grandstand is mostly populated by whites, contentedly consuming beers from cooler boxes. The Queens Sports Club is also full of friendly middle-aged whites in floppy cricket hats. I love this old school vibe; dusty hallways full of fading photos and lists of honorary presidents. A massive photo of Mugabe hangs – Queen Elizabeth-style – next to a stuffed antelope head. Old school class mixes with absurdity mixes with the mustiness of old things. Back outside, the Mecano stands are filling up. Just like in South Africa, it is difficult for me to imagine the brutal white racist states that existed here before. Yes, the infrastructure and reminders of yesteryear remain but, like the Soviet Union, it is impossible to comprehend it as it actually was.

I love my life. I just want to say that. Blacks and whites mix without issue. I get no sense of animosity here. The crowd are roaring at the last stand of Mpofu and Jarvis, chanting "Mpofu, Mpofu" as he craftily steals runs left, right and centre. There is dancing in the crowd. Vuvuzelas intensify in direct proportion to the amount of beer consumed. Mpofu nicks a ball from yet another Windies fast bowler and his fifteen minutes of fame are over. 159 all out.

Ethel is happy for me to stay longer instead of moving into my own place. The MFC will cover my first two weeks here and I will cover my share of the electricity, water, and part of the food bill for the rest. It is a result for me as I never in my wildest dreams expected to come to Zimbabwe and feel so comfortable. When I lived in Sierra Leone, we had no electricity or running water, and as soon as it got dark most evenings, I just crawled inside my mosquito net and sweated for 11 hours.

Ethel tells me that people's names here are often chosen to celebrate what was happening at the time. There are Zimbabweans with names as remembrances to famines and elections. And kids named after what their parents were eating or drinking at the time. Don't be surprised if David Beckham gets to hear about this and calls his next kid avocado! Chuckling, she reels off a list of names that include Margarine, Fanta, Beer, and Ballpoint Pen.

Monday, October 23, 2017

We are looking into the idea of hosting CONIFA's first ever Africa Cup here in Bulawayo. I am working on that as well as the possibility of the 2019 AGM being in Addis.

It is my first experience of local public transport today. Straight from the nearby garage, a minibus to town takes about 10 minutes and costs half a dollar. This is also my first time walking around central Bulawayo alone, rather than jumping in and out of the car, and I have to say I like the vibe here.

Smartly-dressed school kids and tired-but-smiley office workers are knocking off for the day as I meet some of the lads at *Bruce the Goalkeeper's* printing business office. I like the petite girl with the gap in her front teeth who works on his front desk; the first local lady that has really turned my head since I came here.

We are taking the team for fitness training this evening. Khanye is by the town hall as the light fades, but the team are a no-show. A gangly 19-year-old lad is with us but it is basically one player and four staff going for the evening run and fitness session. There should be 20 of them. Alarm bells clanging; it is not exactly an impressive turnout for what is the first official training session attended by the new head coach.

I have been dreading this all day, fearing I won't last. Especially as Busani has the gait of Mo Farah. We jog up to Ascot, an area of opulent looking houses and upscale restaurants hidden away off the main road. We run a slow pace uphill, reaching our destination just as I start to falter. This is another Bulawayo time trap: a former top racecourse dating back to the 1890s, now defunct and overgrown with grass, gigantic weeds, and bushes. The original scoreboard and winning post are still here, rusting away, disappearing further into the undergrowth with each season that passes; like a scene from a post-apocalyptic film.

I make my excuses about running the steps saying *I will do it after a couple of weeks*. Khanye and Co. sprint up and down steep angled steps for a solid ten minutes. Two of those runs would do for me. Four after a month of training. They aren't even puffing and panting from their exertions. I swear that most semi-pro footballers would complete that ten minutes of sprinting then collapse to the grandstand concrete. Very impressive fitness... from the coaches.

If this were South Africa or many other countries, you would never dare come and train somewhere like this: unlit, unpatrolled by any form of security. There'd be junkies at best here, gangsters at worst. At the front of the old racecourse, where a kiosk once stood, it is now a dilapidated social club for a middle-aged to elderly crew of lads.

We walk back to town in the pitch dark, cars flashing by too close for comfort. I am still struggling with the local accent. *Your feet*, I think the young lad tells me when in fact he is saying *You are Fit*. I am happy to win respect off one of the players, especially as I am sure the news will reach the other lads that I can still run around.

As it is so late, I need to get a share bus home which only leaves when it is full. Busani accompanies me this time but says I will need to start doing this alone as he lives on the other side of town. When we jump off at the petrol station, it is as dark as a mine. I can barely see my own arms in front of me. There isn't a single street light in the area. I notice Busani check over his shoulder a couple of times which gives me the fear for when I do this alone. I appear to be the only white living in this suburb. I hope everyone assumes I am a local and not some silly, clueless tourist with a wallet full of cash.

Tuesday, October 24, 2017

I can hardly believe it. I have only been in Zim a week.

To tell the truth, I haven't had a wash in that time as I know how limited water supplies are. Finally plucking up the courage to ask, I get a bucket full of water and have a strip wash. Wow, that feels good. I wonder how many other international football managers have weekly strip washes?

The water is brown by the time I'm done but I literally feel like a new man. Gratitude. Be grateful for all that you have. So many people aren't. They moan and complain and always want more, forgetting all that they already have. I wish all those living in our throwaway culture would live somewhere with limited resources for a while. Be grateful for your doctors and nurses, roads, lights, clean water, heating, electricity, absurd choice of food, a myriad of entertainment options, cheap and affordable flights to anywhere in Europe. Be grateful for your bank card that allows you to pull cash out of an ATM. Be grateful for your passport! And, most of all, be grateful for all the love and friendship in your life.

One of the neighbours collects discarded plastic to help him get by. He's filled the whole back of a lorry with it! Imagine how hard he must have worked to accomplish that! Yes, he is unemployed but he just cashed in $300, a relative fortune in these parts. People here get by; they find a way. They don't give up as easily as they usually do in the West.

Wednesday, October 25, 2017

A blue-headed lizard bops up and down on the shards of broken glass above the garden wall. I have never seen a lizard quite that luminous. The little boy and girl play cops and robbers as we sit on a shaded patch of back porch that attracts a breeze. It is another scorcher today. The little lad is using a wooden airplane as a machine gun, which he shoots at me.

I am longing for the rains to arrive as it is simply too hot between 9 and 3 to do anything outside.

Darfur have pulled out of our December 10 fixture and we've invited Swaziland to take their place. It is a big ask. FIFA member, ranked something like 130 on the planet. It would be a massive, attention-seeking boost if they were to agree. Provided we didn't lose by double figures, which on paper we should do.

We are also discussing getting our best players under contract to protect the MFC from Zim PL clubs and unscrupulous agents. It is in our best interests as well as the lads'. And I am talking to a friend of mine called Roger, who I met up with in the UK before I flew out, who says he is very seriously considering sponsoring the team. Busani admits to being physically and mentally exhausted by it all. He is under big pressure running the under-resourced MFC and dealing with his own stuff. I don't know how he keeps it all together.

Case in point, Busani and I arrive for technical training at the public fields. We are training for free here as our normal pitch is $9 per hour. Khanye has got 4 balls (one of which is flat), 7 cones, and no bibs for us to use. We hope to be playing against countries and ex *Serie A* footballers in a few months' time. Read that sentence again.

Khanye's session is very decent. I have seen plenty of poor, inappropriate sessions in Africa and this most definitely isn't one of them. This lad is clearly a decent coach and can also play a bit. My only criticism would be that none of them has water with them. The concept of rehydration doesn't exist. Yes, it is an amateur thing but I suspect it is also a machismo issue. We train from 5 until after dark at 6.45. It is still close to 30 degrees even with the sun down.

Friday, October 27, 2017

I cannot write this tale without mentioning the one thing that dare not speak its name. The genocide. 50,000 Ndebele were murdered in Matabeleland.

North Korean-trained Fifth Brigade troops went from house to house, unable to verbally communicate with the residents, taking away anyone 'suspected' of being part of the opposition. People were even beaten up and imprisoned for having too much food in their homes, the argument being that they must have had extra food to feed dissidents. Bodies were dumped in giant termite hills and down mine shafts in the rural areas and still remain there today. The opposition is still relatively muted fearing a return to those unspeakable atrocities.

You read and hear all the time about dissidents going missing. Mugabe will never have to answer for his crimes as he is over 80 and therefore won't ever face the War Crimes Court. This is the same bloke the WHO wanted as an ambassador this week, and who is running this beautiful country into the ground.

We meet and schedule our training slots and friendly matches for the month of November, also discussing fundraising ideas, squad and community days, equipment issues, and the South African tour. This feels more like it. A positive meeting that moves us forward.

The weather is taking a massive turn as I walk into town to do my first ever technical session with the Matabeleland team. For this Englishman, perhaps, it is fittingly overcast and windy, and the temperature is dropping like a stone. I am obviously a little nervous in terms of my personal pride, so I am going with a tried and tested session.

Down Fifth Avenue, I pass vegetable market stalls selling potatoes, onions, tomatoes, and giant green peppers. The stalls are stacked high at the end of the working day, and almost nobody is buying.

At the dusty public field, one lad is waiting under a tree with the cones, which I lay out as the boys arrive. I am glad I got here well before them. It is spotting huge drops of rain. The lads do their own thing until we have 11, while my fellow coaches inform me that one of the balls is punctured and actually I have just 3 for a session for which I need 4.

I do a proper warm-up stretching session, a passing combination drill, a possession drill, then an SSG that develops, focussing on possession and switching play. I then finish with a crossbar challenge, with one of the lads, Kiwa, hitting it 3 times from 4 attempts; only two other players manage it at all. He is clearly the set-piece taker for me.

After the exhausting 35 degree heat of late, it is rather hilarious that my first session is in a 20-degree electrical storm. The wind howls, the rain lashes, the lightning flashes all around. The thunder is so loud you'd think bombs were going off in the CBD. A substation appears to blow up in the city just as another bolt hits only a few hundred metres away. Under normal circumstances, I'd abandon a session in these conditions for safety, but that stupid thing called pride prevents me from doing that in my very first session. It is a surreal, scary, and exhilarating experience.

I am caked in mud from the dirt pitch, dust in my eyes mixing with the rain; every lightning strike scaring me and exciting me in equal measure. I think that was a good first session. I am filthy from head to toe. I look like I have been playing Sunday League in November. Thank God one lad is driving and Busani has convinced him to drop me all the way home. His 1980-something Ford Cortina is a sanctuary with heavy rain and lightning from every direction although we can hardly see a thing as the windscreen glass is buggered with air inside the seal.

Saturday, October 28, 2017

I cannot reach our rendezvous point at the city hall. It is cordoned off. There are loads of men in what look like old blue boiler suits holding antique rifles. One van parked outside the pie shop has a dozen of them sat opposite each other in silence on crude wooden benches.

"The big man is in town," the Pie Man tells me. Yes, Robert Mugabe is over there, 250 yards away from me, here in Bulawayo. Some of his security look as ancient as him.

Until yesterday I was thinking:

But after two weeks in South Africa and Zimbabwe, the terrible realisation has hit me that making a success of the Matabeleland project means:

If, previously, I thought we needed to proverbially scale the hilly peaks of the Lake District, then now I realise (having climbed and hiked the first hill) that I can see Mount Kilimanjaro out there in front of us.

Let me explain. The thermometer has dropped an incredible twenty degrees overnight. I am freezing my nuts off on the sideline of yet another awful African football pitch.

I realise that I bought into all that chat, before I came here, about us being good enough to take on African Premier League sides. The 95% passing completion rate on that crap pitch at the first match made me believe it could be true(!) along with Busani's intoxicating personality and chat. This miserable Saturday, however, we are playing in a mini-tournament against what they call locally 'social teams'. In the UK, we would call them Sunday League pub teams. This is a posh part of town and we are hoping to create new friendships with a group of affluent lawyers who are among the few locals who could potentially support our project financially. For starters, it has taken two and a half hours from meeting to actually kicking off the first match. We crammed 12 of us into one car to get here. I wish I'd taken a photo. It is 11 degrees and an icy wind is cutting through us. We disassemble one of those terribly heavy, dangerous goalposts that some pub teams still have to use back home. The kind where a 40-kilo crossbar hangs precariously above two buckling posts, weighed down by huge rocks and metal pegs; a crossbar that doesn't quite fit into the groove of one of those posts. Back in the day, I witnessed one such crossbar drop onto a goalkeeper's head and have always wondered how he didn't die or sustain life-changing injuries. I instinctively step back as the lads try to set up the goal posts. There you go! It has dropped on Khanye's foot and probably fractured a bone or two.

One of the lads is drinking an energy drink as his pre-match beverage. None of them are drinking water. Matabeleland's players are feeling so cold that they change at the side of the pitch at the very last moment before kickoff.

"I'm in the starting eleven, mate," Busani announces, clearly embarrassed. "Professor needs to leave us and run an errand in town."

We are consequently starting the game with ten players, and one of them is part of the management team. Yes, if I thought I was managing a 'national team' of sorts, then think again, because I have got nine players available for a Saturday tournament, a pub team tournament. In fact, if I thought it was appropriate, I could actually start myself today for Matabeleland.

I must admit, I had my reservations about us playing in this. I see no value in playing poor teams. From experience, playing rubbish teams usually leads to playing crap football. But the MFC is relatively short of friends and suffering from poverty, and I don't blame it for trying to alleviate our plight by playing the overweight lawyers.

Gone is the slick passing of last night's training; the ball possession, the imagination, and positive energy of those first two friendly matches. We are nothing more than a half decent pub team playing a man down.

My hands are numb from the cold. I suddenly have a shocking migraine and I am struggling to communicate my thoughts to Khanye, who is barking out non-stop instructions in Ndebele from the sidelines. Our much-hyped centre-forward, Benny, who was a red flag for me at the first training last night, is not following instructions, not playing to the whistle, has bad body language, and is having a shocker. One-on-one with their obese munchkin GK, his first touch is 10 yards too far in front of him. He doesn't come close in two situations where anybody hoping to play in a CONIFA tournament would surely expect to score with ease.

We only score thanks to a brilliant defence-splitting pass from Busani. And when our pub team opponents are awarded a penalty and their 16-stone centre-forward steps up and dispatches it, his belly flopping up and down, I feel like quitting all of this – at this very moment. Yes, we react by scoring a fortuitous winner in injury time but this 'national team' has just edged past a team of overweight lawyers two fucking one.

The lads are sat on the pitchside bench smiling and laughing to one another. They are a very nice bunch of young men. But I cannot believe what I am seeing. If I played in my team in Latvia and won 2-1 against that team of nice fatties, I would have my head dropped in shame wondering what the hell I am doing still playing football at all. Busani launches into the lads. There is no better sense of understanding how good a team is than playing in it. And, as he rightly points out, that was dreadful! Dreadful with an F. We should be winning 4-0 playing with nine men; by seven or eight with ten men. One of the lads from the opposition team comes over and asks if they can play us again, sometime soon.

"You see that! They believe they could beat us next time. FFS lads. You have narrowly beaten a team of fat lawyers who are British local Sunday League Division 3. If we played at the CONIFA World Cup today, we would lose 15-0. If we were lucky. I asked for 10 or 15 passes and to patiently keep possession, and we struggled to complete four. None of you are anywhere near good enough to go to London right now."

Embarrassingly, our win qualifies us for the mini-tournament final where we play an even weaker team. The Professor, a striker, has returned, so we at least have 11. A band has been playing the whole time from the pavilion. They are very good. Certainly, much better than us. Today was supposed to be a family fun day with hundreds attending. The total attendance is about 12, shivering inside the pavilion, necking shots of spirits.

The Professor is easily our best player. He is quick, getting on the end of moves, and we take a 3-0 half-time lead playing just 20 minutes each way. It ends 4-0 and should be seven. But. But. I certainly don't like the fact that the lads celebrate the goals like a bunch of seven-year-olds down the park. I don't want to spoil their fun; their naive natural innocence. But these boys will be eaten up and spat out in London if they don't quickly change their mindset. I feel like a right twat pointing out to them that you cannot be happy beating crap.

Just before the end, we strung together 12 passes. It was easy but it needed Busani there coaching them on the pitch as a player for it to happen. Most disturbingly, our FA President was our second-best player today. There is a lot of comedy in all of this, of course. But Zimbabwe is a long way from home and I didn't come here for the laughs.

It is cringe-worthy and embarrassing hanging around for the medal presentation at the end. Prof is the best player. The only significantly good news of the day is that, as winners, we receive prize money. One hundred dollars which is like a thousand to us. We give the winner's trophy to the team that finished as runners-up.

As if to emphasise the dire straits we are in, our transport back to town is out of action with an oil leak, so we walk back in the dark in pairs through Central and Princes parks. Busani and I collectively fret over the state of the team; Khanye limps way behind with his crossbar injury.

The lads are being treated to a fried chicken supper with part of the winnings. I'm invited but decline as I promised Ethel I'd be home for dinner. In truth, this is a very convenient excuse as I am tired, cold, and don't know what I am doing in Zimbabwe. Humiliation is on the horizon unless we can pull this mob into shape.

I am in bed by 9pm, blanket pulled up over my head, hiding from the world....

... 3am I have awoken with a massive fear on me. I am not up to the task. This either needs years of back-to-the-basics or a UEFA-pro coach to work magic tricks. There is no defensive shape. None. The players are not good enough. I am an amateur. We are now down to two (very bad) footballs. We don't have two pennies to rub together and we need to raise fifty grand! The boys, in all honesty, won't get visas. And if we do pull a miracle and somehow get to London, we will be absolutely humiliated like Darfur were at the last World Football Cup. I will have let down all of these people who have entrusted me. My personal reputation will also be destroyed. This is a complete and utter nightmare. I imagine us trying to scale Kilimanjaro; players perishing on the climb. Busani jumps to his death. Khanye falls down an icy ravine. I sit freezing to death alone in a blizzard.

I toss and turn and cannot get back to sleep the whole night.

Sunday, October 29, 2017

The clocks changed last night in Europe. I have no idea if they did so here. The house is silent. None of last week's gospel. Things need to change. I am going to start with a list of non-football personal goals: Publish a book - Write a trance tune - Take mum somewhere exciting next year to make up for missing her 70th - Cut ties with negative people - Get fitter - Play football in the national league one more season - Help my nieces - Relearn some Russian again for the FIFA WC - Get a second passport - Catch up with old mates - Grow my own food - Make 2019 a year to remember (Copa America, Japan World Cup, Eclipse) - Get my RHR averaging at 57.

I feel much better having done that. I will try to apply some similar focus to the MFC. I believe if you write things down, then you begin the process to enable them to happen. As Victor Hugo said: *Nothing is more powerful than an idea whose time has come.*

I make two separate minibus journeys from home and meet Bruce the Goalkeeper and Busani who are paying $15 with Ecocash for three match tickets at an old school turnstile at the Highlanders Stadium. Wow, this is a trip back into the 1980s. The stadium is completely terraced: giant concrete steps, huge Subbuteo floodlights, all four stands tight to the pitch. We have paid extra and gone for the covered stand, but I have instantly got anxiety as hundreds of lads surge from the open terrace behind the goal, rush a couple of police officers and run – Millwall-style – into our section of the stadium.

"What the hell is going on?"

"Don't worry mate, haha. It is just because of the cold and rain."

Oh. I feel a bit silly now. I appear to be the only white face inside the whole stadium. Every single player and match official is also black.

Officially, alcohol isn't allowed but it is an absolute free-for-all with lads necking 200mil bottles of whisky.

"A white person!" one toothless lad remarks roaring with laughter as he plonks himself down near me. Loads and loads of lads are climbing over a two-metre tall metal partition to get into the VIP section for free. It is one of those situations where if they trip, fall, and do a Humpty Dumpty, they will probably end up dead. But they are all too hard and drunk to worry about such trivialities. And this is Africa. It feels wild in here although I only feel mildly threatened. Mind you, there is the concern that if the Highlanders score, the fans will surge down to the front of the stand, Boca Juniors style, and we will be crushed to death in the melee. What a way to go. The match quality is poor but the wild atmosphere makes up for its shortcomings. This certainly isn't a cheap day out for locals. Four microbus journeys and the entrance ticket totals $7. That must hurt your average punter in these parts.

God, it is cold. I am not kidding when I say this could be Boxing Day 1982 at Northampton Town. I guess 7,000 have braved the conditions today. The winger and the brilliant 21 are mobbed from the sidelines while one of the police Alsatians goes mental. My heartbeat starts to slow. We hang back and leave when the stadium is 90% empty, bumping into the father of one lad who we want to sign. He says he is *happy and honoured* that his son might go to London, although I can tell that, like pretty much everyone else, he thinks we are jokers and doesn't actually believe we will make it there.

Monday, October 30, 2017

I have a very positive chat with Katya. She is finally earning enough money to get by in Latvia and sounds much more positive for it. Not only does that take a massive pressure off me, and us, but just the fact that I can hear she sounds cheerier obviously makes me feel happier. The girl who has never lived alone even admits to not being lonely. Stop it! I know what you are thinking!

Tuesday, October 31, 2017

In Ndebele culture, it is standard for the neighbours of someone who has just passed away to help raise the funeral costs. They also cook food and stay up all night with the bereaved widow and the body. Ethel returns having spent all night helping one of her neighbours and tells me how the son returned from South Africa drunk, and looking for money. He insisted they move the body to another room, scared off at least three of the ladies (who were kindly doing the overnight shift) and then beat up a friend of his who had apparently come to pay his respects. "We were so scared we thought he was going to kill him. He also removed the coffin lid which is taboo."

Ethel, legend that she is, went to the local community leader in the middle of the night with the injured friend. Apparently, the police got involved; they gave the son 'something to remember' and took him away. Everyone you speak to, here, fears those coming from South Africa because of the culture of violent crime there. Some of those heading north, come with weapons and ammunition and the Zimbabwe police are said to make it a policy to crack down heavily on anyone – local or not – who comes into the country from the south and starts behaving in a criminal way.

The community leader resealed the coffin and Ethel was able to come home finally at 6. An hour later, dressed smartly for church, she wakes me to tell me the story, prepares breakfast for me, and says she is returning to the funeral from where she will head straight to church. You sense that it is neighbours and a sense of community that is the glue that keeps this country from falling apart.

I make my own way to training and put on what I think is a very good session. In the process, we attract attention from a local national league club, whose boss comes over to ask whether I am available to work with them also.

I play in one of the drills (two against seven) and I just about break down, my heart rate spiking at 181. I end the session with 50-yard one-on-ones with the goalkeeper and then jog home, getting back as car headlights briefly light up the all-consuming darkness.

In the Northern Hemisphere, it is Samhain. You can call it Halloween if you wish. My mate Kelvin sends me an image of a magnificently sculpted pumpkin he has prepared for his son. I know my nieces will be enjoying a Halloween party. They love this festival. Ethel is understandably exhausted after last night's funeral debacle and a full day of church duties, and is soon snoring in front of the TV. I have got stomach ache for a third time from eating sadze (a type of porridge), which clearly does not suit my constitution.

6: M is in B

Wednesday, November 1, 2017

Once upon a time, Bulawayo was known as the cleanest city in all of Africa. Now people have lost their pride and it is commonplace to just drop rubbish absolutely everywhere. They used to fine people for littering the centre of town. Busani and I are discussing the idea of making our community day the first of many monthly cleanups, with an emphasis on rejuvenating the central park and all that potential it has for the civic community. I tell Busani about *Let's Do It*, the organisation from Estonia and their one-day cleanups all around the world, which make a fantastic impact. Quite apart from the potential for good and positive publicity for the MFC, this can improve the quality of life of the masses and it might genuinely help kickstart a rejuvenation project for the park and central areas. The plastic collected could be sold and donated to a local charity or used to fund the project's development.

It is my monthly CONIFA Exco meeting. Our main topic of conversation is the stadia we will use in London with Charlton Athletic being discussed as potentially hosting the opening game and final. We are looking at ticket prices being 10 quid with 10% of that going to each member.

Thursday, November 2, 2017

I set up a meeting between CONIFA and a potential sponsor and write my own list of recommendations about stadia and ticketing. I also spend an hour speaking to *Let's Do It Estonia*, planning my coaching session, and then find myself in the members bar at Queens with a cold Castle.

"Please take off your cap – no caps allowed in here sir." Love it. Keeping the old standards. I look across the room from my bar stool.

THIS IS YOUR CLUB. DRESS SMART CASUAL. NO TRAINING PLAYING KIT. FULL TRACKSUITS ALLOWED.

Look at this place! Wooden plaques celebrate the visits of Lancashire CCC, Bucks RFC, and Cheshire Cats Zimbabwe Tour 84-85. Dozens of dust-ridden ceiling fans are falling into disrepair. Trophies line glass display cabinets along the walls, fading famous player caricature portraits sit in off-centre frames. Martini and Gordons Gin mirrors look like they have been gathering dust for decades. Cricket bats and old touring blazers gather even more dust in what look like abandoned fish bowls. I can't believe a bottle of beer is still a dollar in here in this day and age. The only sense that this bar exists in 2017 is the TV and a sign displaying the ECOCASH MERCHANT CODE.

The umpires and captains remove the bales, and it is done. Both sides accept a draw and the series ends 1-0 to the Windies. Zim's Raza is apparently only the third cricketer in test history to score 80-plus in two innings and to take five wickets. He understandably gets MOM and says he is honoured to be in the same frame as such famous names.

I must admit to feeling a wee bit tipsy as I depart the stadium ahead of training. Tonight's session is just over the road, behind the Hartsfield Stadium. After hanging around for 30 minutes and nobody showing up, I begin walking back towards town assuming I have got my wires crossed. A couple of hundred yards down the road, one of the players finds me and tells me I did have the correct spot. Apparently, Busani put out a message on WhatsApp saying we were training at the public pitch just to see how many other teams or people came down to watch my session.

"Several teams came down. The place was full with people." I'm told. You have got to laugh really. A crowd gathering to watch me coach! More smoke and mirrors but it seems like it is needed, sadly. We do fear sabotage from outsiders, losing players to other clubs, or indeed me being arrested and deported for God knows what.

The session goes well again. I am amazed by the quality of possession in the 4 v 2, 2 v 4 drill. Fourteen players is my best turnout to date. But the lads look weak when running on goal. Timid is the word. Five lads score directly from corners in my corner challenge at the end of training.

Busani had to spend six hours queuing in the bank today to take out a few quid. Can you imagine? What a state of affairs.

I run, jog, walk, and pant my way home in the darkness and pop over the road for water and a cornmeal drink. My word, crap low-grade 400g pasta has gone from 0.69 to 1.09 to 1.39. It has doubled in price in three weeks. This shit would cost 30 pence in Europe. I find I am eating less and less each day, currently. The MFC don't actually have the money to subsidise my food as they had planned. Tonight, dinner is a potato and half a tin of beans. I am very grateful for it, though. Looking in the mirror, for the first time I can see I am starting to lose weight.

Friday, November 3, 2017

Helicopters whirr whirr all night at the local aerodrome. I find the noise of helicopters at night very sinister. Something is going on in Bulawayo.

ZIMBABWE COULD DESCEND INTO CIVIL WAR a leading newspaper cheerfully predicts today. Apparently, there was some kind of clash between the military and the police back in August. Other pointers are the war going on inside ZANU PF, the recent sacking of 21 members of the opposition, the escalating cash crisis, and the return to hyperinflation. All of this could merge into one perfect storm.

On top of all this, Robert Mugabe is back in Bulawayo for a huge graduation ceremony. The town is full of government agents, troops, and fake supporters bussed in. All this means I need to lie low as there will be security personnel asking for documents everywhere and as a British tourist wandering around with a dubiously weak sounding story, I could end up being detained under suspicion of all kinds of things with Mugabe in town. On Saturday, there is going to be a huge rally at the White City Stadium. Soldiers and police will be in the vicinity for a couple of days as well as, of course, the government agents reporting back to Harare.

Outside, though, the birds cheep, the flowers bloom, kids laugh, and it feels like an early June heatwave in England. How strange to be hiding myself away in a house fearful of going outside and getting arrested when in truth I am not guilty of any crime or, indeed, negative intent.

Poor Busani is under massive pressure. He has burned through all of his savings supporting the MFC and his trip to a UN conference in Kigali could be off. Truthfully, and despite good intentions, they cannot afford to host me as they had intended with rent, a daily food allowance, transport in Zimbabwe, and internet. I am already paying for a lot of things I never thought I would have to cover. If Roger keeps to his word about supporting me and the MFC, then that will really take some of the pressure off. Having to part finance my girlfriend, who is ill and subsequently not earning money, is just another additional headache I am going to have to deal with from afar. Katya's European Schengen visa runs out on March 1st. It is causing us massive stress. I don't know the answer. Whirr whirr go the helicopters. I don't sleep well.

Saturday, November 4, 2017

I feel like I am under house arrest. Town will be infested. There are roadblocks everywhere, including just up the road from the house. Mugabe apparently wants the death penalty reinstated, and an American woman is the first person in Zimbabwe to ever get arrested under new social media laws; arrested for a tweet about Mr M.

I am increasingly paranoid about what I write and to whom. And the problem with paranoia is you never know how close your imaginings are to the truth. I haven't posted a single message on Twitter since I came here. Skype I feel relatively safe using. Emails I am very dubious about, sort of assuming some are read, and with Facebook – I am certainly being careful about what I say. Mugabe is simply referred to as M. And while M. is in B., almost everyone is scared to utter his name or complain about anything more divisive or controversial than the weather.

As a British friend who knows the region and the workings of such states advised me before I came out here: "Keep your footprint on social media to an absolute bare minimum but make sure you are in constant contact with friends and family so if anything happens to you, your silence is spotted very quickly."

Saturday, November 5, 2017

Just as I go to leave the house, I spot two likely lads loitering outside. They don't seem quite right to me. I put off leaving and find myself peeping out of the crack in the gate to make sure they have reached the end of the road and turned out of sight. It is like an episode of Spooks but I could be imagining it all.

At least half a dozen pairs of eyes fix on me as I tiptoe out into the street and head down towards town. I stop after a couple hundred yards, buying some time smelling some flowers and examining my sports watch to see whether anyone is following me. Simultaneously, two blokes cross past each other and both stop. Jeez, they are staring down the road at me. I play with another flower bloom and glance back down to the end of the road. One guy is stood still, still staring in my direction. The paranoia. Normally, I exchange *hellos* and *how's it* with passers-by but, this sunny Sunday morning, I have got my head down trying to make my face disappear into my cloth cap and unkempt beard.

I turn onto the main road and walk for about ten minutes before I start swearing under my breath. *Fuck's sake*. Over to my right, five army trucks are parked up and full of armed soldiers. A load more are stood to attention on waste ground. I cross the Harare Road and an army truck passes. I don't dare look interested or make eye contact. *Fuck's sake*, my heart rate is quickening. There are pairs of police stationed on street corners. I am keeping my head down so much that I trip on a rock and almost end up face down. With Mugabe in town, there is definitely a darker air. People are noticeably less friendly; less affable than they usually are. They seem to eye one another with suspicion or with their heads down.

Our first game today is up at Barbourfields. We pass another five army trucks en route, parked up with troops being drilled. There is also the bizarre sight of two police dogs and fully-armed riot police practicing under the shade of a blooming Red Flamboyant tree. My fear is melon sized.

Busani's Sunday League team, which five of the boys play for, is playing on the decent grass pitch under the shadow of the Barbourfields Subbuteo floodlights. There is actual grass on these pitches! Some lads I get chatting to are saying that some activists have been beaten by the police; arrested and detained at His Majesty's pleasure. I spot one bloke watching our game who appears to be fiddling with what looks like dog tags around his neck. I am absolutely sure he is army. I don't mention it to anyone. Suspicion is a terrible thing. But at least it keeps you on your toes. *Things seem to be deteriorating rapidly*, I comment to one of the strangers. *Yes, it is getting worse, day by day now.* He comments. *It feels like a revolt has started.*

A fistfight breaks out on the adjacent pitch and ends with a mob of blokes chasing a couple of lads down the road. It is the first such incident I have witnessed in Zimbabwe. Can't say it helps my fear. I lie down on the grass so I can be out of sight of the army bloke. What is that shocking, stinging sensation? FFS, I have only been sat in an ants' nest for ten minutes. There are hundreds of them inside my shoes, all over my tracksuit, and up my bum crack. I hop around, swearing. So much for not drawing attention to myself.

Our lads go 4-1 up. This is Zimbabwe Division Three and, in all honesty, is probably a lower standard than the Latvian league I played in last season aged 46. Some of our lads are playing worse because they are playing with considerably worse players. I have got to have a word with the MFC about this bollocks. It just can't be helping. Once this season is done, I don't want our lads participating in 2018.

One of our lads sees red then hits out at the player. He retaliates and is also off, followed by a load of theatrical handbags. Seriously, what the hell am I doing here? The game ends 4-3; Bruce the Goalkeeper lets one through his legs in comical style. A diminutive player called Whisper is our best player but he doesn't even play for the MFC. The same Whisper is the coin collector on our microbus, we have commissioned back into town.

The affable coach of Bulawayo Chiefs asks me down to their training next match. Busani says they are trying to poach me. They'd be better poaching an egg following how I feel about everything today. Our 2pm game kicks off 90 minutes late after the lads have had banana sandwiches and Mazoe squash. It is absolute madness for these boys to be playing another 90 minutes after playing 90 this morning in 30-degree heat. For God's sake, most of them haven't consumed even a drop of water.

Our centre-half, Kiwa, gets sent off after just ten minutes as he deliberately handballs a goal-bound shot. They score from the penalty spot. Playing 80 minutes with ten men is a disaster but, on the plus side, there are many lessons to be learned. Especially as we give them another penalty, which they score from, ten minutes later. I am up in the stands trying to get a better appreciation of the players while Busani and Khanye coach below. The truth is that one lad is excellent, two are decent, three or four have potential, while the rest are poor or worse.

We are 1-2 down and it should be 1-5, but our opponents miss several sitters before Benny releases the Professor who finishes well to make it 2-2. A sublime five-pass move from the back ending up with the centre-forward should make it 3-2 for us, but he tries to go around the keeper. It's very respectable to finish 2-2 against such a decent team, particularly after playing 80 minutes with ten.

Some lads finished their 180 minutes of football today as the stronger individuals in the final 15. But clearly (and it is a big but) most of these lads are nowhere near good enough to play at a CONIFA WFC. And I have rarely seen a side with less defensive shape. We need to play fewer games and get on the training ground instead.

I tell the boys I am proud of how they finished the game and how they battled with ten men for 80 minutes. But I am honest when I tell them that, for me, only three played well while the rest of them were only OK at best. Only 14 lads turned up today. As things stand, we are in big big trouble. Yes, we have got four players who can compete but we have got no money, no footballs, we are scared to go public about the project, and Zimbabwe feels like it is about to completely implode.

7: El Presidente & the Circus

Monday, November 6, 2017

Mugabe is scared of Bulawayo. He came here with so many bodyguards, soldiers, police, military vehicles, paid thugs and rhetoric that he must be absolutely terrified of this place. The old dictator probably fears that he is going to draw his last breath here from a sniper's bullet. I was thinking about the scale of that operation yesterday and what it tried to convey. Imagine Northern Ireland in 1980 and the Queen or Thatcher going to the most Catholic place in the country, a hot spot like Derry and holding a 50,000 rally of Protestants at the football stadium, most of them British troops in their civies.

British troops and police on every street corner, arresting any Catholics brave or foolish enough to protest, beating them up and throwing them into prison. In fact, better still, make it Dublin – a place unlike Derry that seems devoid of state security apparatus on a 'normal day'. Thatcher telling those gathered that Dublin needs to change its game and support her... or else. And most Catholics cannot get a job. Unemployment is 90%. The price of cooking oil has gone up 100% in a month. You need to queue six hours at the bank and, if you are lucky, withdraw a maximum of 20 Punts for spending a day in line.

Ethel's' collection of plastic is really growing in size. Some people wouldn't be seen dead collecting rubbish. Ethel is a proud lady but she has no problem doing it. She says she likes the fact that it helps clean up the streets and that removing all the remaining labels before putting it all in giant bags isn't at all stressful. She is going to use the income raised, when she cashes it in in December, for a Christmas Day party. Respect.

I haven't shaved or trimmed my grey beard for eight weeks. I look like an Afrikaans Roy Keane. Initially, it was for style, then to avoid the need to wet shave in Africa. But after a short time in Zimbabwe, I realised it serves as a disguise of sorts. Not only do I look like one of the local former landowners but the hairier I get, the more my face disappears into the beard. With El Presidente & the Circus (good band name) gone, I have decided to trim it all. I clearly cannot go to a hairdresser, the nosiest, best-informed people around. *So Sir, in Zimbabwe for work or pleasure?* An hour in the mirror carefully pruning and trimming. Twenty quid in much of Europe; I will take that as my day's salary. Ethel does a double take as if a stranger is at the door when she returns home from errands. I also begin my exercise campaign today, barely managing the sit-ups.

Busani, Khanye, and me discuss yesterday's performance before Busani heads off to Rwanda tonight, where he is speaking at a UN conference. Maybe I am being a bit harsh on the lads, but I believe I will need to be hard-nosed at times for us to succeed. What is the point of taking a load of passengers to the WFC who aren't good enough to compete? There are huge limitations on me doing my job here, but I already believe that my input is a big plus for Matabeleland. They need managing as much as they need coaching, and for that I certainly don't doubt my ability to guide them in a better direction.

Ethel takes me for an early evening stroll to meet some of the 'neighbours'. Neighbours in Zimbabwe is a bit like it used to be in my Nan's day in Northamptonshire, meaning anyone you are sociable with up to three streets away. In a country like Zimbabwe, where the words society and community still have meaning, the neighbours we meet are a ten-minute walk away. Our first visit is to Ethen who Ethel nannies. His finger went septic playing with God-knows-what and his very attractive mum is off work taking care of him. A doctor's consultation is still free here, for kids, but he has ended up needing private consultation and medicine and the bill has come in at $60.

Ethan is in pieces, snoring like a lion after taking the prescribed drugs. We sit with his affable mum and Ethan's grandmother in their lovely three-bedroom bungalow. All these places have beautiful mahogany floors. Decades-old, but aside from the odd scratch, still as good as new. There is a lovely shaded balcony which looks out on a lush green garden.

Ethan's gran has a borehole so she can water her veg and immaculately kept fruit trees, which look like Bonsai trees. When lawns can be watered in Matabeleland, they are the most glorious green. Sadly, these days boreholes now cost anything from $3-6k to install, so the days when the middle class could afford them have practically gone.

I realise it is quite weird for some of the older generation to have a white man in their homes. It must, without doubt, bring flashbacks of Rhodesia when they themselves were not much more than glorified slaves to the owners of these same bungalows. They weren't even allowed out on the streets from 6 till 6. I bet a white person hasn't stepped foot in most of these properties in decades.

Our next visit is to a couple who look like they are in their 50s. This bloke cracks me up. There is such a young smiley face hiding behind the grey and wrinkles. As always, it is South African TV that is being watched. Breaking news is that Mugabe has just sacked Mnangagwa, his VP, the man many people had hoped was going to be the transitional leader of Zimbabwe after Mugabe wins next year's rigged elections and his health finally goes after a year or two.

El Presidente is trying to manoeuvre his wife, Grace, into the co-pilot seat for next June's elections. I fear it will be dangerous being here next April in the lead-up to the elections, shortly before we head to London. Actually, I doubt whether anyone will manage to get a volunteer visa for me when we apply next year; the authorities might well conclude I am here to do undercover monitoring or to subvert.

The husband is roaring at the news. Grace M is universally unpopular, even with the Shona, especially after she beat up a female model in Joburg. Talk about the mask slipping. Mnangagwa is well connected to the military, and there must now be the real possibility of the military taking over. Last time there was an attempt to do something like that, a load of high-ranking officers later died in car accidents and poisonings. M has the military infiltrated at all levels, they say, but can a man of 93 – in ill health – really keep the lid on all of this?

Both neighbours are laughing, almost crying, when I tell them that their properties in a good UK city suburb would command half a million dollars or more. You can currently buy one of their houses for $45,000.

Tuesday, November 7, 2017

One of the many reasons I will never go too far in football management is that I am too empathetic. I gave the five lads who were late for training a rocket, and one of them was saying *I'm sorry, sir* and looked like he could cry. He then had a shocker in training. I end up feeling sorry for the lad a whole 24 hours later and wish I had never said anything in the first place.

Some of these lads are no way good enough to get on the plane in May but I can only imagine how much it will destroy them if they don't make the final squad. And I don't want to do that to them; I really don't. These lads are so decent, honest and respectful. Thus far, I cannot even see a rough diamond among them. No nasty bastards despite many of them living out in the projects. For this team to improve, I have got to be a bit nasty at times but I do not want to be.

Only six turn up for the start of training, when it is still 30 degrees.

"If it continues like this lads, I am not coming back next year."

I wish some of the lads were arseholes. I roomed close to the South Ossetia, Abkhazia, Isle of Man, and North Cyprus teams at the CONIFA Euros and, no disrespect to them but, there were plenty of rough lads who might get involved in a fight outside a pub among that collective. Without at least a couple of players like that, we have got no chance. But, that aside, I have to take my hat off to the Ndebele community of Bulawayo for producing such nice, polite, honest and friendly boys. As a human being, I don't want them to change, but as a manager I think it is vital that some do. We might need to import one or two nasty bastards into the final squad.

Eventually, we have 12 at training and I get to do the things I planned with my session. The lads are very conservative when they get near goal. This is going to need a lot of work. Right now, we are down to just one ball. Yes, the Matabeleland Football Team has one football... and no nets.

Wednesday, November 8, 2017

No electricity.

This is an example of what you might call the "challenges" of managing Matabeleland. Today, I have dedicated much of the day to planning sessions, looking at ideas for improving team shape, and writing up extensive notes I keep about the team. Until my computer battery finally fails.

It has taken me a month to really start to understand the team, the players, and the dynamics at play. I can now cater training to what we need rather than putting on more generic sessions. If only I had equipment, support from Roger (who is radio silent) as promised, and money to run things day-to-day. We could be so far ahead of where we are now. Ethiopian Airlines have offered me group rates of around $750 per person for us to fly to London. It requires a non-refundable deposit of $4,000 in the next 27 days. We also need some considerable coin for the South African matches on December 10. That could run to a similar figure. I literally have no idea where seven or eight grand is going to arrive from in the next three or four weeks.

I want to improve my coaching while I'm back in Europe and prepare a folder full of technical sessions for my hopeful return. The coaching system in such bollocks in all honesty. I want and need to do a higher qualification to improve myself but most coaches based abroad, who haven't already got their badges, are in a right mess with it all. I have no practical way that I can do my UEFA B, so I am looking at other options to better myself. I am wondering whether I can go and hang out with a club for a week and just observe. Originally, I was heading to Red Bull Salzburg with Roger in January. There is Riga United's connection to Bayern Munich. Maybe Northampton Town? Perhaps even 'The Master', Chris Wilder, at Sheffield United? Yeah, nothing to lose, I am going to write to Chris and ask. The lad is a gent, and my bet is he will reply to me at the very least.

SACKED FORMER VP FLEES THE COUNTRY

My mate Graham, who lives in Latvia, wants to send some equipment out to us. Very kind. Graham asks me how it's going. I tell him that in comparison, our club Riga United seems like an EPL club when it comes to facilities, equipment, and finances. Matabeleland have got a better squad, though, thank God.

I purposely turn up 15 minutes late for training to make the lads wonder and find nine of them already there. We have 14 by the end. During training, our new goalkeeper – Nonja – pulls off an unbelievable save showing his potential. Praise has been the most consistent player since I came here. He plays centre-half or holding midfield but in the shooting drills today, he comes out top lashing the ball into the net from various angles. The sweeper is also clearly very talented but needs to be coached and play somewhere else on the pitch. Both lads should be on the plane to London. I am trying to encourage the team to shoot whenever an opportunity presents itself. They have this habit of wanting to walk the ball into the net.

A MILITARY COUP IS LIKELY IN ZIMBABWE is the optimistic and frankly realistic headline of Sunday evening's Bulawayo 24.

Thursday, November 9, 2017

Early on when I started living here, I felt a bit frustrated and lost at how I spent my days. Yes, I enjoyed the peace but I felt time was being wasted. Now, I absolutely love having hours to plan my coaching properly. When I was in Europe, most of my sessions were prepared under time pressure and I found that very stressful and, of course, counterproductive. A routine of sorts is evolving. I count myself extremely lucky to have mornings to myself for meditating, writing, thinking, breathing, exercising, working, planning, developing my own things and resting.

As an example, it hits 4pm and the day hasn't as much as flown by as "in-the-zoned-by". Training goes really well. The session is focused on using wingers. I am especially pleased to see the lad who had a howler on Tuesday – Xolani – star with a great headed goal and a superb defensive interception. He also wins my mini competition for who has the longest goal kick. As ever, the champ leads the cooldown and you can almost see him grow as he leads the slow jog around the pitch in the half-light.

So much of football is in the mind. I need each of these boys to find consistency and to become stronger mentally.

Kuhle is absolutely class crossing on both feet. He doesn't play left wing but, clearly, he could or should. I want these boys to learn two or three positions. Many of them are technically brilliant footballers and I can see perhaps three or four of them playing in different roles to which they are accustomed. Having several players who can play in different roles is part of my footballing philosophy.

Most homes in Matabeleland have South African TV. The nightly news bulletins are something. Don't watch them if you are suffering from the fear that particular day. Today we have a story about an ambulance being attacked in Cape Town, the medics held at gunpoint and the poor little 8-year-old boy being rushed to hospital after a car crash, subsequently dying from his injuries during the holdup. Another story is about a bloke who enslaved women and forced them to have sex with dogs in Gauteng. Then there is the scandal about the 150 mentally ill patients who were abused, experimented on, and seemingly murdered by the local health authority. It is all so bloody disturbing.

Friday, November 10, 2017

Hundreds of flying ants are prancing around in the rain as I peer out. Is this finally the start of the rainy season? It was torrential most of the night. In fact, I woke up at one point, forgot myself, and somehow thought I was back in England. Big puddles have appeared in the yard and the birds go mental with excitement as ants crash and burn.

I finally make it to Indaba café, in town, which is the first establishment I have found reminiscent of Europe. I want to read the local press to get a better sense of what is going on. *Pump up the volume* plays as a bloke in a brown corduroy suit strolls past street signs and long since defunct billboards, stuck in time. There are more whites in here than I have seen on the streets of Bulawayo in the past seven days.

Punters order expensive lunches and breakfasts and leave half of it. Classic Western fucking wastage. *Because I am worth it.* Leave half my lunch and move on to a humongous-sized piece of cheesecake. No matter that

I can see mothers with their kids trudging past on the street with barely a penny to their name.

Mnangagwa was dismissed for 'disloyalty, deceitfulness, and ineptitude'. You might not like Mugabe but you have to respect the 93-year-old's use of the English language. His ego, though, certainly knows no bounds. Yesterday, Harare International Airport was renamed Robert Gabriel Mugabe International Airport. He must know he is on his way out.

Back home, Ethel's daughter calls me into the kitchen. "Come and look at this." There must be 100 flying ants circling the light bulb. Others have started to make their way down the corridor and into the lounge and my bedroom. So many are crashing up against the bungalow's windows that it sounds like it is raining outside. And as a car drives down our road, headlights on full beam, the ants create the effect of a snowstorm. I have never seen a swarm of insects like this in 25 years and 125 countries of travel. I am glad I wasn't jogging back from training as I think it would have freaked the hell out of me.

"The Matabele people like to roast the flying ants and eat them," Ethel tells me. "The snakes also come into the garden to eat them. Lots of snakes." A moment when you thought you were living in an exotic, mildly dystopian 1960s version of England but realise you are actually living in Africa after all.

The flying ant swarms mark nature's acknowledgment that the Zimbabwean rainy season has begun. Much bigger flying creatures will appear later. "Tastier ones," Ethel tells me as we watch Bafana Bafana losing 2-0 to World Cup-bound Senegal in the final Russia qualifier. "Scorpions. Yes, they get into the crevices of the house and start to move around. The big ones are dangerous. Black mambas in Matobo. Be careful when you go there."

Saturday, November 11, 2017

Busani didn't get back from Rwanda until 11pm last night and our planned community clean-up day has been cancelled. Unusually, the players have been given a Saturday off.

Four people have been arrested in Bulawayo for the heinous crime of booing the delectable Grace Mugabe.

With the rainy season upon us it is important to get on top of the garden; weeding and tilling the soil. I watch Ethel hard at work and assist where I can. Maybe it is simply the change of season but I feel like everything has caught up with me. I sleep half the day and crash very early, ready for my crack-of-dawn departure for Botswana tomorrow to renew my visa.

8: Windolene smuggler

Sunday, November 12, 2017

What would you know! Ethel is ready with my breakfast tray at 6am. I enjoy a very pleasant stroll into town with a couple of *good morning sirs*, cool crisp air, admiring the fully blooming Red Flamboyant trees; everywhere so gloriously quiet. Bulawayo's vegetable stalls are being busily set up as I reach the streets north of the city hall. Busani very thoughtfully turns up shortly before my departure to make sure I get off OK.

Strange that as the bus leaves Bulawayo, I become sensitive to pangs of sadness, imagining that I could be leaving for good. Is my intuition telling me things are about to kick off in Zimbabwe? I love that there are trees on every street in Bulawayo; growing out of the concrete. The Blue Jacaranda and Flamboyant Red in full bloom really are a sight that should be seen for their aesthetic beauty. There is an honesty to Bulawayo and its people – special qualities that I am not yet able to quantify or give a tangible sense of.

We pass through the city's industrial zone, some of it still functioning, much of it reminiscent of many parts of Eastern Europe: defunct and rusting away. In the early days, after independence, this city really must have been something; very probably the finest city in Africa in those days.

One moment you are driving through a city suburb reminiscent of Sofia in the 90s and the next you are out in the African bush! It is a shock to the system every time you leave Bulawayo and remind yourself you are actually living in Africa. Flat scrub and tree land as far as the eye can see; barbed wire fences segregating land and the odd glimpse of dishevelled subsistence farmers toiling away. The young stewardess interrupts the pleasant drum-backed African gospel on the radio to lead prayers for our journey.

"Please protect this bus and its passengers. We offer gratitude for all the good we have in our lives."

It is a beautiful moment.

Matchstick cartoon birds get disturbed by the bus, then settle on tree branches by the roadside. A large troop of monkeys is dispersed, the alphas standing their ground, almost seeming to mouth *Do you want some?*

Huge rocky boulders occasionally rise from the otherwise flat terrain as we cover the 200 kilometres to Francistown. Close to the border a man who looks like a young Chris Eubank gets on the bus, says prayers and blesses everyone.

"I am the messenger," he keeps repeating, then explains to everyone the rather obvious process that will soon take place at the border post.

Zimbabwean customs and immigration give me zero hassle. There is a No Man's Land of a few kilometres between the two countries which looks rather like a half-abandoned Afrikaans farmstead. We are each required to walk through Botswana customs and open our individual bags to the officials but it is not as if anyone here is going to be smuggling stuff from Zimbabwe to Botswana with the prices on "this side" compared to "that side". It is, however, now illegal to cross the border in either direction with fruit and veg. Eubank floats around making sure everyone is alright (without actually doing anything). His grey dress shirt, buttoned at the collar, looks like a woman's blouse.

As we successfully exit customs, he makes some speech about having helped us all reach "our final destination on this fine Sunday" and then, yes, asks everyone for money. I can't believe that some people are giving him $2 bond notes and he looks to have earned $10 from his rather comical efforts. Fools and their money are easily parted.

I have been to Botswana once before, cycling and hitching through here in 2010 after crossing the Zambezi on a dodgy car ferry. I find it to be a rather odd country with its modern, European-standard infrastructure, and down-at-heel villages, where most locals seem to sit around looking bored. Some of the bush here looks one step away from turning into desert. There are noticeably more electric fences and barbed wire around the houses as we enter Francistown and there's a slight shock to see a minaret. I am astounded by the pace of the spread of Islam around the world that I have witnessed during my quarter-century of travel.

We are dropped off at a petrol station where most of the passengers who are not travelling on to Gaborone jump into taxis. I very rarely do taxis when travelling alone and get pointed down the busy A1 dual carriageway. One of the first sights is a man with his cock out openly urinating in our direction three yards from the main footpath. Classy. Many of the lads passing me are six foot something. Amazing really when you consider how generally tiny the neighbouring Ndebele are. I must have walked a kilometre and seem to be heading out of town. I stop a taxi driver turning at a junction who points me back to where I started.

I am staying at the Peermont Metcourt which shares its space with a casino. Oh wow, air con 19 degrees, super-fast WIFI, plasma telly with 7 channels of Super Sport, comfy mattress and duvet, tea & coffee machine, hot shower, fridge. I am Alan Partridge in a Botswana Travel Tavern! *Back of the net!* I cry as the hot water hits my body, my first shower in weeks! *Jurassic Park!* (with a fist pump) as I discover England v Argentina live. I could stay in this room all day but my visa run is also a shopping trip on behalf of the MFC and Ethel.

Central Francistown is a soulless American-style mix of malls, car parks, and neon-lit fast food chains. It feels like a monolithic motorway service station in the middle of the African bush. JG Ballard could have written a novel about this place. I have decided I am going to buy Ethel all of her groceries plus a few extras. She more than deserves it and it's a small token for how she has made me feel at home in her country. How different this place feels to Zimbabwe. Walking around Shoprite in Botswana, I could be in ASDA in Milton Keynes. My three-hour shop costs $37. I reckon it would cost $100 in Zim.

The Zimbabweans joke that the people of Botswana are incredibly stupid and uneducated. This place does remind me a little of the film Idiocracy. Someone selling you a single banana and onion in Zim seems very smart as they have likely got a Uni degree and bags of common sense. Here, though, many shop assistants have the vacant look of a dairy cow grazing in a field. Mind you, if I was sentenced to a life in Francistown, I think I would end up looking equally vacant.

Monday, November 13, 2017

From my bedroom window, in Francistown, I survey the concrete and glass utopia. We all live in America. They won't be satisfied until they have concreted over the Amazon and we are all drinking Gatorade.

I buy two match balls and six training bibs for $84. I have enjoyed the sanctuary and luxuries of my room but I am delighted to leave this very silly town.

Two would-be murderers offer me the opportunity to jump in their car and travel with them to Bulawayo. I decline and buy an international bus ticket off an affable lady called Agnes sat on a plastic chair in a petrol station forecourt. There is nothing to say she is genuine; never mind a uniform or badge.

At the border, I am a little nervous. If I get knocked back here, it is game over for me as an international football manager.

"I am giving you a month, OK?"

Visa valid until 12/12. Phew.

Every single passenger has to present every single bag to customs who check that every single customs declaration matches the contents of every single bag.

All of us are 'smuggling' goods into Zimbabwe but the actual number of genuine smugglers probably numbers two. When products cost 2-3 times less, who wouldn't try to bring home goods from a foreign visit?

"Pay $200 and you can get pretty much get anything through this border," a passenger tells me under their breath.

Eubank is back helping to facilitate our safe and smooth passage. It's like a game of Supermarket Sweep or Bullseye. *What's in there? Clothes.* Open it up and it's a compact disc player! *Bed sheets.* It's a 24-piece set of matching cutlery. *Groceries.* Two dozen boxes of rich tea biscuits. It is anything from two to fifteen minutes per passenger. I am thinking the whole time: how am I going to explain the 10-pack of super soft toilet rolls as a backpacker? I can't believe I have actually become a toilet roll smuggler. What will happen if they find the kilo of bran flakes, I have tried to conceal under some underpants?

"What do you have sir?"

"Err, my computer, my things, umm some groceries... my footballs." My footballs, haha.

"Please open up your bags."

A tin of beans spills out. How embarrassing. Kilo of milk powder. Suspicious.

"Please show me what is under there."

Crouching, I remove a plastic bag used for concealment and look straight up at him. Our eyes meet and he has got a pained expression of *why on earth would a backpacker have a giant container of Windolene in his baggage?*

"And that?" He asks in a tone that suggests he is about ready to quit his job; a British backpacker finally pushing him over the edge.

"Washing powder."

Yes, I always go travelling with a two-kilo giant-sized bag of Surf washing powder, and an 890g bottle of salad cream. A couple of my fellow passengers gesticulate to him – come on, give the guy a break, he is just a tourist bringing someone he knows a couple of things – and, shaking his head, the official stamps my blessed blue form. Thank God he never found the four hidden plastic containers of fabric conditioner refills or the ladies' deodorants. I might have been detained for just being damn weird.

It is another wasted hour in our collective lives before everyone is finally checked. Eubank has done a good job of looking like he is being really helpful without actually doing anything. If I fail with Matabeleland, I might diversify into what he does. I have counted eight different zip pockets on his very zippy jeans where he must spread his hourly deposits of cash. Someone has clearly panicked and discarded their 3-kilo giant-sized bag of high-grade pasta. What an absurd situation this really is. The state making such a fucking mess of the economy that ordinary citizens have to go through this.

"What must the little (uniformed) school boys make of this?" an Indian Zim lady asks, as she tries to justify her giant-sized box of Christmas biscuits.

"We are supposed to show them how to live and behave, and they see us lining up here for two hours looking and feeling degraded for the crime of buying food with our own hard-earned money."

But we have made it through and I feel mighty relieved as Eubank begins another rendition of *I am the messenger*, pockets a load more cash, and departs saying *he needs to meet another coach quite soon*. Ten dollars per bus, ten buses per day; this lad could be earning three grand per month with this little circus. What a legend.

Zimbabwe.

Storm clouds are gathering; black as night above the bush. I am sat next to a teenage money changer who does the trip to Botswana twice per week, returning home the same day. He says his passport is almost full and he might need to change jobs as a new passport will take 4-5 months to process.

I admire the, at times, alien landscape of huge termite hills, strange ancient rock formations, and traditional roundhouses. I also spot an incredible blue-winged fluorescent bird, a huge swarm of very odd-looking moths, and the absurdly entitled Smiling Cow Abattoir.

Beyond Plumtree, lightning bolts flash only metres away and then the rain comes lashing down bringing flash floods. In just minutes, everything around us is turned into a lake. It is an exciting spectacle if not a little terrifying. This, for me, is travel just as much as enjoying sundowners on exotic, relatively unknown beaches.

I am in. One more month. Hopefully, I can start coming out from the shadows now with the coaching, and also begin visiting a few places as a tourist.

It is good to be back in beautiful Bulawayo. Joshua Nkomo Street's fine buildings are good on the eye. I walk all the way home for the exercise and the exaggerated sense of emancipation and of being a local.

Ethel and her daughter are pleased to see me and I am very happy to present them with the smuggled Windolene and salad cream.

ZIMBABWE ARMY CHIEF WARNS MILITARY COULD STEP IN OVER PARTY PURGE

9: Wenger must go!

Tuesday, November 14, 2017

There are two uniformed police officers tightly holding batons, sat on the grassy steps next to our training field, when I arrive for our 5pm session. My stomach sinks. Are they here to arrest me? They look at me but don't say a word. In fact, they don't speak to each other. I lay out my cones for the session but let the lads warm themselves up.

25 minutes after arriving and the police are still here. This can't be good. They have their phones out and, I can't be sure, but I think they are filming me. I leave and take a stroll. Up on Robert Mugabe Way, an army truck passes.

"Things are getting very tense," a passer-by comments, neither of us daring to glance upwards until the truck has passed and is almost out of sight. My intuition says keep on walking in the direction of home. There is no telling what the police lads are up to. When I walked away from the training field, a man in a truck seemed to briefly follow me and show an unnatural interest.

When I got back yesterday I stupidly fooled myself into believing the paranoid days were over but after last night's army press conference, military helicopters flying over the house in the middle of the night, the police at training, the suspicious van, and now a second army van in the space of five minutes – this one from a different direction – it is clear to me that the shit is about to hit the fan in Zimbabwe.

My heart is absolutely pounding.

Perhaps I shouldn't admit it, but this feels exciting. Like a kind of game. And you know, I am not actually scared about getting arrested and detained, even of going to prison. I fear them coming for me only because it will likely spell the end of the project.

The mood at home is darkened by my observations but lightens over dinner as we watch South African soaps… until…

"Reports are coming in from Zimbabwe that TANKS ARE ON THE ROADS DRIVING TO HARARE."

I knew it was coming, but my stomach still turns when I hear it.

I manage to get about ten minutes of slow internet: the Zimbabwe press, TIME, and the Daily Mail are reporting that a military coup is in progress.

Mugabe is calling the army chief a treasoner. ZBC News, which did not go on air, is said to be surrounded by troops. Mugabe's home is encircled. But almost everything I am reading appears to be rumour and counter-rumour.

It is a strange emotion going to bed not knowing whether tanks will be rolling down the street outside when you wake up.

Wednesday, November 15, 2017

GUNSHOTS AND EXPLOSIONS HEARD IN HARARE

MILITARY TAKES OVER STATE TV

THE BRITISH AND AMERICAN EMBASSIES IN ZIMBABWE ADVISE ALL THEIR NATIONALS TO STAY INDOORS

In truth, it seems, nobody knows what the bloody hell is going on. We hear that there are spot checks in town as well as roadblocks.

What would Pep or Jose do in this situation? I ask myself aloud in my bedroom.

How about you Woy?

Wwell Justin, you wwere part of the bwave two thousand in Ukwaine, so my advice is hang in there!

Most people were not expecting events to turn until after the ZPF conference next month but as an outsider, looking on, things have just been moving too quickly for something like this to be delayed another month. Clearly, this was on the cards.

The consensus is that I definitely should not go into town. Half of the city has decided to stay at home today. My mum will be having kittens when she goes downstairs, brews a coffee, and puts on breakfast news to hear that there is a coup in progress in Zimbabwe. I've got to find a way of letting her know I am fine.

The local internet cafe above the garage is closed, the nearby hotel says the internet has been taken down. Zimbabwe takes up almost the entire BBC World News bulletin as I decide to chance it and leave the house.

Taking the side roads into town, there are significantly fewer people about and those that are gather gossiping quietly on street corners.

Indaba is deserted apart from one old lady. My mum is mighty relieved to hear from me but in return has very sad news that my legend of a great aunt, Lucy, is dying in Ireland. She is one of my favourite people in the world: always fun, positive, chatty, kind and complimentary. Tears well up and I feel a little sick.

Around ten people have sent me messages asking whether the coup is affecting me.

Mercifully, the military has disarmed the military police in Harare, and there is no sign yet of a split in their ranks. Grace is allegedly bound for Namibia. Mnangagwa looks like he will take over from M who, according to his friend Jacob Zuma, is under house arrest. At this point, it isn't so much a full military coup as a military-backed transition of power to one member of the ZPF from the incumbent leader.

The elderly white lady on the table next to me must have seen it all: Rhodesia to the demise of Mugabe 40 years later. She finishes up her finger sandwiches as a polite young black man informs her that her taxi awaits. Time too for me to get my arse home while things remain seemingly quiet. I joke to Tony that our football training has been cancelled... forever!

In Pick n Pay, the mood is jovial, almost as if it is the day before Christmas. I overhear people talk about *this being the twilight of a new era.* How privileged I am – if indeed this is the case – to witness the end of the world's longest-serving dictator.

Ethel proudly shows me the progress in the garden with the sweet potatoes she has tilled the ground for, the mango tree bursting with hundreds of small fruit, and the banana bush and orange tree doing well. I just managed to get back before those black clouds burst and sit under the guttering getting half-soaked watching the rain pour down. It feels marvellous. One of the neighbours' little girls briefly dances joyfully in the heavy shower.

With everyone sheltering inside, and into my second beer, I watch the rain chase the animals, insects, and birds away. Two huge storks swoop overhead. I swear they look stressed by the impending storm. As the lightning rolls in, and the alcohol kicks, I have got goosebumps celebrating Mugabe-has-gone Day. Everything smells so fresh.

I think of Tony who could so easily be here with me if events had panned out differently. He'd love this. It'd stay with him forever. The money won't. He'd agree with me. I'm just making the point that I feel sorry for him that he's missing out.

In my room, I pull back the curtains so I can observe the storm in bed. Hurricane-like, the wind gusts and the torrential rain kills visibility. Fork lightning at every conceivable angle. Thunder booms as if the military is bombing Matabeleland. Lightning strikes are hitting in the neighbourhood, one taking out a transformer a garden or two away and causing it to dramatically explode, and prompting me to instinctively dive down behind the window. The power goes out. Everywhere. There is another explosion nearby. I close the curtains and try to sleep. This is some finale to Mugabe-is-gone Day!

Thursday, November 16, 2017

The storm has caused massive damage. A tree crashed down on the electricity line a few metres down the road which must have been one of the explosions I witnessed in the night. One house nearby burned down, another has lost half of its roof. Trees are down on the road. There is still no electricity, so we put firewood on the *brai* and start a kerosene fire to boil some water. It is sunny but cool, hundreds of black millipedes marauding around the garden, full buckets of rainwater used to soak and wash duvets. Damn, that twig roasted coffee tastes good. It is fantastic to be alive.

Banana skins everywhere, my mate Neil commented about Zimbabwe. Yes, Zimbabwe isn't as much a Banana Republic as a Banana Skin Republic. The challenges of preparing a football team for international competition include military coups, economic chaos, police preventing you train, and massive electrical storms knocking out your communications. A couple of days ago, we were close to finalising opposition for SA, booking flights for London, scouting foreign-based players, kick-starting fundraising, coaching the boys to actually defend, bringing in equipment from abroad, organising our community day... the list goes on and on. We slip on one banana skin, get up, and then go arse over tit over another slippy yellow bastard.

Nobody outside of here will ever know the half of it and certainly never truly relate to what we are all going through on our journey to London, dateline May 29th 2018. There are even things that I can never write down in my diary or tell.

Neighbours report the army has moved into town and have set up roadblocks. FFS. Everyone now needs to carry ID. The situation is so uncertain. For all I know, I could be forced to leg it out of the country in the next 24 hours. With no electricity, our phones are out of power and we have no internet, radio or TV. Aside from local gossip, we literally do not have a clue what is going on.

Oh, my word, yesterday's optimism is ebbing away and turning into fear. Mugabe hasn't resigned. In fact, word is he is refusing to go and this could all turn on its head. Some voices in the British government are saying Mnangagwa should not be allowed to take over, suggesting that would be replacing one dictator with a war criminal. Except Zimbabwe isn't that easily explained or conceptualised. Truth be told, we don't fully understand what went on behind the scenes with the genocide but in order for the country to fully heal from its decades-long wounds, there will need to be a peace and reconciliation process in the coming years.

The army have indeed officially moved into parts of Bulawayo and set up roadblocks. Some countries are advising their foreign nationals to leave Zimbabwe immediately. The British FCO is still saying *stay indoors*, as if imagining the doors are made from titanium. I have discovered this information from the nearby two-computer internet cafe. Clearly, there will be no football training today, so I am continuing my new trend of afternoon drinking to help me deal with my fear.

Busani and Khanye pop over with Nqo, the lad officially representing the MFC in the UK. He is here for a family funeral so it is an ideal time to discuss UK fundraising, sponsorship, a possible partnership with the city of Aberdeen (which Bulawayo is twinned with), cultural events for London, ideas on the cultural ambassador role, social media plans, me scouting players in the UK, etc. Nqo seems spot on; he and I are linked by the fact that his little lad was born in the same relatively unknown town as me, Huntingdon. I go out of my way to stress to him that we desperately need to kick-start things with the huge UK Ndebele community.

Meanwhile, the MFC is calling off our community day and there will be no training until Monday at the earliest. As for my situation, well we reckon that if there is no positive news by the weekend then, chances are, things will begin to deteriorate from there. We are looking at the possibility of me getting out of Zimbabwe on say Monday and staying in South Africa until our December 8 Human Rights meeting and proposed game two days later. Contingencies will be looked into for housing me in South Africa although, ironically enough, I might feel safer staying in Zim (in the midst of an ongoing political crisis) than hanging out in Joburg. If only I hadn't used my second visa going to Botswana, I could have gone to Mozambique for a week and laid low there until things are clearer.

Friday, November 17, 2017

I wake at first light, not long gone 5am, with a sense of relief that we have made it through the night. My moods are flying up and down now with each passing day.

I am up earlier these mornings and I am super grateful for morning coffee at six or seven, Ethel having got the fire stoked at 5.

It is a sunny *Mugabe Isn't Gone Day* in the Banana Skin Republic of Zimbabwe. Extraordinary, but M is attending the Zimbabwe Open University Graduation ceremony. You couldn't make it up. What on earth is going on? Why has the old dictator been allowed out of the house to do that? I don't know whether to laugh or cry. One rumour doing the rounds is that Zambia are willing to send in their troops to support him and their tanks could be here any day.

MNANGAGWA FINGERS GRACE

My clear winner as the best headline so far. If they are not trying to be funny, then that is legendary.

The electricity finally returns at 1pm. The defrosting fridge, with everything going off inside, is a good metaphor for Zimbabwe.

Interestingly, the BBC's Ben Brown has somehow managed to get into the country but barely mentions tomorrow's marches. This is pivotal. If they go as planned and there are 100,000 plus people on the streets... and it stays peaceful... then I think Mugabe is toast. If it somehow turns violent in Bulawayo, then I am packing my bags and leaving the city for Mozambique tomorrow night. If it's not too late.

Out on the veranda, I enjoy two sundowner beers. It is a truly beautiful evening. I best enjoy this because it could be my last ever evening in Zimbabwe. There is a slight nip in the air, and I also spot a light travelling across the heavens at what seems like thousands of miles per hour. Even the aliens cannot believe Mugabe might be on his way out.

I chat to a gentleman from the neighbourhood.

"You cannot even start to imagine how good this whole area used to be, even under the whites at the end. It was such a fantastic neighbourhood. This country has been ground down and destroyed. Mugabe must go. We are all so tired. People who simply spoke up were arrested and never came back. Why doesn't he understand that we all want him to go?"

At this point, I am not so much a football manager as an eyewitness observing and recording the story of what it was like to be here when one of the last remaining dictators of the twentieth century was finally sent packing.

Saturday, November 18, 2017

"The army have armed roadblocks on the road out of town. They were asking us all if we had seen any police stopping people on the road saying they won't tolerate any more of that stuff. They will go and shoot them if they find them stealing money from the people instead of doing their real jobs. There were loads of armed soldiers with even more waiting nearby in the bushes."

I cannot sit around anymore hiding away. It is time to come out of the shadows. I've reached the point today that if I'm going to be arrested and deported, then so be it. Fuck the regime. I have got less than three weeks left and there is so much that needs to be done, which cannot be done with me hiding or remaining under the radar. There are reports of massive crowds gathering in Harare. I want to, and am going to, go into Bulawayo; observe what is going on as this Zimbabwean soap opera enters a new, dramatic phase.

On my four kilometre walk in, men of all ages are huddled together discussing politics or carefully shading their phones so they can peer at social media posts about the latest news – much of it, in truth, made up or speculation. I purposely avoid the main roads and stick to the residential streets to avoid the army.

As I reach 2nd Avenue, I can hear a distant noise, the kind you associate with football stadiums. Cars begin to pass, blaring their horns. The street leading to city hall is congested and the carpark in front of it is mobbed by people. Hundreds, not thousands, but a large crowd is packed on the city hall steps and spilling out beyond the car park onto the road singing, chanting and doing a lot of smiling. Goosebumps have broken out on both my arms.

"I'm tired. It has to change now!" a middle-aged man declares as he strides past.

Vuvuzelas, car horns, over-accelerating cars and vans. Fags, beers, smiles, hugs, cheers, laughter, and a general sense that you cannot actually believe this is really happening.

Young, old, blacks, whites, coloureds, Indians. An old bloke with a massive beard stands atop one parked van waving a large Zimbabwean flag from side to side; near him, mixed-race kids with smaller flags. Many people are wearing Zimbabwean cricket and football tops or colours of the flag. Dynamo Football Club are doing a roaring trade selling replica shirts. An antique Ford truck flashes by. "I can't believe it!" is the second most used term after "I am tired". I am witnessing the first free and sanctioned public protest in 37 years. The last time it happened was in something like 1979 or 1980, and I was a young boy at school in Leicestershire. For now, this is the first peaceful "coup" in Africa's history. I've still got shivers knowing I am part of history – observing it – to some extent taking part in it, as I join the crowd, cheering.

MUGABE MUST GO (placard)

I walk around town enjoying a freedom of movement – a sense of it at least – that I haven't personally enjoyed since I first came here. Nobody is going to stop and question me today.

Revolution is in the air but a couple of blocks away, there is little sense of that as most people just do what they always do: prioritising food on the table for their families, selling or buying, or doing whatever they need to do to get by. All around town, microbuses flash by, horns beeping excitedly. Newspaper headlines displayed on the street read:

MUGABE CORNERED

VIOLENT CLASHES ARMY, POLICE

At home Ethel, Busani and I watch the non-stop coverage on the BBC. Mugabe is adamant he will not step down, but the tens of thousands in Harare and in Bulawayo believe he will. People are calling it Independence Day.

You have to laugh: as it nears kick-off time, many protesters are leaving the streets to go and watch Spurs v Arsenal. MUGABE MUST GO. WENGER MUST GO is a placard from Harare trending on Twitter.

Not today, because Arsenal and Sanchez are brilliant. I am in a local dive bar for the Saturday EPL football and a timeout from the revolution. Zambezi beer, I briefly chat to a mixed-race bloke, probably in his 50s, whose daughter is living in Leicester. *Nothing for her here*, he says.

The bar is boisterous but it is a bit of a result that we've managed to get them to show Leicester versus Man City. A mad Rasta, whose eyes are frankly terrifying, latches on to me. His idea of personal space is about five centimetres nose-to-nose.

"I am tired. I don't care if I die. This can't go on. I just came from Harare. I'm not scared. I want revenge, I want to go to their houses and kill them.

They stole from me. They stole everything. I collect firewood to survive. I dig vegetables. Is that OK? We worked on a farm but the farm was given away to one of them, and no one could run it. Look at me! I don't care if I die!"

I believe him. He looks ready to kill. I am trying to remain poker-faced and maintain eye contact, more than aware that this boy could go at any second.

A security guard tries to reason with him as he aggravates a punter sat near the bar. Rasta accuses the guard of being Zanu PF. Worse still, how did Vincent Kompany not get sent off after upending Vardy clear on goal?!

While Busani is away trying to use Ecocash to get Cashback or some other Zim money madness to pay for a round of beers, Rasta and Leicester boy have got me draped in a full-sized Zim flag taking moody photos of us. I don't know if I am their mate or they are gonna kick the shit out of me after a few minutes.

Man City go 1-0 up. Rasta returns after smoking outside, strides quickly up to the bar and smacks one lad sat there around the back of the head with a full beer bottle. Fighting erupts. I am amazed that didn't knock that lad straight out. Or worse. Busani and I run out the front door, beers in hand, as the fight spills out onto the street. FFS, Rasta is the kind of lad who could turn a peaceful transition into a bloody civil conflict. All you need is a hundred lads like him kicking off, and this country could quickly turn upside down. Busani is such a decent bloke that he thinks we should go back to the bar with our empties, so they don't lose a few cents on the bottle deposits. I am not as nice as Busani and tell him over my dead body.

The day isn't done. I'm determined to take Ethel out to the Cape to Cairo jazz club in town. When Busani said we were going to catch a taxi, I didn't think he meant stand in the pitch dark, stop a random car, and kind of hope the driver spends his evenings driving around for cash. There are almost no licensed taxis in Bulawayo. Why? Because if you license a taxi, you get hit by extortion, huge taxes, and 'fines' every day at roadblocks. I have heard it said that the average microbus driver pays out $5 per day to "the police". The scale of corruption in Zimbabwe from the top down to the bottom is simply astounding.

But, first, we need to stop at a bank to change some money.

The "bank" is five sizeable "ladies", each sat on plastic picnic chairs outside Bakery Inn. Each wears a long, cumbersome dress and has an eastern European-style man bag tightly held in hand. Yes, in 2017 this is the real bank in Robert Mugabe's Zimbabwe. Two hundred of my Rand now get me 19 Bond Dollars – about $13.5 in real money but with the 1:1 status the Bond enjoys with the Dollar in the local bars and restaurants, I have made $5.5 profit by selling this small amount of hard currency. It is clearly good to do business with these local "bank managers"… if you have hard currency.

The streets are as busy as I have seen them at this hour. Plenty of people are out enjoying a new-found sense of freedom. Enjoy it now because tomorrow it could be gone.

Busani kindly walks us halfway to the jazz club before departing for home. Poor sod. Apart from running backwards and forwards to South Africa and Rwanda, he spends almost all his waking hours, currently, in the bloody bank trying to extract his maximum $20 per day cash. Or online paying for things. Or trying to organise MFC stuff. Today, he has hopefully set up the stadium for our trip to Joburg and we have taken steps to create the Human Rights Cup, an idea I have had to turn our one-off friendly match to celebrate December 10th's Human Rights Day into an annual cup event, held in South Africa, and hopefully recognised by leading NGOs.

I am of course the only white bloke in *Cape to Cairo*. I am used to that now. The local whites all seem to hide away together, somewhere. Half the time it is as if they don't exist. It annoys me, frankly.

Ethel, a very middle-class fifty-something lady, accompanied by me, dressed up for the evening in my black formal shirt; we must look like a slightly odd sight, I suppose. The band cannot begin their set on time as a crowd of young men in red shirts are watching Man U v Newcastle on a plasma. Jeez Mourinho, cheer up you miserable bastard! Can you imagine him having to face the daily ups and downs of Matabeleland!? My third EPL game of this revolutionary day. Wow, plasma aside, it is old school in here. All wood furniture, dusty lamp shades, stuffed animal heads, a retro bar. Some of the staff are even more dated. One toothless waiter must, seriously, be 80. Plus. A young six-foot tall woman walks in wearing a tight black dress and our five-foot-three, 80-year-old, waiter here slaps her backside with all the force he can muster in his bones. He lets off a Sid James *Carry on Waitering* laugh as he does it.

A man in a Liverpool shirt asks to sit with us at our table but gets beckoned away by an obese lady-of-the-night, who instantly begins stroking his head like he's a young puppy dog. I was warned that it was expensive in here and am expecting a big bill, especially as the jazz performance is free. A Zambezi beer is $1.20, which in *Bond funny money* care of 'the bank' is actually costing me 72-dollar cents, or 55 pence. The jazz band get ready tuning up their instruments and fixing their trilbies. Man U turn it on. 3-1, 4-1. Turn the bloody footy off! The sound is turned down at 4-1 as four old men, in very jazz band-like clothes, and a token young lad, on drums, begin their set. There is an African vibe to it, a Deep South vibe. Very good. Ethel approves. Back in the day, people used to flock to Bulawayo from near and far to enjoy its jazz scene. The city even had its own genre of jazz: Bulawayo Jazz, which emerged in the 1950s and was famous beyond the continent. Until it began to die along with so many other things here. Like the public parks. The grand old buildings. Like hope.

I am still in awe of Sid James. The boy has got me in tears. He has only gone and slapped a second woman's posterior and then winks at me with those sparkling eyes. Meanwhile, the obese prostitute is off her head. It is fair to say that the atmosphere in here is, ummm, very specific. Not everyone's cup of tea. As a voyeur – of sorts – I think it is brilliant.

A lady vocalist joins the band. It is quality stuff. You would pay a lot of money for a band like this in many places, and they wouldn't be half as good. I finish off my fourth beer – remarkably the most I have had to drink since I came to Zim, and it is time to go home.

Our "taxi driver" is a no-show. WhatsApp clearly has its advantages in this part of the world, but it is no way to run "a business". Ethel wastes her remaining bundle of airtime on the taxi, and we are forced to set off through the darkened streets in search of an alternative. There is so much damn litter everywhere. It is sad really. Africa's cleanest city certainly isn't anymore.

We stand by the main road waiting for "taxis" that don't exist but do exist. I don't like this. Waiting for some random car to pull up in the darkness and offer you a lift. Aren't any of these people murderers? Imagine trying this trick in Joburg! It is pitch dark. "Madness," I whisper to myself, which sums up the entire day as much as anything.

Finally, after perhaps 15 minutes, a bloke stops. His driver's seat is so far reclined that I can only get one leg under it in the back. He's a nice bloke and drops us at our door for the princely sum of one Bond each. Yes, in truth, it has cost about a quid to get safely home.

I have walked 21 kilometres today, my watch tells me. The BBC is still non-stop Zim. Ethel falls asleep in the lounge at midnight watching it. I get up at 2 for a pee and find her asleep under a blanket with Fergal Keane still yapping away.

Mugabe wanted a one-party state, but he's ended up a one-man party.

Sunday, November 19, 2017

It is a two-kilometre walk to the Body and Blood of Christ Catholic Church. I have been promising to attend for weeks. We arrive at eight to find most of the congregation in their best whites. The ladies wear a traditional Sunday uniform that looks like a cross between a nun and a baker's outfit. The affable priest delivers a sermon about nightmare wives. "You come home, and she pulls a face, and you have absolutely no idea what you did wrong". He then scorns husbands who live in the pub drinking the family's money away. I like this bloke. He is hilarious but succeeds in making you think. There is singing. A lot of singing. And three African drums near me. Men mostly sit apart from the women and the kids.

My knees can barely cope with the wooden benches. Surprise, surprise I am the only white here. I take it the whites have their own whites' version of the Catholic Church. The newly-ordained receive presents of cash and gifts. One lucky lad gets a 750g box of Kellogg's Corn Flakes.

Outside, after the final song, I realise the service has lasted a grand total of three hours. And then there is the time spent shaking hands with the priest, newly ordained, and members of the congregation who all seem to invite me back next week. Following on from today's service, there are women's meetings, church council groups, church finance group meetings. During the service, there were also the notices, the accounts, and a discussion about the ongoing issue with the older members of the community still having problems using Ecocash when donating to the church.

I race home past the Jewish cemetery using the trees on that side of the road as temporary shade. Onwards past the North End community swimming baths, and finally to the shopping arcade where cold sugary drinks are being sold outside and are definitely in order this scorching Sunday. Oh, my word, the ginger ale goes down well. Time to hide in the room.

ZANU PF SACK MUGABE, THREATEN TO IMPEACH

6pm THE PRESIDENT RG MUGABE WILL ADDRESS THE NATION, ZBC SAYS

6.30 We sit on the veranda, waiting for M, me necking more ginger ale as I admire the lime trees.

7.30 No Mugabe.

8.30 Still no Mugabe. Is he having a laugh?

9.15 Finally.

The army did nothing wrong. Blah blah. He says he *understands some of the issues people have. Blah blah.* Mumble. A lot of long words. Whoops, lost his place and seemed to skip an entire page he is reading from. Hang on, this speech is off at a tangent. Did he really just say he is going to preside over the ZANU PF national congress on December 10?! Does he even know he has been sacked?

The speech is going on forever and, oh my goodness gracious, the cheeky mentalist is actually NOT RESIGNING. He seems to believe he is still in control of things in Zim and it is all going to fall back into place. This is like one long weird recurring dream. What a mad bastard.

The BBC's Ben Brown can barely keep it together. *Does he live in a parallel universe?* he comments. The British representative of ZANU PF tells the BBC he is heartbroken and slams Mugabe.

"The military takeover has in no way affected my authority." Brilliant. There is a tank parked outside your house!

I leave the BBC's coverage and lie face down with a pillow over my head, roaring with laughter.

Monday, November 20, 2017

I have written to Northampton Town asking to observe training sessions and hoping they will help me with social media support. I have also written to Sheffield United asking if they will allow me to pass on a personal letter to Chris Wilder requesting that I might watch some of his sessions in January.

Katya is unwell and staying longer in Russia which puts more financial pressure on me. I hide in the house. Hide in my bedroom. Uncertain about so many things in my life right now.

Tuesday, November 21, 2017

Jeez, that is the worst scrambled eggs of my entire life. I am discussing contingency plans with Busani in a retro 80s cafe. The eggs taste like they have been here since 1983. I am trying to talk Busani out of cancelling our trip to South Africa. We dearly need it for the fundraising, profile, branding, bonding, experience, and football.

The big news is that if a civil war doesn't break out, we are no longer going to play Zim League One Bulawayo Chiefs this weekend and instead face Premier League side Highlanders' reserve team at their 35,000 capacity Barbourfields Stadium! *This is massive*, as Busani likes to say. The Highlanders first team will play their Castle Premier League match straight after us. We also plan to hold a team day and overnight camp in advance of the game, and discuss the possibility of playing South Cameroon in a high-profile friendly, unsure as to whether such a move might upset several countries because of current political sensitivities.

IMPEACHMENT OF MUGABE BEGINS

Finally, the MFC is back on the training field, and with the police currently off the streets, we know they won't be bothering us. One of the headaches of any amateur coach is preparing your session not knowing how many will turn up. My guesstimate in the midst of this political crisis was 7 to 16, so I have to chuckle when 22 show up. I am coaching defensive 1 v 1. I don't want to teach these lads how to suck eggs, but as good as many of them are, they have never been taught the basics.

Overall, I see an improvement as the drill progresses. Then we do team passing movements and combinations, ending with crosses into the box. Many of the lads are a bit wet with this, and the quality of the crossing and finishing is poor overall. I drill them and drill them hoping to get good habits into their heads. I also practice corner set pieces. I am a huge believer in having a whole set of corner, throw in, and, of course, free kick routines. There were two corner routines we had with Riga United Ladies which we must have scored seven goals from, over half a dozen games.

As well as the 22 lads, Busani, Khanye, the doctor, and myself – the MFC representative, visiting from the UK, is also down at training.

"He's gone!" Nqo comments as one of the lads spoons his shot over the crossbar. A bit harsh I feel and just raise my eyebrows knowingly with a half-smile.

"Mugabe, I mean."

"Mugabe?! Really?"

"Yes, haha, he has gone."

We embrace. The rest of the lads don't know yet. I can barely contain myself.

After an 11-a-side to finish and a cooldown, I gather the lads and have the honour of breaking the historic news. Every single one of these lads has only known a time with Mugabe.

Almost everyone in Zimbabwe of every creed, colour, age and tribal background wants Mugabe gone, but for the Ndebele they still must tread carefully. You sense the lads are all too scared to show how they feel. They are so used to behaving poker-faced about such things. I am the most vocal and the most excited by the news. On the surface of things. And I very much understand their caution. I get a piece of card and write "Wenger is next!", holding it in front of the lads for a team photo. But Busani and Khanye are terrified this image will somehow make us look political and refuse to let me have the photo to post on social media.

Distant car, van, and lorry horns are sounding in every direction as the light turns to darkness. Barely audible cheering, reminiscent of New Year's Eve at midnight time, can be heard beyond the fields. Somewhere.

I want to go into town and observe what is going on. The lads joke that I came to Zim on a mission to rid the country of M. "Why do you think you didn't see me at training last week? Thanks lads! I will now be leaving you, having completed my mission here."

Nqobile drives me into the city centre where we quickly hit a wall of noise as cars undertake and overtake with flags waving, beeping horns, and their passengers hanging out of the windows cheering wildly. We park up on Joshua Nkomo and walk down to his statue where revellers are blocking the road and quite literally going bonkers. They dance, chant, and sing rude songs about Grace and Bob.

Lads lie in the road in front of oncoming cars. Others climb onto the top of passing lorries and dance – one sudden tap of the brake pedal away from an early grave. Ladies dance a jig. Beautiful girls dressed up for the event take selfies and flirt with the boys. I find myself flirting with one or two beauties myself. Every car that passes needs minutes before it is allowed to pass as the mob bangs on the sides. Marine flares are lit up giving the appearance of a Belgrade derby. I join in one dance and find myself mouthing what I think are the words. I am buzzing. I disappear to Baku Bar to buy vodka shots. The bar is doing a roaring trade, spilling out onto the street. At OK supermarket, Nqo and I buy beer and joke with everyone we meet. *See! The economy is already picking up!* some bright spark exclaims in the packed queue. The shelves of beer and cheap whisky have already been half-cleared. Some mixed-race lads stop us and ask us *is this really what you want? Won't it just lead to a new dictatorship?*

Look at this! Nqo says, pointing at the unbridled joyous riot. *The genie is out of the bottle. These people have tasted freedom for the first time in their lives. The old status quo cannot return.*

A twat in a lime green van is driving around in speedy circles and doing handbrake turns as hundreds stand in a huge circle cheering him. One mistake and he will end up killing and maiming a sizeable number of people. Many other lads are driving around like maniacs. I don't know how nobody has been accidentally mown down. A couple of lads from the crowd pull down the Robert Mugabe Way street sign, and I am one of the people who gather to have my photo taken with it. Madness. Dictator for 37 years; now the crowd are defiantly stamping on his name. More girls flirt and ask for photos. If I were single, I think it would be a long night. Clearly, there will be a population spike in August 2018.

Ladies walk past grasping half-finished bottles of whisky. Takeaway pizza, eaten in the streets and very often shared out, is another celebratory treat. For the first time since I came to Zim, kids come to me and ask me to give them money or buy them beers. A couple of people think I am an ex-white farmer and express their desire for me to return to farming. A couple of people take photos with me or any other white person they can see as if they want to emphasise this celebration; this joyous outflowing belongs to everyone.

Surreally, flocks of white birds fly out from the city hall as if one hundred white doves of peace have been released. The crowd bellows with hundreds pointing into the skies. The birds return three times and, on each occasion, the noise grows in volume as do the roars of laughter. It is impossible to put into words how amazing this experience is. The raw, unbridled joy and excitement. I have never ever experienced anything quite like it. Roar energy. Joy. Relief. Hope. Expectation. Change. Love. Unity. Euphoria. They are all here.

I feel sorry for the poor buggers who have got to clean up this mess tomorrow. Or any stranger to town looking for signposts pointing them to Robert Mugabe Way.

I am drunk – surprise, surprise – and take a tactical chunder in the shadows of a shop front. I am trying to take it all in. Remember as many small details as possible. This is history being made. When you speak to Bulawayans, they all mention wanting change, unity, development, getting the country out of its mess. Nobody talks of violent struggle, revenge, retribution, division. Not one person. They have had enough of that already.

10: New era

Wednesday, November 22, 2017

I have awoken to a new era in Zimbabwe. Friends congratulate me on witnessing history unfolding. But tragic news that, in the midst of last night's wild celebrations, eight people died in and around Bulawayo in accidents.

ZIM STOCK EXCHANGE PLUNGES 18% ON GOOD NEWS

Clearly, I am not the only one at training with a massive hangover. My 2 v 2 defending drills go OK, but much of the defending is mediocre at best. I understand why the lads are not in the zone today but, that aside, I am starting to notice a clear division between those who have it both in terms of ability and mentality, and those who don't.

Praise gets injured again. He is such a key player for us, but unless he gets that persistent injury sorted by taking some time off, I'm not sure he will even make it to London. Personally speaking, I'd like him to be our captain if he – indeed we – get on the plane to England. It is difficult convincing any of these players to have time off to heal injuries. I was the same as a player in my teenage years, and it cost me big.

As he sits nursing his foot, I tell Praise that he's been the most consistent player for me and his attitude – everything, in fact – has been superb. He keeps saying *thank you, sir.*

"Will Draxler and Aguero play at the Russia World Cup?"

"Yes," reply at least half the lads at training.

"How do you know that?" Silence. "Quite apart from the fact that they might get injured, neither of those two players is guaranteed a game in Russia. They might completely lose their form or fall out of favour with their manager. Please think about that fact gentlemen. None of you, and I mean absolutely none of you, is guaranteed to go to London."

Mnangagwa is live on TV addressing the ZANU PF in Harare. I hope to God this man, and those around him, will unite and not further divide this country as well as sorting out the nation's economic shambles. The Ndebele need a voice as well as the Shona. The people celebrating in the street last night simply want unity and a brighter, shared future.

Thursday, November 23, 2017

My wonderful aunt Lucy passed away at 9.50 last night. God bless her. Such a brilliant aunt to me. One of the few individuals who approved of how I live my life and told me so!

Even though we are being 'hosted' at the Barbourfields Stadium on Saturday, we must cough up $165 to play there. Imagine how much money that is, in the context of where we are! I want to video the match for analysis purposes. In Latvia, I always found someone willing to do this for free but – get this – here I am being asked for $200 by people.

I have rarely seen someone give so much blood, sweat, and tears to a project as Busani does but his desire to do almost all of this himself is beginning to backfire. I have been in his position before; when you end up doing about 20 jobs yourself because you cannot trust others to reach the high standards you set. A lot of days, he is so busy that I sit around for hours at home waiting for him before he finally cancels. I am good at what I do and all these lost days, when I could be doing work for Matabeleland, is hugely frustrating. When I came out here, I was committed to working full days 8 till 8 for the Matabeleland cause but with Busani trying to do everything, there are lots of days that go by with me doing nothing more than scribbling coaching and development ideas down on paper at home.

I have been warning both Busani and Khanye about our goalkeeper situation since that very first session I attended and, finally, they are bringing in a new young keeper to train with us. Bruce cannot play at the CONIFA WFC. Like the majority of keepers I've seen here, he hasn't got a clue at corners and set pieces, and he dribbles in and outside his own box like he thinks he is Manuel Neuer. Let's be clear: he is a brilliant lad. Arguably the biggest personality in the squad. He comes to almost every training session, he is very decent in one-on-ones, and can be relied on by the team more than almost anyone. He also can't help the fact that he is five foot seven. Teams fall apart without individuals like Bruce in their ranks.

I have been banging my head against the wall for weeks saying we need to be going to London with three very decent keepers and should be looking to create a pool of five to choose from, all managed by a dedicated professional goalkeeper coach. Nonja, our "first choice GK" is under contract with another club, and there is no guarantee we can have him in

2018. Case in point, Nonja is unavailable for the highest profile match in our history this weekend as he is playing for his club side.

Khanye's grandfather is dying and he has gone to the rural areas to see him. He needs to find a goat to sacrifice for him, as is the custom.

Training attendance has dropped from 22 on Tuesday to 18 yesterday to 15 today. Every amateur coach knows of this frustration. I wouldn't describe it as ideal preparation. Star man Gary hasn't been seen in weeks after a family bereavement. We have got four or five lads good enough for Saturday's big game plus a new centre-half coming in (Goddy) who I am told *is the player I have been asking for: tall, strong and athletic.*

I do defending-as-fours. Some of the lads haven't got a clue. I give them a rocket and, as usual, they react by putting it right. The shooting drills expose the truth that we don't possess a single genuine striker, and our two central defenders carry our biggest goal-scoring threat. We practice corners to test out the new goalkeeper and Bruce. It is not pretty.

I also ask the lads to drop crosses into the six-yard box, and surprisingly most of them can't do it. *I want you to do this* and promptly I drop a floated cross right into the middle of the 6-yard box on my first attempt. Both keepers are struggling to get near any crosses. Busani and I don't know whether to laugh or cry as we mutter to each other, and fish out a couple of footballs from the undergrowth for the lads to cross in.

If we played North Cyprus tomorrow, their six-foot-five captain would murder us on set pieces. A shocking state of affairs. The application from the players in the final shooting drill is rather half-hearted, so once again I step in to show them the urgency and energy I want, controlling the ball from a pass and pinning it in the bottom corner; hitting the green cone from outside the box on my first attempt.

It is getting on for 7 when the light finally fades now, so after an almost two-hour session, I find myself jogging home, sucking in the cocktail of diesel and flowers, muttering to myself in disappointment and frustration at the state we are in as November draws to a close. I will try to remain optimistic for Saturday, though. Teams with five or six decent players can actually achieve great things.

Friday, November 24, 2017

Once again, I could barely get off to sleep last night with the heat, anxiety, and post-training endorphins racing around my body. Mnangagwa is going to be inaugurated today in the 60,000 national stadium in Harare.

In some senses, I am going to be inaugurated tomorrow in a 35,000 stadium in Bulawayo.

The past few days have made me realise, if I didn't before, that the emphasis is on me to raise most of the finance we need to get to London and clearly that is how I must spend my time in Europe. For all their hard work and good intentions, I very much doubt the Matabele lads can do it. Better they continue to focus on keeping us rolling day-to-day in Zimbabwe itself.

MUGABREXIT WIPES $6 BILLION OFF EXCHANGE

MNANGAGWA SWORN IN AS PRESIDENT

That seemed to go well. 60,000 buzzing in the stadium, the new president talking about everyone working together, ending corruption etc. etc. Not that I believe a word politicians say. The whole world will be watching this time, Mr. Mnangagwa, so let's hope your promises are kept and that the 2018 elections are not marred by violence and death.

My girlfriend problems continue. I guess I should have known that this time and distance apart would wreck us. If this whole project falls apart, and I end up losing Katya because of it, I am not sure I will forgive myself.

I meet the lads in town at 8.30, buying food for our overnighter at the guest house. The bill for this weekend's match is now: pitch $185, guesthouse $170, transport $50, food, drink and match posters $50+. All in all, a friendly match in our own city is already running to $500.

Seven of us cram into a taxi. Kiwa, the right back, and I cuddle up closer than I have been to any human being since I was last with Katya. East of town, we pass Hillside and continue on to posh Burnside as Kiwa tells me five people died on Tuesday night when a microbus blew a tyre on this road, rolled four times, and wiped those poor souls from this planet. I witnessed a similar event when I was living in Sierra Leone, all because people don't have enough pennies to replace worn rubber tyres while the likes of Mugabe steal billions they can never possibly spend.

Burnside is indeed posh, with huge, gated houses, impossibly green expanses of lawn, and enough razor wire and electrical fence to compete with a posh suburb of Joburg. Burke's Paradise is only a few kilometres out of town but, as we enter its private drive and pull up next to its sculpted gardens and bullfrog pond, it almost feels like a different country.

Some of the senior lads help prep dinner: a huge bubbling and slurping pot of sadze plus meat. Lots and lots of meat. And this being Africa with all its daily twists and turns, metaphorical roadblocks and, let's be honest, almost non-existent timekeeping, my insistence that we should eat at 8pm tonight and the lads be in bed by 10.30 has turned into dinner finally being served at 11pm. But anyway, it is not exactly the FA Cup Final tomorrow and this – doing this together, sharing the experience, bonding yet further – goes far beyond tomorrow's match. It unites us, and prepares our collective minds and souls for what is ahead of us this year, and all the way to London 2018.

There you go, coach. It is a joy to sit outside amongst the exotic plants and lush vegetation, slurping my noodle dinner, as the bullfrogs ribbit, the crickets cricket, and the warm night air begins to cool. The lack of light pollution means the night sky is visible in all its glory.

Saturday, November 25, 2017

Poor Busani is up at 5am to leave us and spend hours queuing at the bank to beg for his own money to pay for us to play at Barbourfields today. Pele (our own Pele) arrived here at 3am after his night shift. Great commitment from both lads.

Two players, though, have failed to show up at all. I can't believe it really. Imagine not having enough desire and appetite to play at one of the biggest and most famous football stadiums in all of southern Africa! Imagine not wanting to be part of a football team travelling to another far-off continent to play in a world cup – not just representing the Ndebele people but, in this current climate of national unity, Zimbabwe! Well, two lads clearly don't want it enough and, having discussed it with Khanye and Busani, we will be issuing a final warning to them next week. Truthfully, though, I am not surprised that one of them is Benny. He's a nice lad, but he stood out at the first trainings and matches as the one person with negative body language. The one with no burning desire to be part of this great adventure. Still, and I must emphasise this point, he has more than played his part, scoring goals that ultimately enabled the MFC to qualify for London. Without Benny, I likely would not be here and there would be no world cup dream. He's not the first and he won't be the last player we lose along the way. Sadly, some of these lads will also need to be jettisoned. I fear Gary will end up being one of them despite him arguably being our best player.

Up at seven, I'm relieved that the lads have managed to sleep in and get the recuperation they needed. Dozens of colourful birds are hopping from tree to tree singing as the boys start to arrive for their breakfast of jam sandwiches, boiled eggs, and juice. There is an excited but chilled buzz in the air. It feels like Cup Final Day at the end of a monumental week in Zimbabwe's history.

Mrs Adam, as Khanye (humorously-for-me) refers to the wife of the owner of this place, says devotions as all 20 lads gather together just before they tuck into their breakfast. Bible in her left hand, wearing a long blue flowing dress under the shade of a tree, she talks of *guarding our hearts* and of the virtues of staying faithful to one woman; of being good men. This group of young men is as nice a bunch of human beings as you could ever wish to meet, so I imagine she is mostly preaching to the converted.

Boys will be boys though. God created us that way.

There is great merit in much of what Mrs Adam says: these lads stepping up and being good role models, faithful husbands, good fathers, not turning into drunks. Whatever you might think of all this, devotions are devotions. We all huddle in a tight circle, heads bowed, holding hands, singing the Lord's Prayer. Religion helps unite and strengthen this team, and I am happy for that.

Post-breakfast, the lads sit with their legs dangling in the pool, joking, taking selfies and, of course, spending most of their time discussing football. It is a lovely scene, and I sense some of the lads have never felt so close to 'having made it' in life. We enjoy an hour by the poolside, the sun mostly hiding under clouds that threaten rain later, me snoozing off for a moment or two on a sun lounger. This is brilliant but I can see the hands on the clock spinning around, and I just know we are not going to be at the stadium a full 90 minutes before kick-off.

Khanye sends the boys to change into their Subway sandwich training tops before reconvening in the garden. A young, motivational speaker – dressed a bit like a St John's Ambulance volunteer – is our guest. He tells the boys how he lost his parents at five, had numerous setbacks in life, but has made it in the US and Europe. He asks the lads if any of them will admit to a failing marriage or relationship and Kaka (our Kaka) steps up, which I respect him for doing. *Kick away the negative people;* he has us all volleying the air, Kung Fu-style. It is uplifting and adds to the positive vibes of a shared breakfast, pool time, Mrs Adam's devotions, and a lovely beautiful morning spent at this little enclave of paradise.

From a pure football point of view, I'm not too happy about us leaving at 10.45 for our noon kick-off, but it has been a super overnighter and morning session, setting us up perfectly to play the Zimbabwean Premier League boys. The lads sing and clap. Khanye chants and sings. He's got a fantastic singing voice. At moments like this, he is our undisputed leader. The bus is rocking as we leave one of the few remaining corners of privilege in Bulawayo and head for Barbourfields. Driving through town, we are so loud that bystanders stop to stare and point at this mystery group of happy, positive young men.

We have stopped in town. A couple of the lads have gone to buy water. When I asked to be at the ground at 10.30 it wasn't just so we could walk on the Premier League pitch and suck in the moment, have a banana or two, discuss tactics, and warm-up for 30 minutes... but was mainly to avoid unforeseen circumstances which, it seems to me, are in endless supply in Africa. At 11.15 we move on, the boys in full voice, getting some thumbs up from Highlanders supporters beginning to make their way to the stadium.

Surely not? We have stopped again. This time apparently because we don't have a captain's armband. "Screw that. Tie some material around his arm!"

11.25. I am anxiously looking at my watch, deducting the time left from what I wanted to say and do pre-match. The driver looks like he is going to pull into a petrol station and inside my head I am shouting: *Surely, surely you filled up before you came to pick us up and you don't want to, now, 35 minutes before kick-off!* Relief, he changes his mind and speeds up before we reach the *robots* on the turning that leads to the stadium. I did have kittens for a minute or two back there as clearly the petrol gauge is down well below the giant E for Empty.

The lads are in full song as Barbourfields comes into view. I'm sure I am not the only one thinking this is going to look brilliant when we pull up outside the stadium with the lads singing and clapping. We must definitely do this in London. In fact, I will demand the lads walk into the stadiums singing. The opposition are going to start doubting themselves today. They have got everything to lose as professional footballers playing a load of unknown amateurs.

The minibus almost stalls. And then it almost stalls again. The driver turns off the main road and stops.

"Now what? Come on mate; it is 30 minutes to kick-off."

"What are you doing?" Busani asks him.

Silently, he grimaces and turns the ignition. There is a dreadfully hollow sound, rather reminiscent of the dentist's chair.

Half of the lads jump out and try to push start the bus. Oh no, you have seriously got to be joking me! Our bus isn't starting because – yes, you know where this is going – we are out of petrol! Busani looks at me with a pained *you told me so* expression. I look at him with a *I can't fucking believe it* scowl.

We roll the bus up and down the road. Nothing.

Quick on his feet, as he often is when the chips are down, Busani stops a passing car and gets them to take him to the nearby petrol station that we passed three minutes before we ran out of fuel. The informal economy of this country, where 94% of people are unemployed, *is* the economy of Zimbabwe. It works on the basis that you can get anything done. You just ask people and pay them in return. Almost any driver will pick up strangers for a bit of coin. In fewer minutes than it seems divinely possible, Busani and two of the players return with a $5 yellow container of fuel. Our driver though, so desperate to redeem the situation, has tried to restart the bus far too many times and likely sucked up all the dirt from the engine. The bus is not going to restart. It is 15 minutes to kickoff, a KO that cannot be delayed on this occasion as the Highlanders play their final Premier League game of the season immediately after us. All kinds of things are flashing through my head. If we don't play this match, it is the kind of public humiliation that could wreck the entire project.

We grab all the kit bags, water bottles, and footballs off the marooned bus and run to the main road where we shoehorn most of the squad inside a microbus while another half-dozen cram into a 'taxi'. I am thinking about that blown tyre and half-dozen dead people on Mugabe resignation night as we hurriedly and horribly overtake traffic on the road up to Barbourfields. With ten minutes to kick-off, we are struggling to convince the old boy manning the turnstile to let us in.

Highlanders are going through their final warm-up but nobody can point us to a dressing room leaving the lads to throw their kit on in the stadium concourse. We run out onto the pitch at four minutes to twelve, with me still insisting the lads do some kind of stretches. I suppose pushing a two-tonne bus was probably warm-up enough.

I have barely had a chance to take any of it in as I warm up the young goalkeeper making his debut for us today, pinging balls at him. My God, look at this! 35,000 stadium, giant Subbuteo floodlights towering above. Imagine playing here in front of a full house! Truly unbelievable. The referee angrily blows his whistle again to make it clear the match is about to start, and I can't help myself as I purposely smack the ball into the top corner for a bit of completely unnecessary self-indulgence.

The ref, so keen to start no more than 5 minutes late, actually kicks off with me still sprinting across the pitch with the warm-up balls. All week I repeatedly insisted we be here 90 minutes before kick-off to properly prepare and instead we got nine! Should I laugh or cry?

Highlanders almost punish us early doors, but our goalkeeper is up to the task saving well with his legs. Clearly, the three-minute warm-up I gave him worked wonders. The save seems to settle the entire team. Our midfield takes control, Pele and Gary winning the tackles and knocking sublime balls over their defence on the angle. Jiro gets sent clear on the left-hand side of the penalty area but, one-on-one, six yards out, screws the ball wide of the target. While we are forcing our professional opponents into shooting from long range, again one of our players gets free in the box and should score, only to shoot tamely wide.

40 minutes in, it is 0-0, and we are the better team. But all it takes is for one player – our left back Khule – to switch off and get caught out of position. With him failing to recover, they have a man over and work the ball into the box for one of their strikers to find space unmarked and fire into the net. That, I suggest, is why these boys play for a ZPL team and our boys don't.

At halftime I go through my usual list of personal observations: Kiwa playing too high and not goalside, Praise not picking up the forward as he tries to slip away from him and find pockets of space, some lads needing to jockey more instead of piling in, etc. But, overall, the best 45 minutes of football ever played by the MFC. "We should push buses as a warm-up more often," I joke. "More of the same please, gents, with more hunger and ruthlessness in front of goal."

No substitutions. The lads continue where they left off and, rather unbelievably, considering the calibre of the opposition, we create two more one-on-ones with their keeper. Miss. Miss. The sky is as black as night as we miss our fifth clear-cut chance of the game and you know, at this point, that the boys wouldn't score if we played until Wednesday.

We introduce three or four new lads into the game. They are giving a decent account of themselves but on 65 minutes we look mentally fatigued. We have started pissing around at the back and some of the lads are out of position. The new centre-half, our best player in the first half, seems to be playing a free role in midfield.

"What is he doing there?"

"He is high with play."

"What? For fifteen minutes?" Well, more like five, but I want to emphasise my point. "Tell him to drop back into defence. Our shape has completely gone."

But I am telling K+B stuff, and they are barely listening to me. I am annoyed. Very annoyed. The arrangement we have is that Khanye coaches the team in Ndebele from the sidelines along with my input to him. Yes, I do shout some instructions in English but as the first language of all members of the team is the local language, I don't want unnecessary confusion. The only problem is that he isn't listening to a word I am saying. We are now playing like a park team – everyone now playing high, out of position (including my assistant coaches), chasing an equaliser, and not worrying about the consequences of a counter attack.

Jiro gets sent one-on-one again. This is it! He rounds the keeper and only has to pass it in… but his touch is heavy and the ball runs out of play. It is all us, which isn't perhaps surprising with eight in midfield and attack. You know if we don't score, we are going to be punished. And you know we are not going to score.

"Look at our backline! They're not even interested in their strikers," I plead, as we waste another corner. With no time for a pre-match chat, the lads haven't tried one of the set pieces I worked on in training with them. 80 minutes, still 0-1 and we have won a free kick on the edge of their box. I video it expecting us to finally get the goal we deserve from one of our training ground routines. The lads try some contrived free kick that we most certainly didn't dream up in training and 30 seconds later Praise, as the last desperately covering defender, puts the ball into his own net.

Any coach will know my frustration at seeing his players fail to leave the cover and subsequently gifting the opposition an overload on the counter. Kiwa, our right back, is playing left back. The central defender, Goddy, is still in central midfield. We have gone to pieces. Khanye and Busani finally acknowledge what I am telling them, but it is too late. Our shape is non-existent. FFS. A tap in from another overload. 0-3. "We are going to lose this five fucking nil and lose all the respect we have gained mate," I shout at Busani. "Stick four in the back and make the holding mid actually hold."

When our best player and certainly a lad, in my opinion, who could and should be gracing the ZPL, Pele, misses a one-on-one on the angle, blazing it a mile over the crossbar into the high terraces, you just know this wasn't meant to be our day. With us practically playing a five at the back late on, it ends in a respectable but hugely frustrating 0-3 defeat as the heavens open up and lightning flashes all around.

Some of the lads are shivering as they sit huddled in the dugout. Busani rips into them. They admit they decided for themselves to shift positions and roles without consulting the coaches.

"Why on earth would you do that? Never, ever take it upon yourselves to change the formation in a game without us telling you to." Embarrassed stares, heads dropped. "We created a total of seven genuine goalscoring chances against a group of professional Zimbabwe Premier League players and we have lost 3-0 because, ultimately, after 70 minutes you morphed back into amateurs," I tell them.

Honestly, though, I'm playing up a bit as I think all of this is going to be a blessing in disguise. Failure offers us the opportunity to look for new solutions. I have been saying we need to find real strikers and now the MFC will no doubt start searching for them. The lads are being taught lessons about bad decision-making in every game. Let that happen now and not in London. Nobody will be under any naive, romantic illusions that we are going to win the World Football Cup. Had we won this 3-1, which we easily could have, I fear they'd all be thinking they are superstars now. Worse still, clubs would have come in to steal Gary and Pele. And perhaps too, Busani and Khanye will learn to listen to me during the game instead of practically ignoring me as they did today. I am not Pep, but I do know what I am talking about. As for the debacle of almost missing today's game, I am making it clear to my coaching team that in London we have to work on the clock. No *Africa Time*. It isn't happening.

The storm is ferocious. Lightning bolts in every direction, the bucketing rain reducing visibility to almost nothing. Ironically, all of this means that the two teams playing in today's ZPL season finale only get fifteen minutes to warm up as it is just too dangerous to be out on the pitch.

After an eternity hiding from the rain next to the riot police under the main stand, and a brief chat with one of the Highlanders players who seems to think I am French, we make our way to the top of the stand.

Green-shirted Caps United fans attempt to take up residence in our stand to shelter from the rain but are told in no uncertain terms to bugger off. Again, it is wild up here as the game kicks off and everyone packs in closely, especially the more aggressive element who usually take up residence behind the home end goal. The only time I ever seem to come across rough lads in Bulawayo is up at this stadium.

It is a strange sensation watching a game up in the terraces on the exact same pitch we were playing on a mere hour or so ago. All of the MFC present, of course, delight at the misplaced passes and spooned shots. A couple of our boys could definitely play out there. I am certain of that now. Another one of the many pluses from today.

I sit next to Jiro and Praise. Praise reads the game, you can see that, and discusses the PL match while sharing a big bag of delightfully wet groundnuts tasting almost like peas. Jiro wants me to analyse his performance; tell him how he can improve, give him a score out of ten. I give him 6. "I won't come back from London," he announces, as if blatantly showing off that he's going to use his tourist visa to stay illegally in the UK.

"Oh yeah?"

"Yes, I won't come back because a club will see me and sign me. I am telling you now, so you remember." Well, the boy missed two open goals today but at least he got into those positions to miss. I am glad he has got the self-belief. Personally speaking, I am not sure he will even get to London but I'd love to be proven wrong.

1-1 at the final whistle. The Highlanders fans, dressed in their Juventus black and white, invade the pitch as is the tradition after the final match of the season.

Sunday, November 26, 2017

I am in the back of a 1970s Mitsubishi with what looks like four middle-aged black nuns. The one that's driving puts me in mind of my just passed Aunt, as she barely sees above the steering wheel and drives chuckling a little like Mister Magoo. How this thing is still on the road is a religious miracle in itself. Nothing has been touched up, replaced or upgraded since it first spun its wheels when I was a child.

The service is safe and lovely feeling and is 'just' 2.5 hours, even with a dozen kids making their first Holy Communion. It sounds so bloody strange, in this heat, when the priest announces that next Sunday is the first weekend of Advent. Christmas is almost upon us.

I spend Sunday compiling a giant Matabeleland 'To Do List' for my time in Europe. I need agreement from the MFC on our strategy. There is too much make-it-up-as-we-go-along for me. I know it is the environment we are in, but anyway. I also want to understand what I am permitted to do on behalf of the team in terms of recruitment, scouting, fundraising, marketing, etc.

While I'm doing this, Ethel visits sick parishioners. Whatever you think of religion, where it serves as a positive force in a community and gives people a purpose, it is surely a brilliant thing. People today mock religion but miss the irony of worshiping technology or fame or money or shopping or sport or science or themselves. The system. People follow the system. They structure their entire lives around this bizarre Neo-Liberal lie in which money, politics, and the media are not at all that they seem.

Monday, November 27, 2017

Dealing with what is in front of you in your own daily life is enough to be going on with but, in our modern world, it is often the endless possibilities that pop up on the internet that blindside us. I find I get more anxious opening my emails these days than dealing with whatever random shit Zimbabwe and helping manage the MFC can throw at me. My aunt dying last week; Katya falling apart in my absence. Three hours online at the Rainbow and my head feels frazzled.

I stroll around Bulawayo snapping photos for posterity. It felt too risky to do this a few weeks ago.

The thing I most enjoyed today: buying a bottle of Chardonnay and sharing it with Ethel in the midst of yet another power cut; me toasting what I hope is the beginning of a new, more positive era for this strange and sometimes wonderful country.

Tuesday, November 28, 2017

The police are finally back on the streets of Zimbabwe. Allegedly, the plain-clothed army is out and about observing them. Some army are even said to be masquerading as money changers in the hope this will put the population off changing money on the streets. Meanwhile, Mnangagwa has created a three-month amnesty for returning funds sent abroad. It certainly feels different here than it did before M was removed by M.

One of the Highlanders' coaches gives me a lift to training. Respect to Khanye and Busani who have, as requested, already found me a new centre-forward. Percy is big, strong, mean, powerful and exactly the kind of lad on my wish list. In less than three minutes, I know he is good enough to join us in London. Today is 90 minutes of shooting drills. We lack lads who confidently shoot and score goals and we need to drill this and drill this.

Strange I should be thinking about next year but we have to have plans (and it is only seven months until my contract is up). My current first choice for 2019 is still going to Micronesia, if they can come up with some kind of package for me. My biggest issue is my badges. Perhaps I can find a way to finance a residential B somewhere. Otherwise, it seems to me, I will need to focus on coaching non-FIFA teams. I do know though that I cannot spend another year without a salary, burning my ever-decreasing savings. I am 47 next month, and I haven't been so poor since I just left Uni.

11: Aim low and work upwards

Wednesday, November 29, 2017

How do I best spread the word about Matabeleland once I get back? It is not what you know; it is who you know. I will add another pearl of wisdom to this: it is not who you are, it is who people think you are that counts.

We need stories about Matabeleland all over the British press, and the easiest way to achieve this is by using the angle about the unknown British amateur coach managing them. I realise that by doing this, it might end up making me the story, but whatever it takes to create awareness of our project. Once supporters and the press embrace the team, I know they will not be disappointed. They will love the team's passion, joy, spirit, and naive innocence.

Khanye joins my session as a player; his foot finally recovered from the crossbar debacle. When I came here, I expected him to be assisting me but he rarely consults me on what I do and, during most of my sessions, he just sits on the sidelines observing the players' performances before getting involved at the end with the just-before-dark kickabout. I am very happy to do all the technical sessions but our individual roles are rather confused at times. We do about six different shooting drills over the evening and end with a ten-a-side. This is the first time since I came to Bulawayo that I have allowed myself to join in any of the practice matches. The bounce on the pitch really is unpredictable, but I manage not to humiliate myself.

It is good to play with your players. I believe you can often learn more from that than from the sidelines. My observation as a player is that Pele is the standout man. By a distance. He intercepts one of my passes for fun, goes flying past a load of us. You just would not want to play against this lad. Especially in the 80th minute when his impressive fitness kicks in. I knew he was class but, out on the same pitch as him, he might be the best I have ever played against.

I tried to make the lads hungrier and less hesitant in their shooting today. The new CB once again stood out as did Kaka and the new CF. It seems to me that Khanye and Busani have, in the space of a couple of weeks, gone out and done exactly what I asked of them: *please find me a centre-half and a centre-forward better than anything we currently have.* Fantastic stuff.

Thursday, November 30, 2017

It never rains but it pours, my Nan used to say. As if I haven't got enough problems, Katya and I have a Riga 'flatmate' who tells me she is moving out and therefore so must we... by December 31. How lovely of her to dump this on me at the very last moment when, clearly, she knew this was her plan some time ago. And what a stupid situation that I am paying for a flat in Latvia with me in Zimbabwe, and Katya in Russia.

Training at least allows my mind to escape all this bollocks. We have 22, and I need to zone in to ensure the session works. First, I tiptoe around the pitch clearing rusting bottle tops, plastic, dangerous rocks, and discarded drink cartons. The theme tonight is crossing. I want to get it into the boys' heads to look up when they receive the ball and again before they attempt to cross. Ieva Bidermane, a Latvian international, is the best player I have seen for this – always getting her head up and assessing before delivering to a player she can actually see. The truth is most players just cross a ball in hope. It is very rewarding to realise I can genuinely develop players. These lads are humble. They want and are willing to learn.

There are some brilliant goals in the progression. Jiro PlayStations one, on the full volley, with the outside of his right boot. Pele smashes another into the top corner from 30 yards with such pace and power that if you blinked, you would miss it. Premier League Highlanders are interested in Pele. I am not surprised after he made their pro players look like small boys in our recent friendly. Alarmingly, we still don't have any players under contract but, as Busani keeps reminding me, doing so has huge financial risks for the MFC. Imagine though if we end up losing 4 or 5 of our best players. Every single player is developing under us. We make them fitter, sharper and perhaps most importantly of all, in the context of Zimbabwean football, we develop their minds and character.

I still want the MFC to concentrate on getting these lads signed up for us even if it only means release clauses committing them to join us in London. The 11-a-side is the best we have had since I came here. Everyone suddenly looks hungry for goals. There is lots of crossing. I made that happen. It is a great feeling. I tell the boys *that is what we need: that hunger and tempo* and they clap themselves knowing I am correct and they have developed this week.

I leave training absolutely buzzing. If we keep this squad together. If we get funding and equipment. If we bring in five foreign-based players with semi-pro quality. If the lads get visas etc. etc.… we are now reaching that point where we have the makings of a very decent side. Buoyed, I do the last kilometre of my run home in four minutes thirty, a full 12 seconds faster than my previous record. I am getting fitter. The boys are getting better. It is all down to hard work.

Friday, December 1, 2017

Wow, it is December. I love December; the build-up to Christmas, the coming holiday. Watching South African breakfast TV, my heart quickens at the very mention of it. For many Zimbabweans, Christmas starts for them today as they begin travelling to spend time with relatives.

MNANGAGWA WANTS MISSING $15BILLION BACK

BRITAIN SAYS IT WILL HELP FINANCE ZIM

Just totalling up my stats for my November fitness campaign started on November 6th: 305,000 steps, 520 press ups, 660 sit ups, and a total of 40 minutes of planks. Average RHR now down to 61. If I had spent November in Europe, I'd no doubt be two-kilos heavier and significantly less fit than I am now. How do you develop something? Aim low and work upwards. That is what I have been doing with my own fitness and, to a great extent, with our football team. Step by step, raising the standards.

It is the World Cup draw today. I stick on SABC, there is a brief power cut, but the electricity comes back just as Gary Lineker remarks: "But we all know Diego has always been good with his hands," Maradona kindly fishing England out of a bowl. Cheers Diego! England have a relatively easy group with Tunisia and Panama; Belgium will clearly progress as winners from the four. Unlike the past few tournaments, I am bullish on England this time to reach the quarter-finals. My one ticket I managed to buy in the blind draw is Spain v Iran in Kazan. Happy with that. Argentina, Croatia, Nigeria, Iceland is the most interesting group for me. France or Germany world champions. Belgium close.

"Two World Cups in one summer, one England will win, the other one seeing Matabeleland crowned as champions," I say aloud, doing a John Motson.

Sunday, December 3, 2017

First Sunday of Advent, it feels homely and calming witnessing the communal glue and individual hope the church gives many of its parishioners. I have to bog off early, though, as I am off up to Barbourfields.

The lads won their social match 8-0 this morning, more evidence I hope that a week of shooting and attacking drills has paid off. It is a scorcher. We are playing on the second-best surface of my time here, a watered grass pitch adjacent to the famous old stadium. Most of our lads are available as we play the recently crowned League Two champions. 1-0. 2-0. 3-0. The boys look hungry for goals and, best of all, two have come from crosses, one a replica of something we did in training. Offside, offside, miss, miss, offside. So much of football is played in the head. We started brilliantly, but now the boys cannot hit a barn door or think to look up to see where our opponent's high defensive line is. It is 4-0 at halftime but should be 10.

"Lads, I know it sounds strange, me being disappointed with a four-nil halftime lead, but I am. We need to be more disciplined and ruthless."

We replace many of our best players with the second string. *Bruce the Goalkeeper* comes in with it 5-0 and 15 minutes later it is 5-3. Benny comes on. He has been out of the fold for a while. "Benny you have never scored in front of me. Please show me one today. I know you are going to score." Not long after he enters the field of play, we break from the halfway line down the right channel. Benny twists then outpaces his man and fires the ball into the top corner from 30 yards out. Match of the Day Goal of the Month. The difference between our best and our worst players is semi-pro versus Sunday League Division Four. The game ends 6-3, 14 goals in one day from our boys. Have it!

The paranoia that poisoned my first weeks in Zimbabwe has become a distant memory. But now, I have learned that the geezer with the dark shades near the corner flag is a secret service agent and is asking about me. FFS, not this bollocks again. He looks like a black, bespectacled East German.

"Are you the manager of the team?" asks a twenty-something lad who appears to have been sent over by him.

"No, I am from CONIFA. I am their Africa President."

"Oh, sorry sir."

Yes, sorry sir, you snake. Surely the authorities have done their homework on me and decided whether I am an issue or not? When Sascha, CONIFA's General Secretary, visited earlier in the year, he was openly questioned by the authorities. But, honestly, I haven't put a foot out of line since I came to Zimbabwe. I am here to manage a football team, not a political movement. I am amazed these people still think we have a secret agenda. Or perhaps I am not. Paranoia breeds paranoia on both sides of the line.

We promised the lads a *brai* today and are treating them at one of the best spots in town over near Hillside. My *Zambezi* is going down well as Kaka comes over and tells me the boys are loving my involvement and feel they are developing individually and as a team. It is great to hear and, in itself, makes my time here feel like it has been worth it. Nonja, our semi-pro goalkeeper, also tells me he thinks we have improved and developed massively since Turk Mine a few weeks ago; he says he is enjoying me being around.

I laugh as I observe a drunk curly-wigged clown in a Union Jack onesie entertaining kids and trying to sell plastic shit. He is all over the place. One of the mums comes and bollocks him for overcharging on the pink plastic glasses and sausage dog balloon.

All is well as the boys enjoy their meat and the very occasional beer. Praise tells me he never played football until recently which is rather a shock. Kiwa also says very nice things to me about my time thus far with the Matabeleland team. It has been a great couple of hours including a very positive chat with Busani and Khanye about future plans. Sometimes you need a change of environment such as this to discuss the important things in life.

One of the players has a dance with a girl from an adjacent party, and a couple of photos are snapped. One mess of a woman goes mad. You know the type. The kind of idiot who ends up getting a dozen blokes into a fight over something she imagined. Even having deleted all the images we have with her, or her friends in the background, she is still going mental. We are in a public space.

I can't say she spoils our day, but she certainly ends it. A blessing in disguise perhaps; it clears the MFC out just as night falls at 7pm. We are so sensitive to any bad press related to the project that this creature's needless theatricals are enough to send two dozen of us packing.

"South Africa is definitely off. We just don't have the funds. Let's go in February instead mate," Busani nervously informs me. Well, I knew that was coming so I don't overreact to the news. "Plus, in the last few days, the South African press have been calling South Cameroon a terrorist organisation."

"Bloody hell. Yes, that's probably not the best choice for our branding and fundraising launch, haha."

A pickup truck is found for our lift back into town. As ever, in the interests of limited budgets, most of the lads cram into the open-air back. I have sat in such trucks in numerous places from El Salvador to Botswana, but I am sticking to my guns and refusing to travel in the back in Zim. The older I get, the more unsafe I realise it is travelling back there. One of the lads squeezes in the front in between myself and the driver, who, despair, is swigging from a bottle of beer and is clearly a bit tipsy. Small mercies, he is driving slowly at least.

"So, you are a football team or something?"

"Yes, a football team."

"What is the team's name?"

"MFC."

"Matabeleland Football or something like that?"

FFS, he is a spook. I best pretend to be sleeping. Time for some light, fake snoring.

"Of all the words in the world, how did you come up with Matabeleland for M?"

"Well, it can't be Mashonaland, hahahaha" (baddie laugh) "Or Manchester City."

"That is MCFC."

"OK, Mashonaland then, hahaha."

Ladies and gentlemen, the giveaway in this conversation is it is all being conducted in English rather than Ndebele.

"Who is the manager then?"

"Are you police?"

"Yes."

Fortuitously the conversation has shifted to Ndebele. Clearly, our drunken officer-of-the-law thinks I am asleep.

When we pull up outside Greens Supermarket, I save my best acting for last as I fake having to be woken up, before rolling out of the truck and slipping into the dark shadows.

I had been planning to finally announce my role as head coach of Matabeleland this week but now it is back to full mistrust mode. Clearly, in the last few days, the powers that be have taken a specific interest in me. I am still amazed I have never been detained and questioned... or worse. The problem, though, is that if I don't announce my official involvement soon and start using social media and my network of contacts to get us money and media, then we simply won't have enough time to pull it all together for London.

My opinion is that unless they pull me in before I leave, then we are good to go. If I get deported third time around, then it isn't the end of the world. The technical trainings have been developed. These boys will be without me for quite a few weeks anyway. And, by the way, if I were to get deported next year, then I will use the negative publicity from such an action against an 'innocent' foreigner to pressure the Zimbabwe government into leaving the Matabeleland team alone. I don't believe such bad press would benefit the government just ahead of the 2018 elections.

I jump out of the sardine tin microbus in the complete darkness of North End. I feel relieved that I am going home next week. The smoke and mirrors paranoia is back, and I have had enough of it.

Monday, December 4, 2017

Busani and Khanye are blocking my plan to bring in Matt Perrella from the US as our dedicated goalkeeper coach for the team. They are insisting we recruit locally but I am all too aware that when I tried to do this a few weeks ago, the list of suitable candidates totalled zero for one reason or another. I think we are absolutely desperate for a goalkeeper coach although I also obviously realise that having two foreigners here, helping out, might cause 'issues'.

The MFC is also opposed to my UK player trials. I don't get it. My intention is to bring in a maximum of five foreign-based players, mostly from the UK. They could be semi-pro or just good amateur lads from the Ndebele community. It is a no-brainer for me, particularly as I can use this to connect with the UK Ndebele community and boost awareness and funding. I don't know whether Busani and Khanye don't fully trust me, fear losing control over aspects of their project, or they are simply spooked out by the incidents of the past few days. There are even wet excuses for not giving me the MFC high-res logo so I can produce a polo top and business cards to use in Europe.

One of the few things they do agree to is me hiring volunteer 'world cup placement' medical staff and sports science students for London. It is a long, mostly open, honest, and sometimes-heated-meeting but I cannot help feeling very disappointed when we adjourn at five with them having knocked back at least half of my development plan. Sometimes I wonder why I bother at all.

It is the latest monthly CONIFA Executive Committee meeting. I am determined to attend all of these, despite being down here in Zim. Busani kindly gives up his evening, spotting me with his phone's mobile internet and I am able to use my laptop. He is still mad with me at my insistence that I won't have a smartphone. I understand his annoyance. I just hate the things. It is 2017, and I've still never owned one. Truth be told, it would have made life here much easier. For me, the MFC, and for the secret police.

Our accommodation bill for the World Football Cup could run as high as 250 grand. CONIFA now has a marketing agency.

Per, the President, asks me straight whether our participation is in doubt.

"Six hours at the bank to pull out $20 cash," I explain, "is the kind of daily issue that is holding us back... along with the small matter of a military coup. At the moment we have raised almost nothing for London... but it is unthinkable for all involved if we don't make it to London. I know we will be there because I will make sure we are."

Busani and Khanye have had to sit out in the garden until 9.30 while I finish up. When I tell them I discussed Matabeleland's possible absence from London, the lads go mad. I have never seen either of them so angry.

"Now you seem to be double-rolling. We need to redefine roles."

Oh, my word, these boys are really pushing my buttons today. I am fuming.

"Understand that as Africa Director I have to say how it is and that is how CONIFA operates. We are completely candid and honest with each other. Double rolling? Surely you have understood what I have put into this: nine months without a salary, away from my woman for six months, probably lost the place I was going to live, scared shitless all the time that I am going to be arrested or deported... I was going to hang around for you boys even if the coup turned nasty." To be honest, I am almost in tears.

"We know all that mate, and we are grateful, but in future, you will need to get official word from Matabeleland's board for Excos."

"Are you being serious?" I almost tell the two of them to fuck off and stick it but somehow, somehow bite my tongue. I am a split-second away from my part in all of this story being over.

"CONIFA doesn't work that formally. We don't read official statements from FAs. We are told stuff, and we report in, no personal agenda. CONIFA has to have contingencies for us being a no-show and, we..." I argue, "...must have contingencies for all situations. If only half of the boys get visas, which I think is very likely then, as I told you, we should have players lined up in the UK as cover. But you just don't get that at all."

"We should only work with boys from here." Khanye pipes up, as if completely missing the whole point of what I am saying.

"What if only ten of our boys manage to get on the plane, but we have seven who can suddenly join them in the UK? That way we still have a team. I agree that we should prepare a team almost entirely from here. That is the whole point of the project and why I am here. But we need contingencies and, sorry, but so do CONIFA. The truth is the only double rolling that is going on is me reporting back to you what was said in the Exco. Next time I won't tell you anything at all."

Busani tries to lighten the mood with a joke and then says, "All of this proves we are able to have open and honest discussions." Yes, but disappointingly I definitely get the sense that as I finish my first stint here, I am contracted by the MFC and not an integral part of it, as I deserve to be considered. I am still an outsider despite everything.

Sometimes relationships cross a certain line which they can never return to. These boys knocked me back on most of my development plans today, even seeming not to trust me on such arbitrary matters as having access to the MFC logo. They have also called into question my loyalty. I like these two lads. I have massive respect for what they have achieved so far and how incredibly hard they work. They are good company, and look out for me. But not trusting me I won't forgive very easily. Maybe that is what Zimbabwe does to everyone that sails in her. When you live in a police state, you even start to doubt yourself.

Tuesday, December 5, 2017

4.45am. I can't recall getting up this early for training in my entire life. It is so delightfully fresh, quiet, and the light is magical as I stroll into town. I crouch to collect fallen petals from colourful trees: Jacaranda blue, Flamboyant red. I'd like to give them to my nieces, although part of me still imagines spending Christmas in a Zimbabwean jail cell. As always, it is shocking to get out of bed at this hour but wonderful to be up experiencing this tiny beautiful slice of Africa waking up.

21 DEAD IN HORROR CRASH

The newspaper stand headline turns my stomach. There with the grace of God. All shoehorned into the back of an open truck together with heavy machinery equipment and a speeding driver. Twenty-one souls lost and dozens more in intensive care. You just cannot get your head around it. If it were a terrorist bomb, the military of this (and almost any) country would put their nation under lockdown, but 21 dead in a truck crash will be forgotten by this time tomorrow and will barely enter people's consciousness when they drive this very day.

I find the team on the sixth floor of the Rainbow Hotel. This is very positive. The MFC has struck up a deal to use the gym here. This is a respected brand, has a great location and facilities, and seems to say: We are serious! The burly fitness trainer takes the lads through interval training on the roof. It is at times like this that you realise you really are old; the lads sprint back and forth for 20 minutes, barely panting. This would literally kill me.

Bulawayo is a sea of green, below, with its endless canopy of trees and mostly low-rise skyline. It is 6.45 before the sun becomes uncomfortable; twelve of the lads are doing interval training, the rest inside doing gym work. On my request, we pull out three of them for me to give feedback to before I leave Zimbabwe. The young striker who never looks in the zone in matches but encouragingly is one of the most focused this morning; the number 10 with the skills of a pro and the upper body strength of a young woman; Benny clearly considerably less fit than the others and in need of pushing himself and proving (like he did with his MOTD goal on Sunday) that he *is* the man. There is a really nice vibe to this. It will be positive for me to imagine these boys training up on this roof when I am trudging through snow and ice in the Baltics.

After that tough, physical session this morning, I've decided to make training 'fun' with a passing rondo, a team shooting at cones competition, and my favourite 1-2-1 plus free man drill – a routine that I made up a couple of years ago. I give the lads a lot of stick for the passing quality in the rondo until, impersonating a church pastor, I shout *alleluia* when they reach 17 passes.

It has been so hot these past few days that no matter how much water and tea I consume, I am still as overheated as an old car after a mountain road trip. I stick my head under the cold tap, but I am still struggling. Honestly, I am dreaming of snow and fireplaces and drinkable tap water. And I am also dreaming of roast potatoes, cauliflower cheese, Yorkshires, Brussel sprouts, cranberry sauce. And chocolate. And cheese. And cognac. And British bitter. And good TV. And no creepy crawlies. And the cinema. And good 24/7 internet. And normal money. And paid work. And footy on the TV. And, most of all, family and friends. Much I will miss about here, but I am ready to go. I want Christmas. When I first came here, I slept brilliantly. But now I reckon I am getting 2-4 hours most nights with the heat, anxiety, mozzies, flies, and my spinning head. And my dreams are increasingly strange.

Wednesday, December 6, 2017

I was planning to return here in mid-February but I have changed my view on that in the past couple of days with my flat dilemma, time apart from Katya, disagreements with the MFC, constant paranoia, etc.

Yesterday, I calculated it is 16 weeks from February 18th to when the World Football Cup ends on June 10, plus another ten days on top of that perhaps before I will get to see Katya in Kazan. That is just way too long for Katya and me to be apart. I am beginning to think I need all of January and February in Latvia before Katya is forced to leave when her Schengen expires. Then two weeks in the UK, including one week I hope with football clubs, before I return here. I fear, though, that the security services will prevent me getting a volunteer visa.

If I return in late March, that would leave me with six solid weeks in Zim doing four technical sessions per week, plus a week-long camp in South Africa, a pre-WC camp somewhere in the UK, and two weeks at the tournament. That would be a grand total of 10 weeks together with the team. I don't believe any of the other CONIFA teams will come close to that level of preparation.

Only eight turn up at Crescent training, having prepped it for 12-20. I join in to make it nine and the session goes surprisingly well, considering the shortfall. I enjoy some quality banter with the lads at the end over who scored the best goal – me with my sublime volley into the roof of the net from 20 yards out (yes, really!) or centre-forward Percy's sizzler. I know Percy's a real striker because he insists his goal was the best. And it was, haha.

It really does have the feel of end of term here with the schools breaking up and people travelling to loved ones. Ethel's daughter came 600 kilometres today from the Zambezi to be here. We enjoy dinner together, and there is a huge Swiss Roll for dessert to celebrate the homecoming.

Thursday, December 7, 2017

I am losing it with arseholes driving their cars straight at me when I am crossing the road in Bulawayo. I love this city and its people but, oh my, the bloody driving! I am one week too long here in my opinion.

When I get back to Europe, I have been told I definitely need to vacate the flat on New Year's Eve, and I also have a massive argument with Katya on Skype. My time here has certainly caused me a lot of problems financially, emotionally, logistically, and relationship-wise. I really hope it is all worth it in the end.

One of the reasons I have continued playing football into my 30s, 40s and now heading towards 50 is that when I am in the zone – playing – all of my troubles are forgotten. I arrive at training feeling properly down but once again join in the kickabout. One hour later, sweating, panting, laughing and covered in African soil, I realise I have temporarily forgotten all the negatives in my head. And even afterwards, when they start to ebb back, you are never quite as pissed off as you were before. I love coaching and watching football but nothing ever (ever!) beats playing.

My general mistrust is so great in the black East Germany that it is best I don't tell the boys the day and time of my departure just in case one of them is a government informant. So, I do my farewell speech, thanking the lads for making me feel welcome and for them developing during my time here. I issue a rallying cry to train hard on the football pitch as well as pushing themselves in the gym and at the abandoned racecourse. I want them to realise what an opportunity London 2018 is for each and every one of them; us. The boys break into a click song and dance to send me off with each and every person required to dance in the middle of the circle, including me. Fantastic stuff and something I hope they will be showing off at the World Cup. I want the lads to sing and dance and show off their culture in England. I have toyed with the idea of them creating an Ndebele war dance before our CONIFA WFC matches. I present Busani and Khanye with an early Christmas present: my tactics board made from a cardboard cornflakes box and 20 beer tops (plus two Ginger Ale tops for goalkeepers) and then shake hands with all of the 14 lads present before leaving. Praise is the kindest and most complimentary, "I have learned so much coach. I don't have the words to thank you."

Strange to pace off alone in the dark and rain for what, for all I know, could be my final time with Matabeleland. Off along Robert Mugabe Way, one of the street signs still missing from that revolutionary night, cars zipping by – way too fast – with their main beams on and clouds of diesel fumes. I jog that last kilometre home as fast as I can, as is customary, sucking in the aroma of flowers, burning rubbish, and diesel, through that creaky front gate, puffing and panting, Ethan at the front door exclaiming *Gogo* while he waits anxiously for his mum to pick him up, Ethel's sister cooking. I go into my room and crash on my bed.

Friday, December 8, 2017

My last full day here. It is the coldest it has been aside from that crazy cold snap when we played the podgy lawyers. It is raining, and grey, and the water is switched off. Ethel, the master of all eventualities, has two-litre bottles of water stored away for emergencies.

I pack, compile a comprehensive to-do list, listen to Duran Duran's first album, and continue to formulate an action plan for 2018. I am very, very excited about going home, enjoying Christmas, and lots of adventures with (and without) Matabeleland in 2018. Buzzing below the surface, you could call it.

Saturday, December 9, 2017

Everything comes around. It is time to say farewell to Zim today. I am up at six. I give Ethel some Christmas money (I have kept back some euros) and she is embarrassingly grateful. Words fail me about her hospitality and friendship. Three whole days of travel await me to get back to my home village in Leicestershire. 14 hours to Joburg, one hour to Kempton Park, a day there, 4 hours at the airport, 5 hours to Addis, 5 more hours there in the airport, 9 hours to London, 3 hours in that airport (waiting for my connecting bus), nearly 3 hours to Leicester and then 30 minutes to home. It looks like 20 hours on the road, 12 hours in airports and 14 hours in the sky. It would all be so much easier to fly straight from Zim to London but travelling this way allows me to slip in and out of this country under the cover of darkness, so to speak.

Sunday, December 10, 2017

We spend the whole night – six hours in fact – getting through the two border posts. Zimbabweans are headed en masse in both directions for

Christmas and the customs officials are clearly over-burdened trying to deal with Windolene and toilet roll smugglers. There is relief for me, though, in making it out of Zimbabwe without any problems.

Thank God, I listed to Busani's advice. I was going to make the journey from Bulawayo to the airport the same day. He told me I shouldn't rely on the bus getting me there in time, even with a safety buffer of five or six hours. Sure enough, after a quarter of a day on the border, we spend an additional eighth of a day stuck in the middle of the South African countryside as our bus breaks down and we are forced to hitchhike lifts from other passing buses. A 14-hour bus journey becomes almost 24. God, I can't wait to get home.

Thabiso kindly picks me up in Joburg and after a layover in Kempton Park, I am homeward bound.

Monday, December 11, 2017

It is minus-five in London, and there is snow on the ground in Leicester. By 2pm I am by a roaring fireplace in my local, enjoying a pint of Pedigree, and reliving tales with my mum. Africa already feels like a very long way away. England has rarely felt so Christmassy. I can't believe I am home. I can barely believe that I have successfully completed part one of my Matabeleland mission.

PART 2

12: International cat sitter

Wednesday, January 3, 2018 | Riga, Latvia

I've gone full Alan Partridge. 2018 begins with Katya and me splitting up, and me being kicked out of my apartment and residing in hotels. I returned from Zimbabwe in December longing for stability and for things to work, but it wasn't to be. The time and the distance between Africa and Russia took its toll on my relationship with Katya, and we split up over New Year. One of the costs of coaching Matabeleland is five years with Katya coming tumbling down. Both of us in tears, she departs for Russia on January 3, the very same day our horrid flat owner forces us to move out of our Riga apartment. I shift 27 boxes, one-by-one, 800 yards to a friend's place, and head off to North Cyprus for the CONIFA AGM.

Saturday, January 6, 2018 | Kyrenia, North Cyprus

The weather is gorgeous in beautiful North Cyprus, and my trip is a timely escape from the darkness, snow, and ice of northern Europe and my mental gloom. Yorkshire has officially joined CONIFA. Philip Hegarty, Matt Thomas, and the lads who run the Yorkshire setup are absolute diamonds. Truthfully, *the Vikings* joining us is the biggest thing to ever happen to CONIFA in terms of publicity.

The draw is made for this summer's World Football Cup. I don't tell anyone, but my heart sinks a little when Padania and Szekely Land are pulled out in our group. It is a big ask getting past those two sides. I am sure we will see off our other group opponent, Kiribati, but qualifying for the quarter-finals requires finishing above both the Champions and the third best team in Europe. But, let's see. There will be a million twists and turns before May 31 in London. Our priority, for now, is simply getting on the plane to the UK.

Monday, January 8, 2018 | Vilnius, Lithuania

There's a stupidly drunk Lithuanian bloke on our flight, out of control and abusing staff and passengers. We are an hour on the tarmac in Vilnius while the police come and arrest him. Consequently, I have missed my Ecolines bus to Riga and will have to hang around Vilnius' not-very-delightful bus station for a few hours. Not having my woman, or a home to return to in Latvia, compounds a general sense of *what the hell are you doing with your life, Justin?*

119

Thursday, January 11, 2018 | Riga, Latvia

It is the last of my four nights in the Konventa Seta Hotel as I move into Justin & Sophie's place tomorrow to begin my latest career as a... cat sitter. Part-time international football manager, part-time cat sitter. Actually, I am quite enjoying living in hotels in North Cyprus and Latvia. And at €26 for a four-star room, including buffet breakfast, who wouldn't?

Sunday, January 14, 2018

This lovely apartment is an absolute lifeline. Justin is a golf pro and is spending the harshest months of the Baltic winter in the Canary Islands. He and his wife needed a cat/house sitter for about seven weeks, so this works out perfectly for all involved, including my new beautiful feline friend – Chloe. I am rent free and just need to pay the heating bills. This luxurious three-bedroom apartment will therefore be mine, and Chloe's, until I return to England at the end of February.

It is roughly a month since I returned to Europe from Zimbabwe. The Matabeleland Football team and its head coach have been hibernating since then. Today, it is time we put our proverbial boots back on and get back on the pitch. Quite aside from my cat sitting responsibilities, I go full-time on *Operation Get Matabeleland to the CONIFA World Football Cup*, starting today.

I am well aware that what we need to achieve is nigh on impossible, but I am going to give it 100 percent. To make the invisible visible, you have to imagine it and believe it first. But where do I even begin to start? I don't believe we will be able to raise $50,000 never mind the original target of $100,000, and have convinced the MFC that we aim for $20,000 for all the flights, visas, and general costs. I think it might just be enough money if we can acquire most of the other things we need from sponsors and the kindness of strangers. Twenty thousand is a huge but realistic target. And, for not the first time, we'll just have to go soup and water if necessary. During my time in Zimbabwe, I created a ten-page action plan for the coming weeks with detailed lists of what I think we need in terms of additional staff, equipment, coaching, nutrition, training camps, media, branding, crowdfunding campaigns, etc. etc.

The very first people I speak to are Paddy Power, who might potentially travel to Zimbabwe to make a documentary about the team. Paddy Power are the title sponsors of the World Football Cup, and the more Matabeleland can somehow get them onboard, helping us, the better.

My other priorities, at this early stage, are contacting as many indie football websites and Twitter accounts as possible and seeing if any of them are willing to run our story. In turn, I am hoping to use Twitter to push initial awareness of myself coaching in Africa principally, and then, of course, to build interest in the team. *British football manager going to World Cup* is my catchy email title I send out to two-dozen football sites. Within 48 hours, 25% of them have replied, asking to interview me.

Sunday, January 21, 2018

I have sent literally hundreds of emails in the past week, especially in the past couple of days. I am aiming high, targeting BBC World, CNN, Al Jazeera, etc. At the end of the day, they can only say no or ignore me. It is like beautiful women: you'd be foolish to assume that the best-looking ladies aren't interested in you, and instead settle for something second rate. There's no accounting for taste.

My other big emphasis is currently on universities. I have set up relationships with Bath, Portsmouth, and half a dozen others. I am looking to bring in up to ten sports science students on World Cup placements to make Matabeleland Football Team as professional a set up as is possible. The response thus far is overwhelming with more than 100 applicants.

Meanwhile, it is minus 15 in Riga and blowing a blizzard most days. Chloe is fantastic company and curls up next to me when I go to bed. It is so cold that the bedrooms are impossible to keep sufficiently warm without a crazy heating bill and I am sleeping on the lounge sofa, next to the radiators.

I reckon hanging around with the African boys and all that jogging at altitude in Bulawayo has rubbed off on me as I think I'm playing the best at Riga United training in years. I am an old man, but I actually feel noticeably faster and – strange to say – younger in football training. I certainly need the escape of playing two nights per week as I am now doing about 60 sedentary hours per week on Matabeleland.

Wednesday, January 24, 2018

I have swapped the coaching of international footballers in Africa for six-year-old boys and girls at the international school. The switch only feels strange for about the first ten minutes. As ever, coaching young kids is hugely rewarding and a lot of fun. For me, as well, I feel I have benefited as a coach over the years by working with footballers as they progress from small children to adults. It is a 10-kilometre roundtrip by foot to the school, which I also use to keep myself fit.

I have written to 40 English football clubs asking whether they will host me for half a day, watching their first teams train. Don't ask, don't get. I want to learn from the best and better myself as a coach. Northampton Town are happy to support me on social media, in the matchday programme, and on the training ground. Nothing is going with the club in Finland I thought I'd join for a week. Aside from the three-dozen clubs I have written to, my main targets are now Aberdeen FC, as the city is twinned with Bulawayo, and Sheffield United, as my favourite coach, Chris Wilder, is their gaffer.

Sunday, January 28, 2018

Here goes... I have just emailed Bruce Grobbelaar. *Why*, you might ask. Because, Bruce is a Matabeleland legend, having begun his career in 1973 with the Highlanders and having played 32 times for his nation, Zimbabwe. If I can get Mr. Grobbelaar onboard, I think it will help take us through the gears both on and off the pitch.

Between the hours of 8am and 11pm, I barely move to eat, go to the toilet, or let alone go out. Email after email, tweet after tweet, begging letter after desperate begging letter. I am exhausted. It is depressing sitting up until almost midnight, on a minus ten Sunday night, searching through endless websites, trying to find relevant personal email addresses, then specifically catering letters to said individuals. But I believe it will pay off. There is an unlimited world of opportunity out there. You have literally got to email and message a million and one people!

I escaped all this last night for the epic Mairis Briedis v Oleksandr Usyk fight in front of 10,000 at a wild Arena Riga. I couldn't believe my good fortune when my mate Paul Featherstone said he'd got a spare ticket for me. What an incredible atmosphere. What a fight! The buzz of it all mentally re-energizes me.

Monday, January 29, 2018

Hello Justin,

Thank you for your email regarding the Matabeleland Football Team.

I am aware of this competition for some time now and its message to the world.

As my position in the new Zimbabwe political system I would like the opportunity to be involved with the team in some way or another.

I will be in the UK from the 8th Feb-27th April so maybe we can meet to iron out what my role in this team will be?

Bruce D Grobbelaar

YNWA, JFT 96

I told a couple of mates I was going to write to Bruce Grobbelaar so, when this email from him appeared in my inbox this morning, I initially assumed it was one of my friends winding me up. I am absolutely made up that Bruce wants to get involved. I obviously won't be counting my chickens just yet but, having him on board would be a huge boost in countless ways and make others sit up and take us seriously.

Talking of taking us seriously, Emily, the Business Engagement Manager of Bath University has phoned me, and I will now have one of the UK's most prestigious Unis supporting Matabeleland with sports science students.

Friday, February 2, 2018

This could be massive. CNN have phoned me and are interested in travelling out to Zimbabwe to film me and the lads. I am not sure if they will ever get the clearance but, if they do, the exposure and endorsement will take this project to another level. Rachel, the CNN Producer, is very positive about what we are trying to do. The New York Times has also expressed an interest in visiting!

And things just get better and better as it looks very likely that I have got Paddy Power to agree to provide the home and away kits for Matabeleland. They are planning to hold a kit design competition on social media. This will create a huge awareness of the project. In turn, we can use this to sell dozens, possibly hundreds, of replica shirts to boost our fundraising. The head of the UK's Zimbabwe committee has also set up a fundraiser with his mate Xolani Viki; the two of them will be running a 10-kilometre marathon in a few weeks' time. I call it leading by example.

Meanwhile, tickets have officially gone on sale for the CONIFA World Football Cup. This feels like it is happening now.

Friday, February 9, 2018

Finally, finally, we have gone live with the new crowdfund page on *Generosity* today. The original page, set up by the MFC, is asking for 100 grand and I am sure few people are going to donate, assuming we will never hit that figure. I have also been waiting for the MFC to put together a short video for us to use, featuring the boys. I think the two-minute film is absolutely spot on! Respect to Busani and the lads! We now have a bit more than three months to raise $20,000.

Almost immediately, an anonymous donation of $200 hits the back of the net. I know the person, but he does not want to be revealed publicly. We quickly hit $606 in the first 48 hours, and our page is featured by *Generosity* as a 'popular fundraiser'.

Ex-Latvian international Māris Verpakovskis has agreed that I can go and observe his Premier League Liepāja train later in the month. These Football Times have done a feature about Matabeleland. Only WBA have bothered to reply from the 40 British football clubs I wrote to. And that is to politely say *no*.

I am not sure why but I have gone from fit and healthy to feeling dreadful. I have got a constant cough and sore throat and, in football training, the batteries suddenly feel flat.

Monday, February 12, 2018

I walk out of the upstairs shower with a towel over my shoulder. Chloe thinks it is a game and jumps. Instinctively, I duck out of the way, and she lands on the stair banister rail. Except it is too thin and narrow for her to maintain her grip. To my absolute horror, she freefalls 15 feet from the second floor of the apartment to the ground floor. It is so far down that I have time to manoeuvre myself to see her hit the floor, her tiny head millimetres away from the edge of the bottom step. She seems to scream. I panic. Please don't tell me this lovely creature is going to die.

I run down the stairs as she half crawls off and hides.

I try to grab her from under a table and somehow, she half limps up the stairs, past me to under the bed. When I do finally get her out, she doesn't seem in a good way. I'm hysterical, *Please Chloe, no!!* I couldn't live with myself if she dies while I am looking after her. One of her hind legs appears to be broken. I force her into a pet carry case and set off into the street. Rush hour has just hit, and the snow is coming down in cotton wool-sized pieces. Chloe meows both in pain and, no doubt, in stress at the noise, lights, and chaos of the traffic. Giant snowflakes land on her.

The vet does a full check as well as an X-ray. Talk about nine lives — Chloe's diagnosis is bad ligament damage in one leg, no suspected internal bleeding. I need to nurse her for the next week and administer painkiller injections. I cannot believe she is going to be OK. In the moment, I thought she was going to die. I whispered a prayer, asking to trade my part in the Matabeleland project for Chloe's life.

Tuesday, February 13, 2018

Katya returns from Russia to find me nursing a sick kitten. She needs to spend the last two weeks of her Schengen closing down her temporary residency, bank account, Uni, etc.; her life here. I am happy for Katya to stay with me as it can serve as "a second chance". Perhaps our relationship can still be saved?

I am now targeting podcasts, UK TV channels including regional ones such as Anglia, print newspapers, and magazines. Cobblers' Gareth Willsher is being a great help, as is Dan Morfitt who has me on BBC Radio Northampton's breakfast show. There's even bigger news as BBC Five Live's Caroline Barker wants to do something with me.

Showing the spirit of CONIFA, fellow members Yorkshire, Isle of Man, Szekely Land, and Northern Cyprus have all donated to us. Orcun Kamali, the head of North Cyprus has been a brilliant support and is getting polos made for the whole team to wear in London as well as having his team donate boots to our boys. James Herbertson kindly donates a couple of hundred quid for the privilege of training with the team in London. Not surprisingly, as yet, no one has taken up the hundred pounds crowdfund option to *have dinner with the Matabeleland manager.*

Each time I receive an email from *Generosity*, notifying me that another kind individual has donated to the team, it is like a hit of dopamine. It is also like a scratch card, as I wait to discover how big each donation is.

Saturday, February 18, 2018

When we are young, there are numerous things we dream of being and doing. Naturally, I dreamed of playing football for England. As part of the MTV generation, watching those first pop videos in the early 1980s made me want to one day appear in a pop music video. Well, strangely, today that dream has come true, although it's not quite Duran Duran's *Rio*.

To celebrate the football club's tenth anniversary, Riga United club secretary André Kliese came up with the idea of teaming up with a local pop band and creating a club anthem. That initial idea grew legs and has turned into the release of a pop song and a music video. Aarzemnieki represented Latvia at the 2014 Eurovision Song Contest in Copenhagen. The band's quirky little number "A Cake to Bake" finished 13th in the first semi-final but notched up an incredible 1.5 million views on YouTube. Today, Riga United and Aarzemnieki officially release "United" and I find myself in the video, which we filmed in a recording studio a couple of weeks ago. You never quite know what life is going to serve up!

Tuesday, February 20, 2018

The shirt supplier, who will create the team's match shirts, is just too expensive in my opinion for our replica kits, so I have begun looking elsewhere. It is not a case of going with the cheapest bidder; I want a top-quality shirt. After all, many of those who buy it will be my friends. But I do want a better profit margin for us on each unit sold, so we can get nearer to our fundraising target. As a ballpark figure, I reckon we will be able to sell a couple of hundred.

Frustrated by the lack of support I have received from British football clubs, I put out a Tweet on this subject, and suddenly dozens of people are trying to help. Tranmere Rovers and Woking Town invite me to one of their respective training sessions. I am also now in contact with the well-known journalist Andrew Harding. Africa on the Ball and Million Seat Stadium are doing a lot to help us, as are the lads from YIFA. More generally speaking, I am in talks with nutritionists, sports psychologists, match data analysts, masseurs, physios, fitness trainers, sprint coaches, and social media helpers. We might end up having more backroom staff than Chelsea by the time I have finished.

I also assist with team matters from afar although 98% of what is happening on the ground in Zimbabwe is, of course, in the very capable hands of Khanye and Busani. Busani says there are some issues with the lads' contracts but the players continue to develop and are performing well in friendly matches, which they are winning comfortably.

My health seems to be further deteriorating. As well as the constant cough, I feel totally exhausted – both mentally and physically.

Thursday, February 22, 2018

Sheffield United have finally given my letter to Chris. He reads it and the Blades are back to me in 15 minutes saying Mr. Wilder would be happy for me to come in. I can't tell you how much it means to me being able to go in and spend a day with my favourite coach of the current era.

Luke from Paddy Power has got Matabeleland on the world's most read football website (goal.com) – 17 footballers in a truck. That should really put us on the map.

It is one thing creating a crowdfunder but running one of this magnitude and complexity is damn hard work: sourcing merchandise, stock, liaising with donors, etc.

Little Chloe seems to have almost totally recovered and is now sprinting around the apartment behaving like a curious, mischievous, and fun-loving kitten once again. Tears well up as I give her a last hug and I move out of Sophie and Justin's place.

Monday, February 26, 2018

André and the men and women at Riga United training put their hands in their pockets as they raise a few hundred euros for Matabeleland. The Zim million-dollar notes are especially popular at five euros a time. They also kindly donate Matabeleland's first ever professional match ball.

I'm trying everything with Aberdeen – the city council, the football club and the local press – but it is going nowhere, to be honest. I am really disappointed as I was convinced Bulawayo's twin city would partner us and prove to be a great boost for our efforts.

Katya and I spent the weekend snowed in and snuggled away in a winter cottage deep in a Latvian forest. I still need to work most of the time, but a rocking chair by a log fire is the perfect place to find myself before I leave Latvia this week. I have crafted and posted 200 tweets on behalf of the MFC this month. I also continue trying to scout players for the MFC in the English Non-League. I am looking at four players, with Halifax Town's Cliff Moyo being my main person of interest.

Quite aside from all these things, on a personal level, I am trying to find a potential book publisher. One of my dreams is to be published. I actually wrote a novel in 2004. I believe that this crazy roller coaster of an experience should be told and shared with others.

Tuesday, February 27, 2018

It is time for Katya to head back to Russia once again. I really believe we both love each other but, due to a number of factors, especially related to this project, it just isn't working. It is four months before we can possibly see each other again and I feel that, unselfishly, I have got to let her go to get on with her life. We agree to split up but also express a desire to meet in Kazan in June and give it another chance if we are both still single then.

I have a last night out with my mates which, as ever, is a stupid move, guaranteed to leave me in pieces tomorrow, for my departure to England.

Wednesday, February 28, 2018

It is a bitter minus 22 today, with a wind-chill of 30 something, as I end my time in the Baltics, chasing all the media and money I can find for Matabeleland. Yes, I am in pieces.

13: Hilton Park Service Station

Friday, March 2, 2018 | England

I had planned to pay visits to London, Northampton, and Birmingham on behalf of Matabeleland by the end of this week but heavy snow has rather embarrassingly 'paralysed the UK' and put paid to that. So, my focus instead, is to do as much media as possible.

Dan Morfitt has me on the BBC Radio Northampton Breakfast Show and then there is an interview with Caroline Barker for the BBC World Service. This is huge for the project. The many doubters in the Zimbabwean community – near and far – can now start to believe that our project is genuine. Being on the BBC World Service, and word about our Matabeleland team being transmitted all around the world, is enormous prestige. I find the whole thing nerve-racking, and I have to ask Caroline to drop the more political questions. This lady is clearly a very smart and consummate journalist. I nervously listen to the piece go live and I am relieved to hear that I seem to come across well. In fact, I think it is the best interview I have ever done.

BBC Leicester also have me on their African & Caribbean Show. I am gaining super momentum now, and the donations are starting to fly in. I also go live on Luton radio station, Pamtengo. Those guys are being really supportive of my efforts and are doing whatever they can to push awareness of us to the local Zim community. Neil Jensen, The Set Pieces, and These Football Times have all featured Matabeleland this week.

I am a bit guilty as my CONIFA Africa and CONIFA London committee stuff is just falling away now. I was trying to organise an Africa Cup, but I have dropped my efforts for the time being.

There are also lots of hours negotiating with airlines now. I am trying to nail this deal and get the deposits paid.

Monday, March 5, 2018

We finally have a sponsorship document to send to potentially interested parties. A student volunteer is responsible for that. I hope she does a better job than my student World Cup Volunteers Coordinator who has pulled out saying he is *too busy*. Actually, I regret putting so much energy into the volunteer-students thing. I have spent more than 100 hours on it in total, and I have found the majority of students to be unmotivated, unreliable, self-entitled, often clueless, and lazy. Thankfully, the Bath and

Pompey students, and the handful of other candidates I have remaining, have been quite the opposite.

Tuesday, March 6, 2018

I have travelled down to south London to pay a visit to Sutton United. Matabeleland's opening World Cup game is here on May 31 and I want to get a sense of what the pitch, facilities, and general setup are like. My very good friend Graham Foster joins me as we do lots of video for social media. Someone later comments that our style is a bit like the Chuckle Brothers.

Sutton's Bobby Childs gives me a quick tour, including the changing rooms where Sutton's opponents, Woking, are getting ready for tonight's Conference match. We are accompanied by cameraman Jonathan Binks who is filming us for one of the Paddy Power documentary videos. The pitch is very decent but none of our lads has ever played on artificial 3G in their lives. There isn't a single 3G pitch in Zimbabwe we can even go and prepare ourselves on. Once the lads get used to 3G, it will suit their quick, passing game but I fear that it will take them two or three matches to get used to the completely different bounce and speed of the surface. And by then, we might already have failed to progress to the quarters.

Grabbing a beer with Graham, John, and some very affable Sutton United fans, we spot Sutton United's famous ex-goalkeeper and coach Wayne Shaw. Wayne is a very good laugh, and it is a shame that his image has been tarnished after the Arsenal pie episode. I get the sense that he feels very sad about it all. One thing Wayne definitely is not is tight. He insists on buying all of the beers both before the game and at halftime. Sutton United is a super little club with very decent facilities. Stood on the terraces watching the Woking match, I find myself dreaming of May 31. Sawusani gets sent clear, is upended, and Kiwa slots away the winning goal against Padania from the penalty spot.

Wednesday, March 7, 2018

I am in an old-fashioned laundry shop near St. Pancras, where I'm meeting the charming Kemal Soyer, who runs the Turkish community FA in London, and has been doing so for decades. Orcun, from the North Cyprus FA, put me in touch with Kemal, who very kindly asked his members at last night's monthly meeting to help the Matabeleland team. He slips me an envelope, which I am expecting might contain fifty pounds but, inside there is four hundred quid!

And he apologises *that it isn't much!* One of his members – Gaziantep – have also donated an entire football kit to us as well as two footballs! Unbelievable. Football can be such a force for good! I do a quick spot of video for social media and I am roaring with laughter inside as I realise Kemal thinks my name is Josephine and calls me that on camera.

I wanted to visit Haringey's stadium, where we will play our second and third group games but there just isn't the time. In the hour before I catch my train back to Nuneaton, I meet a potential sponsor at Euston Station. They are very interested in putting their name on our team shirt. If they do, it will bring in substantial coin. I get home in time for the CONIFA Exco, followed by an MFC Skype call with Busani.

Thursday, March 8, 2018

M6 Services, Wolverhampton. I am crossing the pedestrian bridge from northbound to southbound, where ten minutes from now, I am going to ask one of the biggest personalities to ever put on a football shirt in the history of the game, whether he will join Matabeleland as my goalkeeper coach... and potentially come out of retirement at 60 to be our third-choice keeper.

I try to keep it together in the queue to Greggs. My phone rings. "Justin, it's Bruce. Where are you? I am in Costa Coffee, but I can't see you." I turn 180 degrees and spot him. Immediately. There is Bruce Grobbelaar twenty years older than I remember him being. These next few minutes will likely make or break the chances of Matabeleland ever getting to London.

I sit down with my coffee, so keen to appear unfazed by all of this that I burn my lip while nervously taking my first sip. *This is Tony*, he says in that familiar soft Zimbabwean accent, introducing me to his friend Tony Morton. *So, you are coaching in Latvia? I know some people over there. Do you know...?* Bruce reels off three or four names. I have never heard of any of them. Some of the names sound Balkan, to tell the truth. I am a bit embarrassed that I know none of them, particularly as I am familiar with the people – some of them personally – whom I consider to be the main characters in Latvian football. Pahars, Gorkss, Ashworth, Verpakovskis, Indriksons... I know them all but none of these names. There is no way I am going to pretend I know them though. Strangely, Grobbelaar seems relieved when I confess that I have never heard of any of them.

Tell me about the Matabeleland team. I explain it is mostly second division lads and youngsters who have hardly played more than a few friendly matches in their barely adult lives. But we are doing everything we can to develop the lads and they are strong in spirit and commitment. For the first ten minutes of our conversation, Bruce has been more intense than a one-to-one with Alan Sugar, only allowing his eye contact with me to slip when he has a bite of his cheese toastie or a sip of his pint of cappuccino. It is extremely intimidating, but I was expecting that. Everything I am telling him is genuine and, at the end of the day, if he feels that joining us is not for him, then I will totally respect that.

"We actually gave the Highlanders reserve team a good run for their money," I proudly declare. "We were the better team for the first 60 minutes, and all their lads were obviously pros."

"See!" Bruce says to Tony. "See what I have been telling you, Tony! There is so much quality in Zimbabwe. It just needs good coaches working with the players and developing them."

Suddenly, Bruce seems to relax and the intensity has completely gone. It occurs to me that those first minutes were him casing me out, ascertaining whether I am the real deal or some charlatan trying to get him involved in some nonsense. At the end of the day, I could even be a journalist winning his confidence before screwing him over.

Not only has the atmosphere and tone of our conversation become friendlier and more relaxed, but Bruce also confides in me:

"With my position now within the new Zimbabwe, I'd like to help with this. President Mnangagwa called me and asked me to return. Mugabe took away my passport. He wanted me to be the manager of the national team and I told him I wanted to be paid in US Dollars. Mugabe said there weren't any dollars left to pay me with so I told him that's because you have stolen them all!"

The three of us laugh in unison, and I almost snort my coffee up my nose and back down my throat.

"He told me I'd never return after that. So, I am travelling to Zimbabwe after a few days to get my new passport, a diplomatic one. He wants me to be involved in building a new Zimbabwe. Anyway, how would you like me to help?"

"Honestly, in any way possible, Bruce. If you were happy to be our brand ambassador that would really help us get people to take us seriously and spread the word."

"Sure. And you need equipment? I can get you gloves and stuff like that."

"Really anything. That would be fantastic. Obviously, I am a nobody as a coach, but would you consider joining us and helping with the goalkeeper coaching?"

"Absolutely, no problem. When is the tournament?"

Bruce looks at his diary and, aside from a couple of speaking arrangements, he expects to be in the UK and available to join us for most of the period from May 29 until June 10.

"If Liverpool get to the Champions League Final, I might be working and attending that in Ukraine around that time."

Thankfully, the UCL final is the weekend before the tournament.

"I am happy to work with the goalkeepers and give you a bit of help with the general coaching stuff."

"That would be fantastic. I have got to tell you though, Bruce, that I am very underqualified for all of this. Truthfully, I have only done my first badges. I haven't even got the B."

"That doesn't matter. We will get you on the B and A in South Africa after the summer. I might return to work with the national team."

We discuss the huge potential in Zim football and a need for the game to be run by those who understand and care about the game. You can see that Bruce loves Zimbabwe and wants to return to his homeland. He clearly has a passion for developing football in his home country and taking the sport to a point where Zimbabwe can start qualifying for African Nations and World Cups.

"What you are doing with Matabeleland is what I want to do. I have been telling them. Get the best in Mashonaland and Matabeleland playing each other, get the coaches out in the countryside developing the young players. When are you flying back out there?"

"Next week. I am flying into Joburg and then spending a few days in Mozambique before I go back to Bulawayo."

Bruce looks at his diary again, and we agree to meet each other in Joburg where we can speak to some guys who might potentially help us with sponsorship.

"How do you want me to announce this?"

"Let's take some photos, and you put it out saying that I am joining you as the Matabeleland goalkeeper coach for the CONIFA World Cup.

There could be a reaction from some people in Zimbabwe but you can expect that. Don't worry about that."

We take half a dozen photos of Bruce and me posing together, shaking hands and giving the thumbs up, and then it is time to part company.

"Thanks for your good efforts working with Matabeleland and developing the boys," Bruce says quietly as Tony nips off to the toilet.

"Thank you very much. And thanks for agreeing to join us. See you in South Africa."

I am punching the air as I cross the pedestrian bridge back to the northbound services, where my mum has been sitting in the Costa there, patiently waiting for me.

Driving here with my mum this morning, I told her that I felt this meeting was make or break for the project. I am physically and mentally exhausted, and we desperately need Bruce to come in and help pull us towards the finish line. Actually, I almost missed the meeting as I nearly took the slip road to the M54 and had to swerve across two lanes at the last moment to stay on the M6.

My head is spinning as I sit on the front row of the upper balcony at the beautiful 1903 Buxton Opera House watching a performance of the Little Matchgirl. From the M6 services, we drove over a very snowy A53 hill pass to get here, to the UK's highest market town. Even that felt surreal, looking almost otherworldly. Have I imagined it or did I really sign Bruce Grobbelaar as my goalkeeper coach today?

Friday, March 9, 2018

After a morning well spent in the Pavilion Gardens, and the Devonshire Building, I announce Bruce Grobbelaar joining us on my personal Twitter as he wanted. The MFC follow it up immediately. The response is significant but you can just tell that most people seeing that tweet think I've lost my marbles and I am making it up.

Lee calls from Paddy Power and is furious that I didn't tell them I'd signed Grobbelaar so that they could break the news. I am furious that Lee is furious.

"But we could have done this properly and got infinitely more media than you are ever going to get releasing this on your Twitter page. I don't understand what you were thinking."

Lee is right. But my thinking was this: if Paddy Power announced this news, then to many it would look like Bruce was in their pocket, on their salary. The point is that I met him and he is helping the place he considers home – Matabeleland. Grobbelaar wanted me to announce the news. I suspect if I'd let PP do it, Bruce would have gone mad and would no longer trust me. Yes, none of the major press are contacting me to enquire how on earth we have got the world-famous Bruce Grobbelaar coaching an amateur group of Zimbabwean footballers, but I know they will eventually.

The Matabeleland Cultural Ambassador, Sisa Senkosi, is holding a live Facebook event to build interest in the team here in the UK. Busani and I are on, live, from Zim and the UK. A few people phone in and message that they approve of what we are doing although the Grobbelaar factor is not a major part in that.

The Zim who approve – some of them Shona – see the positives of our team participating in London from a cultural, sport, and humanitarian point of view. But, oh my, the number of negative people out there. There is a toxicity to parts of the Zim community. People are accusing us of being fake to steal money, smuggling lads into the country, and being politically divisive. Others mock us, saying we will be crap; the squad is too young, too old. These are comments I have been hearing directly and indirectly for months, and I am sick of them. I don't know what more I can personally do to legitimise us in the eyes of the doubters. The most famous non-President Zimbabwean in the world has just endorsed us but, for many, it means nothing.

Saturday, March 10, 2018

I had dreadful toothache all night. I barely slept despite being away in the lovely Old Hall Hotel for the night with my wonderful mum. There were dreams, almost hallucinations, about being trapped in a giant email inbox, unable to escape. Emails kept dropping in while a miniature version of me was running up and down their texts. I feel like I am falling apart. I would dearly like to hide away here in the beautiful snowy Peak District for a few more days and get my energy back, but I fly next week.

I get back to Leicestershire and meet the lads in Burbage, but I am struggling.

Sunday, March 11, 2018

Mother's Day. I would be nothing without my mother. She is my rock in this world.

Monday, March 12, 2018

I am driving around the middle of Sheffield, struggling to track down Sheffield United's training ground. It is at times like this that my insistence on not having a smartphone drastically backfires. I am basically having to guesstimate my way to the training pitches and then ask petrol station staff if I am getting warmer. Blades Football Secretary Donna Fletcher is the one who saves me in the end as she guides me in on the phone.

The very first person I set eyes upon is my favourite lower league player, Ricky Holmes. Ricky was the most exciting and talented player to put on a Northampton Town shirt in decades before he left the club for Charlton and now Sheffield United, where he recently teamed up with his old coaches and the man I am meeting today, Chris Wilder.

Ricky, and a dozen or so of the Sheffield United players, are on the tea and biscuits and enjoying the usual banter that you expect from footballers. I think of the Matabele boys and how, in truth, none of them will ever get to play anywhere near the level of football these lads play in the English Championship.

The next person I spot is the gangly Alan Knill. Alan is to Chris Wilder what Peter Taylor perhaps was to Brian Clough. I feel sorry for Alan sometimes as his huge input into the success of clubs like Northampton and Sheff U is often overlooked. You could see that Alan and Chris were very much a two-man team during their time together at the Cobblers.

God, I feel so ill. I am barely holding it together as Chris comes and warmly greets me. He then introduces me to Alan and the backroom staff as the manager of Zimbabwe, before correcting himself, which I find amusing, briefly imagining myself as a real national team coach hanging out with England's finest league club manager.

Chris takes me to his office where I explain what I am doing with the Matabeleland team and that I am here today just to understand a bit more about Chris's philosophy and to watch his session. This is the second time I have met Chris; the first (very briefly) was at the Bramall Lane Hotel the night before Cobblers played Sheffield United last year, when I thanked him for all he had done for Northampton Town during his tenure. The club had been hours away from going bankrupt and folding; Chris, the players, and staff hadn't been paid in months. And yet, despite all this, the team went on to win the League Two title that season, playing the best football Northampton had played in 20 years.

We talk a lot about his time at Northampton Town. Clearly, he is proud of what was achieved there and has a great fondness for the club, its supporters, and the players he worked with.

He is even more honoured to be leading Sheffield United, his boyhood club, whom he started his playing career with and holds a place deep in his heart for. I feel honoured just being here. One day he will be an EPL manager, perhaps even England boss.

Chris talks of the quality of goals that the Cobblers scored that title-winning season, especially a couple of worldies from Ricky Holmes, whom I can hear in the other room cracking a joke. That volley against Leyton Orient away is one of the best goals I have ever seen. *Sheffield United are perhaps playing better, creating more chances than the Cobblers did, but they are failing to put games to bed.*

Chris says he is old school but likes to take advantage of the latest data analysis technology. They thoroughly analyse opponents and they also meticulously analyse themselves. *I like to look at the percentage of time we spend in the final third and the number of crosses from those dangerous areas.*

Sheffield United are just off the play off places and will move up to seventh if they beat Burton Albion tomorrow.

We've got 56 points but we've drawn several games we should have easily won. Chris is scribbling down a quick sum on a piece of paper, calculating the difference four or five wins – instead of frustrating draws – would have made to their current league standing. Yes, as he suspected, they'd be about third now. I have to laugh, because *the where we should really be in the league table points total,* scribbled down on pieces of paper, was something I often did in Latvian league club management. It isn't so much fooling yourself with a fantasy of what could have been, as trying to appreciate just how good you think your current team really is.

As I would have expected when speaking to Chris, positivity is a state of mind he believes in when it comes to playing football. One of his philosophies is that the team must try to play attractive football when they are at home in front of their fans at Bramall Lane. We talk about the different systems he used at Northampton and now at Sheffield United, about player recruitment and other things I won't repeat that I feel he says in confidence. Chris *treats his players the way he would expect to be treated himself.*

I totally agree. Being a football manager doesn't give you the right to treat others badly or to disrespect them.

I really do feel terribly ill, and it has prevented me from engaging more with Chris during our meeting. There are lots more things I want to ask him, but I'm going to have to let him go so he can get on with his training session and prepare for Burton.

It is torrential freezing rain. I am regularly out in weather like this in Latvia, but I just feel too shite to be out there today. I'm sure if I get soaked, I will be even more ill and miss Thursday's flight. Instead, I push my face up against the window of the warm players' lounge and then watch from the changing room front door; the rain pouring down in bucket loads.

I am driving home almost in a trance. I have got the heating on full blast. Classic FM plays to keep the mood positive in the constant torrential rain and heavy traffic. I feel so, so ill. I have just got to concentrate on getting home … then I can go straight to bed.

Tuesday, March 13, 2018

Regrettably, I need to cancel my appearance in the BBC radio Northampton studio. I also contact Northampton Town and ask to rearrange my trips to the academy and Sixfields until tomorrow. Next, I am cancelling tonight's trip to Halifax to watch Cliff Moyo play against Dagenham. It turns out he is injured anyway.

I have got an emergency dentists appointment. Once this is out of the way, I return to bed for the rest of the day.

Wednesday, March 14, 2018

I am back in the surgery. The dentist says I have been grinding my teeth from stress. One tooth is probably compromised and I have now got quite a severe tooth infection.

I know I probably shouldn't, but I drive over to Northamptonshire afterwards to watch the NTFC Academy play and to spend an hour with academy boss Trevor Gould, who is a lovely guy. It is best I swerve first team training as boss Jimmy Floyd Hasselbaink is under a lot of pressure at the moment and the last thing he needs is to entertain me. Academy player Seth Patrick has Zimbabwean heritage. He is definitely one of the better players out there for Northampton and could definitely do a job for Matabeleland as a squad player. Speaking at half-time to Seth, I discover that his parents are Shona so, sadly, I cannot bring him into a

Ndebele/Matabele team. I almost faint at one point, chatting to Trevor about his philosophy and work at the club. *I am so sorry Trevor but I am going to have to leave you early and go home to bed. Can you please tell Gareth that I won't be able to make it to Sixfields?*

I am in such a bad way driving back that I have to pull off the dual carriageway, push the seat back, and have a quick sleep. I am due to fly to South Africa tomorrow. There is no way I can leave in this terrible state. I have no choice other than to cancel tomorrow's flight. I have rebooked for March 20 at the painful cost of £150.

Thursday, March 15, 2018

I am gutted I have cancelled my flight today although I feel so ill that the emotion is numbed somewhat.

Sunday, March 18, 2018

Pat's Football Blog is the first donation I have received by post. Local lad Chris Etchingham does an interview with me for the Football Pink and the Captain's Armband. I am also honoured to be the V2 Blog's *big interview*. I have now abandoned my involvement in the World Football Cup working group. I am in bed the whole time so I am still tweeting and emailing, but what I am achieving seems to be diminishing by the day. UK Zim committee boss Nqo is being a complete star, really helping to boost things here in the UK.

Tuesday, March 20, 2018

Instead of being on my rescheduled Qatar Airways flight, en route to Joburg, I am in Coventry A&E. These places give me the complete and utter fear; an existential fear. My health is deteriorating instead of improving. The doctors are quite concerned by my symptoms and are testing me for (or are considering the possibilities of me having) a wide range of illnesses including malaria, lung disease, and sepsis. I am wondering whether this is not just the end of the world cup dream but also the end of me.

The good news is that they don't think I am suffering from any serious illness. The doctors are saying it is a triple whammy of an extremely nasty virus, a very serious tooth infection, and thirdly – near-exhaustion.

I am in such a state that they advise I put back my flights to Africa by a further two whole weeks until April 3 and that I go on a two-week course of antibiotics. My jaw is now locked. I am consuming food through a straw. I only ever recall feeling worse than this once before, and that was when I had my emergency stomach operation a couple of years ago. All of this means I can no longer meet Bruce Grobbelaar in Joburg to go on a fundraising mission there. This is bad news for the project.

The support we are now getting on Twitter is phenomenal. So many people are messaging me wanting to help. But I have come off the rails. I try to keep up with it all but I cannot.

Thursday, March 23, 2018

The past week has been sweating through the mattress, headaches, almost constant pain (even with painkillers), bad sleep, food through a straw, and exhaustion. With the cocktail of strong drugs I am taking, I am not myself at all. My brain feels numbed. I wonder about all the millions on long-term prescription drugs and what it does to their mental state.

I have ordered bibs, cones, and a dozen footballs from ProDirect to take out to Africa. I have to believe I am still going. I am also trying to set up a friendly match against Zanzibar. The Daily Mail and Sky are in touch wanting to speak to Bruce but I tell them he isn't available for comment at this time.

If time to think gives you an appreciation of how good your life is, then illness makes you realise that without your health, your life is nothing.

Monday, March 26, 2018

Message from Pascal Ito: "Dominik (you met him during Copa America in Chile) and I (who didn't meet you in person as you flew to the Easter Islands with Hannes when I arrived) would be willing to sponsor you (the manager) for the Conifa Cup (the 500 $ option on the generosity site). But we don't want our names on your shirt."

Wow. How nice is that! The kindness of some people is astounding.

Wednesday, March 28, 2018

If my mum wasn't my full-time nurse, blending food for me, bringing up *endless* cups of tea, making sure my three courses of tablets are all taken at the exact correct time, and telling me I will recover from all this and return to Africa, I think I would be done for.

I am visiting a dental specialist in Leicester who can remove teeth with only part of the jaw open. He tells me that considering the antibiotics I have taken, this is the worst tooth infection he has seen in 20 years. And he cannot operate.

Monday, April 2, 2018

I am having some treatment done on my tooth. This is my seventh dental visit in the past month. The dentist does not have sufficient time to carry out the whole two-hour treatment so, instead, he has removed part of the tooth and put a temporary filling on top. If the tooth holds out until I return in June, the treatment will be finished. If I were staying here another week, it could be completed but I need to leave for the team. I guess my tooth is another thing, along with Katya, that I will end up losing for Matabeleland.

My mate Andy Dav drives over and very kindly donates a ball bag and team kit bag for the team. And then, I spend my last evening (and my first evening out in weeks) in the *Cross Keys* village pub with mum. Coincidentally, it is Sheffield United v Cardiff live and, what would you know! Despite the Blades dominating the match, Cardiff's Anthony Pilkington has gone and scored a 91st-minute equaliser. It is another draw for Chris, instead of the win he wanted. Mr. Wilder will no doubt be doing calculations on the back of an envelope. He will conclude the playoffs are no longer realistic but – in the matches they should have won – his team are still pushing for automatic promotion. Next season Chris!

As ever, I am packing at the very last minute, leaving half of my personal items I wanted to take at home so I can fit all the training balls, cones, and bibs into my new team bag check-in luggage.

14: Diesel and flowers

Tuesday, April 3, 2018 | Arabian Peninsula

Oil flare stacks burn brightly, adjacent to Saudi industrial towns; four or five spots of orange light are flickering beyond, out there in the desert. The escaping flames are consumed by the heavens, mixing in that moment with the desert sand to turn the Arabian night sky an otherworldly orange. Truly, it is a dystopian scene right out of Bladerunner; a moment when ugliness takes on a strange beauty.

Truthfully, I am amazed I am actually on this Qatar Airways flight. I was so damn ill that I genuinely concluded my World Cup was over. I feel far from properly recovered but, with so little time left until London, it is now or never for me to return to Zimbabwe.

This flight from Birmingham is less 5-star and more Ryanair-esque. A grossly obese bloke one side of me, the emergency door and no window on the other, a fiddly pop-up table, a constant queue for the now stinky toilet adjacent, and a plane full of drunk British cricketers, who sound more like a stag party. I have never been this uncomfortable on a long-haul flight, and I cannot remember many worse short-haul flights. In this day and age, when everything is broken down into different commodities, you would think the airlines would sell the no-window-next-to-the-toilet seat at a heavy discount.

Doha to Joburg is 9 hours. I move to a row of free seats behind the most gorgeous Arab girl I have seen in my entire life. We exchange a couple of smiles, but I notice a photo of her with her boyfriend on her mobile and switch my attention back to the film I was half watching.

Coming in to land at Joburg, I have got butterflies. My heart is racing. My stomach is not good. The last few weeks have really knocked it out of me, and I am dreading this instead of excitedly re-embarking. "I don't want to be here," I whisper to myself.

South Africa

Back in Kempton Park, the lad on reception remembers me from last year. The air smells fresh, the red roses are in full glory, and it is that perfect 23 degrees that the altitude of this huge city often bestows it. Is any of this real? In bed, ill at my mum's for all those weeks and now, here I am, face down in Johannesburg on the other side of the world, eating my Qatar Airways leftovers.

The Paddy Power shirt design competition has concluded today and, luckily, the white shirt with the Matabele pattern has won. It seems to have received something like 7,000 votes, which shows you the brilliant awareness this whole thing has created for our team. Meanwhile, the Paddy Power crew have arrived in Bulawayo, 24 hours ahead of me.

CNN are asking who the team's sponsors are, as the Zimbabwean authorities want to know this before granting the necessary paperwork needed before CNN visit us. Very few people can believe we aren't financed by some shadowy, politically-motivated individual or organisation.

Thabiso very kindly drives me to Joburg Park Station.

There was a time when I chose the cheapest seat on the dodgiest bus to get myself from A to B. Make the funds stretch. In my 40s, ground transportation is something I never go cheap on anymore in this regard. A 16-hour coach journey through the night, over mountains and sometimes pot-holed roads, could be more perilous than walking home half cut through the streets of east London at 3am on a Sunday. These days, I even pay that bit extra to sit on the safer lower deck of the double-decker.

9pm departure, six pickups, two coffee stops, two maintenance stops and we are at the SA-ZIM border at 5.30am. You have got to hand it to the South Africans – seven bus-loads of punters likely totalling 500 people and they appear to have a grand total of two immigration officers stamping passports.

Two hours queuing in a single file line. A young spook accompanies me, asking a million and one personal questions. I have got to laugh because he occasionally turns to his phone and types in some of my answers. If he is not a spook, then he is bonkers. I decide the best policy is to try to bore him to death with stupidly long-winded answers that go off at complete tangents. I even do my old pretend-to-be-asleep trick; this time while on my feet.

On the Zim side, I'm obviously a little nervous of getting my double entry visa. Without it, it will effectively mean me turning around and going home. The crisp $50 and accompanying $20 note are almost snatched from my hand with enthusiasm. I am in. There is also no problem with me bringing 11 new footballs into the country.

Four hours at the border. Job done. I am back in my new adopted home.

Zimbabwe

It is still four hours to Bulawayo. I am in bits. Everywhere is lush green and overgrown. Zim has transformed from semi-desert to tropical green paradise in my absence.

I wasn't expecting balloons, jelly, and ice cream but I also wasn't anticipating nobody to be waiting for me in Bulawayo. I don't have a functioning phone or indeed anybody's phone numbers. A slight oversight. I am carrying 30 kilos, so I am not exactly mobile. I sit in the Greyhound Office for half an hour, then begin walking towards the Rainbow where I can use Skype. "Oh my God, haha, how happy and relieved am I to see you!" It is the Doc, Matabeleland's team doctor.

I am due to stay in a nearby hotel but it is overbooked. So, one taxi later, I am back at Ethel's hoping she will let me stay. Her daughter is the only one home. No rest for the wicked, I have got one hour before we need to walk the four kilometres back to city hall to meet the team and the Paddy Power film crew.

Summer has turned to autumn but, after a harsh European winter, you'd actually think this was spring turning to summer. You can smell the aromas of different flowers and fruits. Birds chirp and sing. I feel like I have arrived somewhere exotic for my holidays. It is wonderful.

"Paddy! Hi!" I call out as I spot the frontman of Paddy Power. "Oh hello. How are you?" he says as he turns on his heels and starts to stride off. He seems to think I am a super friendly local.

Paddy Power are certainly taking this seriously and have travelled with a sizable team. Along with their local fixers, there is Lee, Tom, Luke and Ben. One of the lads tells me he has met me before, but then realises he just cut video of me at Sutton, and my familiarity is actually virtual.

I meet Lee, the project boss. We had that bust up about Grobbelaar a few weeks ago, so we are both understandably a little coy. We have both been under massive pressure with our respective parts in the CONIFA World Football Cup. All seems fine between us.

Ah, there are the lads! I am delighted by their response to seeing me: beaming smiles, hugs, kind words. There are two or three new faces in there but it is, of course, lovely to see the likes of Kaka, Pele, and Kiwa.

We are jogging the three kilometres uphill to the former Ascot horse racing stadium. Five weeks since my last exercise, three weeks ill in bed, a 52-hour journey with two nights without a bed, no meal. I know I shouldn't join this run but I feel I must – to show the lads I am back, mucking in, a part of the team.

We jog along the main road, chanting and singing, taking in the usual heavy cocktail of diesel and flowers. Passers-by look bemused, especially at the sight of a white van driving alongside, a cameraman balancing precariously, filming us. I mostly jog with Kiwa who asks me about Katya and my time home. He is a smashing lad.

At Ascot, the boys sprint up and down the abandoned grandstand for the film crew, almost superhuman-like in their collective fitness. Half a dozen rounds of star jumps, it is exhausting just watching them. Then, behind the main stand, Paddy joins us for the click dance, which is a great laugh, led passionately by Khanye and ending with a Paddy Power chant. I am sure it will make brilliant TV. I am spaced out. This all feels like a very, very weird dream right now.

It is a nice feeling handing over the new bibs and balls to the boys. Busani tells me they are using this new spot near the racecourse for regular 4-a-sides as it has floodlights. Tonight, it is wet and slippery and I am grimacing at some of the dangerous 100% committed tackles flying in. I obviously let Khanye and Busani lead. It would be a bit crass for me to come back and immediately start throwing my weight around, especially just for the cameras. I take the opportunity to hint to the Paddy Power lads about money and our desperate need to acquire it. Soon.

The boys look stronger, sharper, and fitter. You can see that in Khanye himself. Having trained all these weeks with them, he is significantly stronger; even his handshake is rock solid, firmer. Respect to Busani and Khanye for taking the boys forward a few more steps, a few more percentage points, in my absence.

I stroll back into the city alone with Busani. There is literally a bloke following us in the shadows. I try the old speed up, slow down thing and he manages to stay equidistant behind us, just within earshot. I know I am not imagining this.

The transport is the worst one yet. The driver is drunk, they have two-dozen of us crammed inside, and there is an overpowering smell of fuel; the young lad next to me is carrying an open container of petrol. It is 30 minutes before the lads on duty tonight feel that enough of us are sardeened inside.

Friday, April 6, 2017

Bang bang bang. Bang bang bang. I have woken up with literally no recollection of where I am and what I am doing. My mind is a complete blank. I jump out of bed and by the time my brain computes that I am in Bulawayo, Zimbabwe, I am unlatching the back door to the sight of two tiny boys of about six asking for a wheelbarrow.

A new dog has taken up residency since I was last here. I have a coffee and chat with the neighbour as one of the feline residents trots past with a mouse in its mouth. Wow, the smell of flowers, I forgot just how gorgeous these mornings are.

In our management meeting, I tell the MFC that it looks like I have now raised $7,000. *But we need at least treble that, and we now need to concentrate on deeds and actions rather than continually talking of hope.* I have no problem with my bosses trusting in God, but you also have to trust in yourself. I list all the potential areas of fundraising I can still think of. Each requires tonnes of work, but I believe collectively it could all net us up to 17,000. We need most of this cash in the next four weeks.

On my way to training, I film a short video of me back in Zimbabwe to post on social media. Last time I was here, I didn't dare film myself in public, let alone post stuff. Walking through the as-ever-peaceful suburb, it feels like I was never away.

For the first time ever with these boys, I have the luxury of having enough footballs for what I want to do in the session and get two dozen lads started with pair work. Some of the passing is absolutely dreadful. And I mean dreadful.

I am pleased to see that Xolani has improved. His father was a Highlanders legend. Both his dad and his mother have passed, and life is difficult for him. He broke his leg when he was a Zimbabwean international youth player. You just want him to be good enough to get on the plane to London. Then again, he still doesn't have a passport.

Leaving training with the lads playing on in the half-light, slow jogging so I don't stumble into a pothole and put myself out of business, I spot an overweight bloke, stomach spilling out, at the rear of the stadium spying over the wall and through the undergrowth. He's watching our lads playing, and busily talking to someone on his phone.

Diesel and flowers jog home; I forgot quite how shocking the air pollution is here. I received disappointing news about the squad tonight. Percy, the quality centre-forward who joined us back in December, has left us and signed for a 1st league club. Nonja, our first-choice keeper, is also likely going elsewhere. Busani believes we can still get our hands on Nonja for London, but the loss of these two players is a mini-disaster. Jeez, I am struggling to manage the jog home. I am 80 odd seconds off my best time last year.

My former bedroom is being used, so we push a single bed into the dining room and it becomes my new place of abode.

Saturday, April 7, 2017

Cartoon clouds and chocolate hills, we are out in the rural areas for a tournament Busani and the boys have organised for the visit of Paddy Power. I am being asked to address the healthy-sized crowd that has gathered on behalf of Paddy Power, who are still on their way back from filming in Vic Falls. I actually feel like a right plonker making up a speech on the spot in front of 150 people.

The pitch has the world's biggest penalty spot, the sidelines are marked out with ash, and sticks serve as corner flags with traffic cones atop. None of this is unusual in this part of the world, but I am happy that those who view the documentary will get to see it.

Paddy Power arrive, interview me behind the goal, and film me inspecting the pitch with Paddy. It is damn hot. The local crowd of 150 goes absolutely wild and invades the pitch when they score against our second string. It is a wonderful moment. The first team, meanwhile, is starting to look like a real unit. Six first-teamers are missing but the first 13 all look decent. I am so impressed by how far Khanye and Busani have taken the lads on.

The pitch is abysmal, but we are playing good football for the cameras. The cameraman films me sat on the bench. As I am just back from Europe, I am not shouting out coaching instructions because I believe it is inappropriate. I am not going to do it just for the sake of the cameras. Sawusani, who is 200 percent better than when I left, scores for the documentary.

The PP lads are understandably exhausted and leave at halftime for Bulawayo, but this means they miss us turning it on in the second half with cleverly crafted overloads and three more goals, two of them top corner stunners. The MFC lads feel a bit disappointed the lads didn't stay until the end, but I try to explain that PP will probably only get to use about 30 seconds of action from today, tops.

Sunday, April 8, 2017

The noise of car horns and vuvuzelas is deafening. Everywhere you look, you see Bosso's black and white Juventus-style shirts. Highlanders is full. With the queues and the traffic, we are 15 minutes late getting inside. Bulawayo's finest have started the season well, sticking up two fingers to their senior players by using much of their youth team. Honestly though, they look no better than us. Honestly. They now play a 4-1-4-1, which is very positive and floods players into the box. There are fights in the crowd. The last match I attended, the crowd was a pathetic 2,000, but now it is more like 15,000. Highlanders win 1-0.

Back in town, on my request, we meet Nonja, who is sat with his little daughter in an ice cream parlour. I am trying to convince him not to sign for the richest side in league one; cautioning him not to miss out on the opportunity of playing in London, scouts seeing him, and working with the legendary Bruce Grobbelaar.

"A good tournament for us, and all the Zim clubs will be interested in you!"

He says he has been offered a substantial signing-on fee plus – what would be regarded in Zim – as a decent monthly salary on a one-year contract. Khanye has known him most of his life and played in the same team with him in Gwanda. We all want the best for him and for us. Nonja offers a possible compromise of us paying his rent and food. It is very dangerous offering one player money when the rest of his teammates get zero. I take a view on it and find myself offering to pay half of his money out of my own pocket if the MFC can find the other half. We will be a much stronger team with him, especially as an experienced 32-year-old.

Nonja goes outside into the Bulawayo streets for a *two-minute think* and comes back 15 minutes later. Quietly spoken as always, he says he will accept our offer. I suspect though that his new club will come back with a better counter deal or he might go home, talk to his lady, and change his mind. Am I doing the right thing asking him to walk away from his contract offer? He speaks maturely and in a considered way. He says he would be *honoured to play in London and that even Zimbabwe national team players are saying they feel like they are missing out on our great adventure.*

Monday, April 9, 2017

Back at the Rainbow, I discover that a close family member has a pretty serious illness.

149

Al Jazeera blares away with news of a Western-contrived false-flag chemical attack in Syria. Clearly a crock of shit but reason enough for whatever comes next from the likes of the UK. For the second time this morning, my stomach turns.

It is my first stint of internet since Joburg, and I have got BBC Sport and a French journalist asking to do interviews. Busani has gathered the boys to work on the visas. British visa applications are a bloody nightmare. Try having a Russian girlfriend. It dawns on me that the supporting paperwork is all geared towards us arriving on May 30. I have asked our friends in Luton to provide accommodation and training for us, and we have flights held for May 23. I could see potential problems with the visa issuing date.

The Churchill Hotel is a world away from the lives that most of our players know. Dressed up in their suits, the lads look class for our press conference. Paddy, Busani, and myself face a room full of poker-faced journalists and TV cameras; microphones and dictaphones are laid out on the table, which is decorated in Irish colours. My God this is surreal. I have been to many press conferences where I was the journalist doing the asking, posing questions to the likes of Slaven Bilic, Gary Speed and... the Dalai Lama. Now the tables are turned. Literally.

This being Zimbabwe, we are of course treading on eggshells, particularly scared of saying the wrong thing that will then be jumped upon and used to sink the project. One snake in the room is definitely on a mission to seek out things he can use against us. I tell him we'd be happy for Mashonaland to join CONIFA, which we would. Most of the questions posed are a tad on the negative side. And nobody asks about Grobbelaar endorsing us, so I point that out.

I grow in confidence.

The snake goes for Busani, who easily contends with him. Paddy and Busani both perform very well. I think I also do OK. Four or five journalists approach me afterwards. The ladies had very decent questions about female football but were too scared to ask during the male-dominated press conference. We plan to have a Matabeleland Ladies Team playing international football very soon.

Our lads enjoy the buffet dinner in the courtyard. For many of them, they will never have experienced this before. People waiting on them. Even the hand dryer in the toilets is a novelty for a couple of the boys. Three-quarters of them are on soda drinks while the coaches and the Paddy

Power lads (minus Khanye) are all necking beers. I move and join the journos to show no fear and play at being their mate.

Matabeleland present Paddy with a signed team shirt and Khanye and Bruce make a football made from discarded milk bags, plastic, and string. Most kids cannot afford to buy a real ball, so this is what local kids grow up doing if they want a kick around. The Paddy Power lads look damaged by all of this. Humbled. Inspired. They were out with the Rhinos yesterday. Those wonderful creatures that will soon be driven to extinction. Paddy says it was one of the best experiences of his life. It seems to me that his whole Zimbabwe experience could be life-changing for him.

Beer, whiskey, whiskey. We send the boys home, then retire to the hotel bar where we drink until 11. Lee and the lads say they have ideas of how to help us fundraise (that don't involve Paddy Power), while the local Zim fixer, who has been with us these past few days, keeps telling me how *fantastic it is that you are helping these lads*. They have 45 minutes of good film cut for their 20-minute documentary. Paddy tells me he plans to return here for a holiday and sends a 10-second video to my mate Michael, who used to work with Paddy in Dublin. This is the one and only time I have been drunk in Zimbabwe.

Tuesday, April 10, 2018

I have been invited to do a breakfast interview live on local radio but have decided to swerve it in case they are interested in creating problems for us. It just isn't worth the risk. I also swerve the snake from the press conference when he tries to contact me.

On the central market, a woman wants money for me taking photos of her chillies.

TIME RUNNING OUT FOR MUGABE

PROPHETS COULD BE BANNED

I am gutted as we have no option but to drop the UK training camp. My time spent on that and the months of emails and phone calls for the flights were a complete waste of time. It is dreadful that we will now fly in, the day before the tournament. This decision, forced upon us by the mindless bollocks of visa applications, means that I am now due to go home nine days before the others, instead of with them.

More bad news follows as the potential shirt sponsor I met in London, contacts me to say they have pulled out. Everyone pulls out in the end, scared shitless that they will somehow offend the omnipresent invisible force ruling Zimbabwe. On a positive note, it looks like we might have secured the finance from South Africa for our deposits. And my mate Sam Lee, who works for Manchester City, is willing to help us; as is Warren, whom I did the Tackle Africa marathon with, hopefully joining us in London as a voluntary fitness coach.

Ethel is back from the countryside with okra, cucumber, ground beans, avocados, and green peppers; so perfect, they look plastic. I am suffering from a hangover extraordinaire.

Wednesday, April 11, 2018

I seem to be dreaming about the project now every single bloody night.

Caroline Barker and BBC Sports Hour want to interview me during the Padania match on the sidelines. They appreciate it is an unusual request. I have gone full Jim Carrey Yes Man and am answering in the affirmative to every request, no matter how stressful it might turn out to be. Click want Matabeleland's players to take photos with a disposable camera from the tournament. These Football Times have published a story about British coaches abroad including me and two other lads. VICE want to make a documentary film. Massive. A former player of mine, Berit, pops up in Bogota, very kindly donating $100, while two more former players – Ieva and Slava – buy replica shirts. Their kindness is a shot of dopamine in the arm.

The crowdfunders now stand at 4300+1300+1000, plus a few other bits and pieces I have promised to us. That's fantastic, but it means that with seven weeks remaining we are probably 14 grand short.

There is talk again that the cash crisis is worsening. Prices are inflating once more at an alarming pace. People talk of *sabotage from Mugabe's people*.

Overall, things continue to feel much better here than they did before the 'coup' but are they really? Unintended consequences. With the police having had their wings clipped back in November, there has been a significant spike in road deaths. Thousands of them have been sacked and, those that are left are not handing out the made-up road fines of yesteryear, nor dealing with dangerous driving. There was also a prison amnesty with many inmates released. From that very day, there was a spike in break-ins, muggings, and fake taxi drivers committing crimes.

Back to the actual football. We are playing a third division team in a practice match. It is cool and spotting with rain like home. Thirty minutes each way; Las Palmas press us like a pack of Yorkshire Terriers. I've rarely seen anything like it. I switch us from 4-4-2 to 4-2-3-1 to give an extra man in midfield after going in 0-1 at halftime. A few boys like Praise and Kuhle are off their game. It is Busani and me today. I still don't know the names of some of the lads. We miss some easy chances before Kaka crosses for Pele who smacks it in the net. As I have often mentioned, I hate playing lower division teams but sometimes needs must; and we have our suspicions that our opponents might have drafted in some League One players. Regardless, our opponent's young coach is a lad who deserves to go far in the game. I am always really impressed by how he conducts himself and how his team plays.

Nonja has only gone and signed for the league one team after telling us, to our faces, he wouldn't. He also didn't involve us in the contract negotiations so if they know we tried to keep him, they might not want to release him for London. We actually had no goalkeeper available this evening and Xolani, one of our outfield players, had to volunteer. One of our other four goalkeepers has also gone and signed for someone, meaning two remain, one of whom is the out-of-favour Bruce. I was worried, when I offered to pay half of Nonja's salary, that he'd talk to the other players. You can't make him not do that. I asked him not to speak to them, but I am hearing rumours he did. He might only have mentioned it to one of his mates but I guess, in turn, they have told the others. I want to believe players are just guessing what has happened rather than knowing. A lot of black clouds are outside and inside my head. I truly hope things are more positive tomorrow.

Thursday, April 12, 2018

My RHR is the lowest it has been since I was last here, back in December. I suggest it is down to natural food, light meals, going to bed early and getting up early, significantly less time looking at screens, and jogging. I feel like I am getting my mojo back, finally, after weeks of feeling crap.

With another power cut at home, I am in Rainbow fulfilling my role as a digital market stall trader as I negotiate flights, accommodation, paperwork, talk to journos, sell shirts, crowdfund, and do social media. I phone mum but I have got to be careful what I say – this hotel is known to be monitored. Today, for example, the UNDP and Zimbabwean State Finance have conferences and meetings in here, and we all know that the omnipresent *Thing* is watching and listening. I am sick in my stomach listening to CNN in the background banging the war drums. I am supposed to come from a democracy and yet 'my government' can bypass parliament and attack a sovereign state on the basis of a Jihadist video. Mark my words: one day it will be established that there was no chemical attack.

Rather surreally, in a world of absurdity, we are in an ice cream parlour doing visa paperwork with the boys. I really fear how late this has been left and the fact that, for example, five of the lads didn't have bank accounts until yesterday. Personally, I wanted this done and dusted and the paperwork sent off by March 1st.

'Training is off for the visas' but, this being Africa, comically it is suddenly back on at 5pm. I need to be excused though to go and deal with more pressing issues. Back home in the UK, I have got an Alitalia flights deal signed and sealed, awaiting final MFC clearance, with the Zim-UK roundtrip at a decent 489pp. Importantly, the contract is flexible with us able to make a final decision on the names as late as ten days before flying. I have even got us a 10% free cancellation clause. Every single complicated task is like a mini-education course. Now I am an expert on flight group bookings after weeks of discussions and negotiations. I have also organised extra accommodation in London for the team, so we are good to go on our visa and flight paperwork. Today alone, I have spent more than $10 of my own money on internet and phone calls. No wonder I am broke. Volunteering is one thing. Subsidising is another.

"I have got disturbing news," Busani announces on the phone. My mind flashes. They are coming for me, aren't they? Someone from the government has contacted Busani and I am about to get deported. My heart rate spikes, "Go on, what has h-happened?"

"We got the money in from South Africa."

"Surely, that's good news?"

"The South African guys went ahead and booked the flights."

"What flights?"

"The Ethiopian ones."

I can't believe it. Why on earth? The conditions are dreadful compared to Alitalia. We have got to name all our passengers within about fourteen days of now. And pay the balance then. In fact, I had already agreed provisionally with ET some weeks ago to get four free flights if we went ahead with them, which this separate agreement clearly does not include. Madness.

"Fifty thousand Rands has been paid."

FFS, that is more than $4,000. On the plus side, we have just gone from nine grand to more than $13,000 raised. The disturbing news is actually very very good news. Hope is back in the building.

Friday, April 13, 2018

48 days to go. Even with a blanket, the room is cold. I am overcome with worry; my sick relative, Syria, visas, flights, player availability, the sheer number of press who want to film me in England and follow me around. I have done one technical session and haven't match-day managed a senior game in… four months!! Needs must, but I am currently a paper coach and the thought of being filmed by VICE, CNN, etc. fills me with anxiety upon anxiety.

We sold a very impressive five shirts overnight. We have now got good momentum on shirt sales. I have done three interviews today. Phil messages me from the UK. He has very kindly been supporting our efforts since way back in January. His band have played an event at the local parish church back home in Hinckley and loads of kind-hearted individuals turned up and donated to the Matabele boys. The million-dollar Zim notes sold like hot cakes. Effectively, one of our boys is now on the flight to London because of the altruism of Phil, Father Frank, and a load of people from Leicestershire.

Saturday, April 14, 2018

We are playing the third division boys again against my better judgement. Busani and Khanye want redemption – and I get that – but I'd prefer fewer matches and me at least doing some technical trainings. Things are very different since I returned here. I got my way on these things much more last year, but now the MFC is going over my head on the football matters while, ironically, I am going over their heads on all the logistical stuff for the UK. I would also prefer we played top teams at this late stage in the preparations. Losing 6-0 to Caps United would teach us much more than beating Fat Boys United 5-1.

Khanye and Busani are rather assuming we will come here and win 5-0 this time, I suspect. Today, neither of them has consulted me before the match about how we set up and who is selected. Yes, there is something of an understanding that, having only recently returned, I am happy for them to do most of this, but I would appreciate a pre-match run down. Just before kick-off, I suggest we try 3-5-2 against these lads and crowd out the midfield. They out-vote me 1-2. That is democracy for you. Yet again they are going with 4-4-2.

0-1.

1-1 Kiwa scores a brilliantly executed free kick from the edge of the box.

Busani is overcoaching. Shouting at every touch, every error. It is good for some players but you know, as a coach, that it screws up other lads' heads. I honestly reckon Kuhle and Pele's sudden dip in form is partly explained by this.

At halftime, I speak first and point out the shortcomings: not picking up your man when we are without the ball, the old ball-watching problem is back, their opener came from their left winger being unmarked at the back post for an easy header. Shylock, our main striker, is static most of the time when we don't have the ball. I want my centre-forward to be Jamie Vardy and move the defenders around. Keep them mentally busy. Take one out wide if you have to. The boys are also jumping in to every challenge. Even the 20:80s. The big centre-half makes himself look stupid and amateur on a couple of occasions doing this; their young nippy striker flashing by him. Szekely will kill us if the boys do this. Padania will also torment us from set-pieces as the same issue is leading to us gifting dangerous free kicks around the box.

The lads in possession also don't protect themselves and the ball enough. And still nobody goes near the opposition goalkeeper when we have crosses. It is too much for them all to take in during a halftime team talk. I want to get on the training field and work on these things.

Their keeper makes an unbelievable save down to his bottom corner. We hit the post twice and Sawusani flashes just wide, twice. Busani and Khanye wanted to take Kuhle off for the second game in a row at halftime.

"If you do that, he will look like the scapegoat, and he isn't." Thankfully, they listened to me on that one. 1-2, our opponents are playing 4-3-3. What a great team goal; I can't believe these boys are playing fourth tier.

Ciro drives the ball out wide on the angle 40 yards to Kaka, who takes a good touch, looks up, and curls a ball with pace to the back post where Shylock heads in. That is the best team goal I have ever seen us score. Superb. Sawusani makes it 3-2. The improvement in this boy is remarkable. If a decent team took him, manned him up, got him in the gym on his upper body, he could really play at a much higher level. Even in the UK.

I run at the final whistle as I have just about got enough time to get home, have a cup of tea, pack and return to town.

I walk one hour with my backpack, covering five kilometres just before it gets dark. Bulawayo's old school train station is my destination; it is next to the cooling towers. The nearby station bottle store is a little rough and drunken but I am used to it all and chat to a couple of decent lads who advise Chibuku over my Pilsner choice for the train.

The station is a little reminiscent of Nuneaton. There are 1950s trains with dining cars. Dirty, ageing. Announcements are made in English. The timetable is in chalk and the staff remind me of Thomas the Tank Engine. The Ticket Master quips that I can have ten tickets to emphasise the lack of demand. There is one other backpacker on here and a handful of sun-bleached South Africans. We wait to be boarded at the top of the platform, where you can buy airtime and cold drinks, then 200 surge to second class with sacks of food. 200 Africans at Nuneaton station. Inside the first-class sleeper, it is pitch dark and I am sharing with two typically friendly local blokes. The train leaves dead on 7.30 with a station master whistle. That first jolt as we leave. I love overnight trains. The sense of freedom, setting off into the unknown darkness.

It is very bumpy. I've got Pilzeners, tunes and *Minnows United* for company. This compartment looks like a themed prison. RR – that is Rhodesian Railways! It's all original 1958 fittings from Birmingham. There are even original faded photos of lions and the Falls next to the mirrors. Everything is almost as good as new. Just dirty and faded, a bit like me. Minimal spending, a lick of paint and a spit of polish and you could turn this third-class first-class sleeper into an absolute beauty. This was manufactured by professional craftsmen at a time when things were made to last. Before the plastic bullshit era. My sweat, a fellow passenger's fags, my beer, the burning smell from the train, acrid train fumes, a whistle, flies, and moths attracted to the light. Lost in time.

Sunday, April 15, 2018

Thud. Stop. Hiss. Distant shouting. People scampering across stones. Railway walky-talky. Whistle. Thud. Shunt. Rattle, rattle. Snoring blokes, one lad leaves. 6am.

I carefully climb down to the lower bunk so I can enjoy the national park in the half-light. One spot we pass, just before sunrise, is stunning with thick, lush wilderness, which one might expect from somewhere like the DRC.

I am chatting to a Zambian lad whose family live in Byo. He was involved in a 2016 bus crash that left three dead and him without all the fingers on his left hand. "The bus hit a pothole during the night and the steering wheel broke. I lay there five hours waiting for an ambulance to arrive. One person bled to death. I thank God I am alive."

He complains that he can't change a light bulb now, has lost his self-confidence, and is always in pain. He is trying to sue the bus company but doesn't hold much faith. Except in God. You can see that, even now, repeating the horrific tale takes a lot out of him. I want to give him a hug.

Liverpool beating Man City is a much-needed change of topic. Football, as ever, uniting two strangers.

"There used to be thousands of animals from the window. They have gone. Now there are none. Not less but none," my new friend emphasises.

Minutes later he points out at what looks like smoke from a huge, distant fire, rising high into the heavens.

"What on earth is that? A fire?"

"That is Vic Falls!"

Vic Falls station gently rolls in, reminiscent (to me) of a Sri Lankan hill station. There is a lovely simplicity to everything. The hand-painted sign says we are 911 metres above sea level and 450 kilometres from Bulawayo. I wish my friend farewell and follow the train line into town where there are a handful of small restaurants, gift shops, and tourist hotels. Some drunken souvenir sellers are a bit in my face but change their tact completely when I say I live in Bulawayo.

I love this place. Thatched roof, noisy birds, swimming pool. I check in early to Shearwater's, paying 25 quid for a private domed tent with bed sheets, piping hot shower and, of course, that pool. I didn't eat at all yesterday, and have got the appetite of a tramp. Yoghurt, fruit, Bran Flakes, 3 coffees, 2 orange juices, sautéed potatoes, beans, tomatoes, eggs, toast. My stomach looks a bit larger than usual, as I lie by the pool afterwards. I swim with helicopters buzzing overhead, temporarily drowning out the distant roar of Victoria Falls. Birds chatter as red dragonflies glide over the pool and small, brave lizards scamper up the perimeter walls. I have been working so hard and taking all of this so damn seriously. I need to remember to try to enjoy it. That is what we are here for on this planet. I am computer- and phone-free, and how I need that!

This is the first time since I started with the MFC that I have felt like a backpacker. Suddenly, I am liberated, with a sense that absolutely anything is possible. I last felt like this in Gondar. I had forgotten this feeling but how is that possible after all the years of travel?

Of all the hotels in the world, I think I have dreamt more of walking through the hallowed hallways here and having a cold sundowner than anywhere else. I am visiting the Victoria Falls Hotel. My word, how magnificent is this? In the distance, Rhodes Railway Bridge to Zambia spans the banks of the Zambezi River, water spraying into the heavens like an angry Icelandic geyser, rainbows forming from time to time. Monkeys and a family of warthogs are strolling around the beautifully tended gardens below a huge oak tree.

I nearly didn't have a beer – fearing it'd be $10 – but at $3 it is actually cheaper than a dive bar in Riga. Staff in immaculate white shirts and pressed brown trousers busily and politely attend to customers.

Huge portraits hang in the lounge; ceiling fans waft air seemingly in slow motion. A piano player makes me think of Humphrey Bogart.

I so wish I could bring my mum to this colonial time trap. Once again, I feel like a millionaire. On this occasion, I am actually surrounded by them. If I were rich… I'd just spend all my time staying in places like this, trying to combine it with grassroots charity projects that bypass the big NGOs. It always amazes me how the millionaires and billionaires continue working, amassing more wealth and power, instead of utilising their wealth and living La Vida Loca.

As the sun sets, the air is beautifully fresh and damp, like freshly cut grass after rain. Unbelievably, this is my first proper day off since January 8. And it feels like it.

Monday, April 18, 2018

An ex-marine is doing 50 lengths in his swimming cap. Enjoying my breakfast near the pool, birds singing, a lone hang glider above, who must be experiencing the most epic of views, I feel far removed from the MFC and CONIFA; everything in fact. A sense of freedom, I had temporarily forgotten, has returned. Freedom after Unfreedom, Nietzsche might have called it. Clearly, this was needed and will benefit all the things I am free of for these couple of days.

Although I am not going mad, this wee soiree is running down my FOREX to the point where I will be out of cash in about 7-10 days. I

159

seriously underestimated how much I needed to bring, not factoring in this trip or paying rent. It is truly bonkers that in 2018, I cannot use an ATM in this country. I last had that experience in Burma in 2009 and almost ran out of the US dollars I was carrying. Back in the day, when I was backpacking, it was the norm of course but, here in a country which is, in many ways, the best in Africa, I can't withdraw money. I am the only one paying in Bond dollars, and it occurs to me that the majority of incoming Vic Falls tourists will never know there is a dual currency here. The young blonde German girl still keeps stealing a smile. I miss the short-term company of young, beautiful women.

I walk the kilometre to Vic Falls, past annoying kids trying to fob people off with badly photocopied trillion-dollar notes and offers of weed. New York's annual water consumption flows over Vic Falls in two days! Imperial Airways used to fly tourists here in six days via Luxor, Khartoum, and a handful of other African stopoffs. Today, the whole world can visit, but tourist numbers in Zimbabwe have been a mere trickle for many years.

There are 16 viewing points, beginning at Cataract Island. I sit alone at the first of these, watching the tidal wave of water rushing towards the sheer drop. The immense energy. The impossible volume of water. Mind-blowing.

I won't even venture to two viewpoints, which are insanely dangerous with near zero visibility, slippery rocks disappearing in a cloud of water spray. People must die here, especially members of the selfie stick massive. I read, recently, that 260 have died worldwide in the process of taking selfies in six years. I was intrigued and discovered that, on average, a total of six people on this planet die annually from shark attacks.

Jeez, I am amazed by what a rush people are in. I am slower than the pensioners. It is monsoon-like conditions at the final viewpoints, except this is not rain. Brilliant. I am soaked and find myself whooping aloud.

The final viewpoint has a bungee jump. You must be kidding. It resembles the entrance to hell. Beyond us is Rhodes Bridge with an old school train crossing it. Some walk across. It's a little like Clifton suspension bridge plonked next to one of the Seven Wonders of the World.

I stroll back along the border road, past a line of lorries and am almost dry by the time I reach the camp. I sunbathe, meditate, read Mat Guy's book, swim, stare at the sexy German girl when I think she isn't looking.

Oh, to be young. Oh, this sense of freedom and the feeling of the weight coming off my shoulders for a few wonderful hours.

Vic Falls owes much to David Livingstone. Incredibly (or possibly factually incorrect, like most history books), he was the first white man ever to set eyes on Vic Falls in 1855, aged 41, when local tribesmen guided him here in canoes. "Scenes so lovely must have been gazed upon by angels in their flight," he wrote. The Scot worked for the abolition of slavery and had a big hand in the development of this place. He wanted to spread the word of God but, first and foremost, it is apparent that he was a great explorer. I can relate to that. I love spreading the gospel of football but, first and foremost, I love exploring the world.

My name is the first on the passenger list for the overnight sleeper as I return to the Vic Falls Hotel for a final sundowner. There's banter with the hotel's security guard, as I leave for the final time, about my lifestyle. He asks me how I can live this way and I tell him I have no mortgage, wife, or kids. "You are a white Rasta!" he says chuckling. I'll take that.

This time I really do have a compartment completely to myself on the train. I can't tell you how good it is to be internet free for 72 hours. Once, in the Pacific, I went weeks without the internet and a phone. Talk about feeling free. I've rarely felt so happy as I did then. The train leaves dead on seven. I have just spent two days lost in time in a place lost in time.

15: Tracksuitache

Tuesday, April 17, 2018

Crash bang. Ssshhhh. Clatter. I am up at 7.30, conscious that we are due to arrive at 8… but… 9… 10… 11… 11.30. Most punters get off at the last major stop before Bulawayo central where an army of road-weary microbuses are waiting.

Finally, the cooling towers come into sight. It is good to be home, even if Bulawayo feels more urban than my mood wishes after Vic Falls. Five kilometres later, I am back at Ethel's where breakfast waits for me.

The planned team visa trip to Harare never happened. I did warn the MFC that Katya's Russian visa application took us at least 5 hours to write over the course of many days so, clearly, 20 or so lads isn't something that can be completed quickly. I am sure 100 hours+ of work is involved.

Wednesday, April 18, 2018

Today, it is final ticket sales for the FIFA World Cup in Russia. I am in a queue from 11.30 for five hours. The only game that greatly appeals and fits my vague plans is Senegal v Colombia in Samara but only Cat 1 is available. In theory, I could be in Nizhny Novgorod for England v Panama. There are Cat 1s available but I just cannot justify that much money along with potentially struggling to find any affordable accommodation. I'd rather be down in sunny Samara visiting Katya and taking it easy.

I am trying to warn Busani that we have a stack of bills to pay by April 28, and we need a plan with contingencies. He responds by kicking off, telling me he's been doing the visas non-stop and has had no sleep. *I told you to start the paperwork on March 1, not in April.* It is fair to say that the stress and great responsibility we feel to others is now getting to both of us.

I am nervous returning to my first full technical training session since December. The lads are 20 minutes late bringing the balls, bibs, and cones and I only get an hour of light. It ain't easy coaching 18 lads by yourself, especially with the light fading. I totally bugger up the space needed for two drills and although the session is just about OK, generally speaking, it is probably the worst one I have ever put on in Africa.

Dare I say it but, I feel like my relationship with some of the lads has weakened in my absence. A bit like not seeing your girlfriend for four months and sensing something has changed. A load of new faces doesn't help. There is a little bit of attitude from one or two such as Pele and an immature streak in some of the boys doing the drills. Something is wrong, but I cannot quite put my finger on it. I will sort it out, but my poor session hasn't exactly helped.

It is Independence Day but I miss all the events in town. My friend Tony, I am pleased to hear, has taken on my old coaching role at FK Aliance.

Thursday, April 19, 2018

There are 20 minutes to kick-off, and I can't find the changing rooms at Enfield Town. The Cascadia players can't help. I cannot believe what a mess this is.

Justin! Are you OK?

I have overslept and it is Ethel's birthday. She's stripped the kitchen bare, put down cockroach killer in every nook and cranny and is boiling groundnuts on the roaring fire outside. It is so hot that I reckon the nuts could roast themselves in the open.

I have finally re-established contact with Bruce Grobbelaar. *I have secured gloves for the keepers and am in negotiations with New Balance for kit sponsors.*

He has been trying to sort out a kit deal and I have to explain that, fortunately, that side of things is sorted thanks to our arrangement with Paddy Power. He asks to see the shirts and exclaims: *That is absolutely fantastic Justin. I will have a few of those.* It is a huge relief knowing that nothing has happened to put Bruce off being involved in the project. I spend 30 minutes trying to send him the away shirt design, which he says he also wants a few of.

CNN are also saying they are good to go, but need some logistical stuff from us.

Another training match, this time against a 1st league outfit on the pitch next to Crescent. I spot Gary playing for one of the local teams. He says *hello coach* and I feel sad he is no longer with us. Gary, a left-sided midfielder, was the standout player for me when I first came here. He is a class act. He had some personal stuff going on, back at the end of last year, and was already putting the coaches under pressure because of training attendance, communication, etc. I made sure I had a private word with him before I left last year. *Gary*, I told him. *You were the best player for me when I first came here. If you are on form, fit, and keep us happy, I believe you can be one of the standout players in London.* I could see he appreciated being told that but, after the Christmas break, he apparently went AWOL again for three weeks. The MFC warned him over and over again but, in the end, they had to let him go. And, so, a very talented young man will not feature in London. I am tempted to ask the lads to reconsider, but I know it wouldn't be fair to the players who have been coming day in, day out, for months – some of whom won't even make the final squad.

Busani is in a much brighter mood having finished the visa paperwork. With the days ticking by, we have had to pretty much decide the rest of the squad. The good news is that Nonja is in. Sadly, Percy is out. The first-choice striker for me. He smacks the ball like a pro. He'd break a young keeper's wrist with some of his pile drivers. No Gary. No Percy. Down to bad decision making on their parts. And while we are on that subject, there will be no Benny either. Matabeleland's best striker in CONIFA qualification, as I suspected from the start, just hasn't got his heart in this. And no Jiro, the lad who told me at the Highlanders' game last year that he would *go to London, be snapped up by a club and never return.* His relationship with the coaches deteriorated in my absence and he definitely won't be on the plane; if indeed anyone is. Now we are down to 27 or 28 players and possibly my wild card in England, Halifax Town's right back Cliff Moyo. His chairman Mike Sharman has pretty much agreed clearance for Cliff on the phone, but I still need to speak to Cliff himself to see if he wants to join us.

Busani takes a backseat and allows Khanye and me to manage the lads alone. It is an improved performance and it is working well together with Khanye today. The new stand-in keeper, who – surprise, surprise – is called Bruce, upsets us both by coming out of his box, brilliantly chipping over the oncoming striker and then setting off on a skillful dribble. The crowds would love it and I feel bad in a way scolding him, but I don't want any showboating like that. One of our new strikers, Thabiso, is back after losing his sister a couple of weeks ago. I reckon by playing, it might allow him to clear his mind for 90 minutes and, sure enough, he scores the only goal of the first half from a slick five-pass move. When these boys play the quick, clever passes, they are properly good. They would even unlock a good pro team. Goddy, the big centre-half, can apparently play attacking mid or goalkeeper and is being given a stint in midfield. The only area where we look lightweight is now our left flank. We don't offer a lot going forward, and we are suspect defensively on that side.

Dinner with all the family at Roosters for Ethel's birthday is great fun but comes with an absurdly expensive price tag of $168. The huge slice of birthday cake and Malarone just before bed guarantee a restless and nightmare-ridden night.

Friday, April 20, 2018

The cicada in the garden sounds louder than a rattlesnake but it is just a tiny creature flicking his hind legs, trying to attract a repulsive-looking female-beetle. I have never knowingly heard an insect make so much noise.

The neighbor shows me a strange fruit I have never come across before. Meanwhile, a dozen green bananas from the garden sit on the kitchen table, the last of 200 this season. On that theme, it is sticky, gooey okra from the garden for dinner.

Daniel – one of my UK-based opposition data analysts – has done a really good job analysing Szekely Land. They usually play 4-4-2, like to go long, play it behind the opposition defence on the transition. Their defenders aren't great in possession. They like getting their fullbacks high. Clearly, when we play them, we will need to take the game to them from the start, put them on the back foot, take a lead and then shut up shop, so we don't play too high and allow them to punish us. I have seen them play myself. They should be too good, too experienced, and too smart for us, but one or two early goals against them and we could beat them for sure.

Saturday, April 21, 2018

The malaria dreams leave me feeling like I have barely slept. Overnight, a load of friends have committed to buying shirts. My good mate Andy H has donated 200 quid. The support from my friends is unbelievable. Without them, there would be no World Cup for the Ndebele lads. I am truly blessed. Dear friends around the world. My extended family. So many have supported me in this endeavour. So much kindness. I would be nothing in this world without all these people enriching my life.

I am in the Northampton Town matchday programme today. The Cobblers also tweet me after I wish them good luck in today's match from Zimbabwe. I run five kilometres for the first time in my life as a set, intentional distance, running the backroads of North End; the only white guy in town, plodding away. But it feels like an accomplishment and I feel good afterwards.

BRITAIN WANTS ZIMBABWE BACK IN THE COMMONWEALTH

15,000 NURSES STRIKE, SACKED

Sunday, April 22, 2018

I can't explain why, but this morning feels like the day we begin the last leg of our pre-tournament adventure. Back in church for the first time since December, it is the usual beautiful melodic gospel and, of course, a super long sermon; this time about mercenaries.

My mind is spinning the whole time, thinking about all the things I need to do to get this bunch of African lads to a life-changing football tournament in London. The CNN visit, sell shirts, find a sponsor, rebook my flight home, right midfielder double up and drop back against Szekely Land, Bruce Grobbelaar... Actually, I spent an hour reading up about Bruce last night so I can better understand the man if I am going to be working with him. Fantastic to see his Wikipedia profile saying he is the GK coach of Matabeleland. But I was on my back reading a recent interview with Bulawayo24 about his time serving in the Rhodesian army. People have stereotyped views about Bruce but, for me, that interview completely redefines anything you might think about him.

Also, his quote: *I went to Britain with $10 and left with $5*. I read he has an autobiography coming out this year. I wonder if Matabeleland will be the last chapter, full circle in his career from starting off playing for the Matabeleland Highlanders to being GK coach and perhaps player of Matabeleland. It is clear from the interview, and my discussions with Bruce, that he wants nothing more than to return to his home country and lead Zimbabwe to African Nations and World Cup qualification. The potential here is incredible and if ex-players like Bruce and Peter Ndlovu are able to take a leading role in ZIFA, I am certain the country's football team will begin to rise to the top.

Monday, April 23, 2018

I wake up mid-brilliant Usain Bolt dream. He is signing a ball with the names of his 11-a-side team and telling me he knows all the stuff, all the hard work, that goes into coaching an African side.

I believe I have sorted a much more beneficial merchandising deal for the MFC which will make us a grand or two more, perhaps. Sadly, the pennants will be made at a loss. I am doing everything possible to find sponsors but it feels like a lost cause.

World Soccer City ask me to nominate a female coach for their annual awards, which is a great honour. Then, bigger still, VICE ring and ask to go ahead with a documentary that will include us. Fantastic news. I am such a cheeky bastard, currently, that while they are on the phone, I ask them to sponsor us. They say they will consider it.

Otherwise, I prepare a series of rondos for training as well as in-game stuff that I didn't do last year. Energised, mentally as well as physically, I run five kilometres two minutes faster.

Tuesday, April 24, 2018

"I miss my dog. His name was Buster," the little pig-tailed girl with pretty eyes is telling the dog who thinks he is our dog.

I'm waking up nervous in the mornings. I don't like it as it is too far off the tournament to be suffering from this anxiety.

Grobbelaar says he is going for a meeting with New Balance about boots for the team. He also orders seven replicas for himself. I am driving shirt sales as I feel the general crowdfunding is almost dead now. I spend endless hours on the computer; it's quite unlike last year when days felt chilled, far away from home, healthier.

PP say they cannot openly promote us on social media as it will look like favouritism. Plus, they (understandably) don't want to endorse replicas that won't be as good as advertised in their competition. But they don't know me. They will be better, not worse, just you wait and see!

Million Seater agree a shirt RT competition to help us. We get 100 RTs although 20 of them are me messaging people privately asking them to do it. Lots of mates are reserving shirts but the Zim community... nothing. FFS.

Ethel bags the biggest avocado I've ever seen with it – I have to laugh – 'technically' overhanging our garden from the neighbour's. The dog is getting brave and tries to move into the house. The cockroaches are now completely out of control.

From city hall, we walk up to Ascot through the increasingly litter-strewn central park. The lads run up and down the old stadium stand and do 400 squats. People come to nose. Busani is in a good mood about the visa meeting in Harare. The lads went suited and booted in a hired van. Thabiso, the centre-forward, doesn't have a passport. The three of us agree we will front the costs. We desperately need this talented footballer to join us.

It is 10 by the time I get home and see the message from Grobs saying New Balance have agreed, and he needs the boot sizes by Saturday. That is great news.

Wednesday, April 25, 2018

I am trying to book pitches for us to train on in London. I'm still constantly posting on social media to push shirts and create interest in the team so that we will be the hot ticket in London. I know people won't be disappointed when they meet the boys. More potential sponsors have dropped out.

Halifax Town's boss says Cliff Moyo has already represented Zimbabwe but he can play for us if Cliff agrees. I Skype my mum shopping in Tesco. I now have five journos who want to interview me on the phone but I literally cannot cope with all that I need to do, and I have to put all of them on the back burner.

At training, I get the lads to clear the pitch of crap. Some of them look at me like they think I am losing the plot. Praise fills an entire carrier bag full of stones and various crap. Some of them barely manage a handful. This tells its own story, and they don't realise I realise this.

I do an evening of rondos and passing into end zones. It is never easy keeping 21 lads busy by yourself. Our best players, aside from Sawusani, are off form. I think we are 3-4 players short for London. I am starting to get my coaching mojo back, but I am still some way off where I need to be.

The dongle has stopped working so I miss my first ever Exco at the 15th time of asking. I covered 20 kilometres running around on behalf of the MFC today.

Thursday, April 26, 2018

I will miss Ethel. Sitting out on the back porch, drinking coffee, I am overcome with sadness that this wonderful African woman won't be in my life anymore after a few weeks. I will also miss the simplicity of these mornings.

I have another coffee and buttered bread at a cafe under a police station in town. I am meeting the head of the Save Matabeleland Coalition. It has taken some persuasion but, I have managed to get all present to agree to me buying 150 home and 25 replica shirts to sell. If we sell them all, we will raise about $4,000 in pure profit. The cost of visas has cleared us out. The lads agree to a training camp in Zim and in SA before the WFC. But suddenly go all James Bond, saying people are listening to our conversation and insist we leave.

We visit a sports clothes manufacturer. The lads are mad with me when I point out what I consider to be inferior work from the potential manufacturer. Sometimes, I just don't get these lads. They'd rather I kept the status quo than say the truth. I know they like to maintain politeness and, to them, I am a bit *bull in a china shop*. The tracksuit designs and quality on offer though are bloody horrible. Why inspect the merchandise if I can't give my honest feedback? They should have let me order them in the UK, when I had the chance, to be honest. And, it is my mate Graham Williams, who is very kindly funding most of this out of his hard-earned money. The manufacturers want $35 per tracksuit. If we get the money wired in, it will cost us 35% less using Ecocash, so about 500 quid all in all. We must have them produced and ready for CNN's visit next Friday.

With so much to do, I ask to be excused from tonight's training session. Social media, shirt negotiations, messages, merchandise, etc.

Smart business types are arriving en masse for this weekend's trade fair, and Busani is talking up a night out to coincide with this.

I get home around the time training should be starting. Military helicopters buzz North End. The ladies are out at choir practice. I am down to my last $40 and am trying to organise a Western Union transfer through Nqo in the UK. My tooth is starting to feel dodgy. Five weeks today, it all starts. I need to do a visa run soon. Students, bloody useless millennial students. I wish I hadn't wasted so much time trying to recruit them in the winter. All those dozens of hours, so many have dropped out or are hopeless. I am down to half a dozen who seem competent or bothered, and sufficiently qualified. Why on earth would you employ your average Uni graduate frankly?

Friday, April 27, 2018

Armed Baboons on Rampage, reports the B-Metro.

I've got *Wonderful Life* by the Hurts and *Tunnel Vision* adding to the sunny morning vibe.

I ask the boys to take a photo of me together with the hilarious Baboon headline and they refuse.

"It's for me."

"No. Don't in any way associate that with the MFC."

Oh, my word, the paranoia of these boys is off the scale. And there is more. Apparently, on the subject of Khanye's auntie offering to pay for a flight, I "pressured too much that side" and now the support is in

170

question. This is not a great start to my day. The players bringing in $100 each – agreed a few days ago in our three-man crowdfunding meeting – is now "You don't understand these boys. They don't have money."

"I will be honest lads, I am getting really pissed off. I have brought in ten grand. You are telling me not to push the Americans. Not to push the British Zims. But most of them are doing bugger all!"

Oh, my word, they are telling me again that *the Matabeles are going to flood into the project when they believe in it*. FFS, it is April 27! I have been doing this now for 200 days. The Zim community in the US, UK, SA, and here in their homeland, have mostly been invisible. I'm trying to push some responsibility back in the direction of the various Zimbabwean communities but they are kicking off. Agggggggghhhhhhh.

In Bruce's office, I discover loads of brilliant images that no one has thought to publish or share or give to me for marketing purposes.

On many levels, I feel the same as these boys. In many instances we get each other; we share language and culture and humour. They are very smart and funny; good company. But, on some levels, these lads are from fucking Mars. Or I am. There is some odd behaviour I will never get. Clearly, they think the same about me.

Tracksuit tailor number two. This lady is real but the concept of her actually marketing what she does is lost on her. Her horribly cluttered office is like a Channel 4 *Compulsive Hoarder* documentary. She is apparently the tailor for the Zimbabwe National Cricket Team. What a gig! Personally speaking, I think her gear looks like something from 1983. Indeed, this could be a wee clothing manufacturer in Leicestershire…. in 1983. I have my serious doubts. Back to shop one. I wish I had videoed this. The tops they are offering us sit horribly on people. Like a tyre around the waist. The Matabele boys are telling me they look great. And people back home in Europe laugh at me, saying I have bad taste in fashion!

"We need slim fit lads. Our boys are all thinner than Mister Bean. And we need zip legs so the lads can take their shin pads on and off. Please just trust me on this."

B+K want to order XS for most of the lads. Oh, my word. "Please let me just say this: if you fuck them up, you can't change them. Better to be too big and reduce the size. Grobbelaar wants XL lads. Whatever you do, please don't give him smaller."

This whole process is dragging on and on and on. Lucky, I suppose, that none of us have real jobs. If this were Norway, with all of us on 30 quid an hour, this whole circus would cost thousands. The deal is the tracksuits are done by next Thursday. We get $900 from Western Union, transferred down from the UK by Nqo. $300 for me and the $600 for the MFC, most of that from the kind-hearted Graham Williams.

I have got toothache, headache, and now tracksuitache. I blow seven quid on calls to my mum and Cliff Moyo. That hurts. Cliff seems like a top lad.

"I'd love to play for the team. I am honoured you have asked me."

I am thinking, *Yess!* Until, like some girlfriend about to split from you, he utters that BUT.

"But I have been called up to play for Zimbabwe and it is the exact same dates." My heart sinks. I have just lost my best player because he's playing against South Africa when the WFC is on. To be fair, it is a pretty solid excuse. I suddenly lose Skype and stress that Cliff probably thinks I've put the phone down on him. When I do finally reach him, we agree I will send him all the info, he will talk to his agent and, if his new passport doesn't turn up in time for international duty, he will join us. During my time with the MFC, I have got used to the idea that what looks like happening often doesn't, and what seems impossible can often be pulled off.

It is 5.30 as I pace alone down a quiet stretch of road and past training, which I've missed because of my tracksuitache and Zimbabwe national team player shenanigans.

Sirens are wailing, a pair of police motorbikes come flying down Mugabe Way (in the centre of a residential district) at what must be 60mph! What is this madness? One is doing a wheelie, pointing people out of the way as, suddenly, the fucking president comes flying past in his official car with what looks like two trucks full of soldiers ready to fight the Mexican drug cartels. It is at times like this that I wonder whether I am in Purgatory or lying in a mental institute imagining it all. The crack team of Robocops are wearing bulletproof vests, fingers on automatic rifles, pointed at the sidewalks. Imagine if one of them accidentally shot me now and I no longer had to worry about our UK visas. And then, behind the two robo trucks, is a fleet of four by fours, which hurtle by, weaving in and out of each other's tracks. It is quite simply the most mental cavalcade I have ever seen. Infinitely more hardcore than that of the European president and NATO leaders I have seen, and even topping most silly Hollywood films. I have got to laugh. There is an Assad Senior-sized billboard of Mnangagwa that must have gone up overnight by the roadside. Meet El Presidente. The king is dead, long live the king.

After almost an hour by the roadside with Ethel, no microbuses have passed; so I am in an unmarked taxi en route to meet Busani and Khanye in town.

They wouldn't take me to *the Vista* last year because of spies and such like. Now I am inside, I don't know what all the fuss was about. A mildly amusing comedy club stand up is playing to a crowd which is 90% blokes. It is friendly but dull.

The lads know I have been single for four months and would be happy for me to find deliverance in this Zimbabwean desert. Bar two, 90% blokes. It is just my opinion. At the end of the day, it is all opinions, but the ladies frequenting, are in no sense of the word *fit*. The bar is overcrowded and we plonk ourselves in the corner with vodka and beer; Khanye is a teetotaler. A rather large girl approaches me and asks whether her friend can speak to me as *she likes me*. I say yes. I always say yes out of politeness. Her mate introduces herself saying she is from Botswana. The first thing that pops into my head is Botswana's 20% HIV rate. The next thing is: she's alright. The second-best girl in the club. I am a bit taken aback as Khanye is super rude to her and the lads tell me I *can't dance with her*. Are they having a giraffe?

"She is press and you will appear in the yellow press next week being accused of sleeping with a prostitute."

"I am 47 lads. I don't have a wife or kids. Why on earth would anyone care anyway?"

"You don't know how it is. They want to destroy the project with fake info."

"Do you actually know she is press? Perhaps she is actually a woman who likes me. I am not being funny, lads, but from what I have seen, barely anyone knows the MFC exists in this town."

"They want to destroy us."

Zimbabwe does horrible things to people. I know these lads would never behave like this if they resided in England. They are stupidly petrified of the state.

"Is she press? Can you actually categorically tell me you know her and her mates are press? Or are you just trying to spoil my fun for the hell of it?"

No, they actually have no idea who she is. Dear, oh dear. These boys take the biscuit for paranoia. Why did they hype this evening if I am not allowed to speak to women? I despair of this bullshit. It has got to the stage where I am fantasizing about a night out in Hinckley like it is Moscow.

Thank God we finally go home at 2am. What a joke of a night that was. What on earth are these boys on about, thinking they can tell me which women I can or cannot speak to? And it is lost on them that I am not about to disappear off home with some random girl from a club in Bulawayo anyway.

Saturday, April 28, 2018

The worst kind of hangover: the what a waste of fucking time and money last night was, and what a shame today will also suffer as a result kind.

Having barely slept, and on coffee overload, I accidentally manage to fix my computer and work until 2 for the MFC before a power cut puts pay to that. I lose Cobblers 0-0 away at Walsall on internet radio with us needing to avoid defeat to have a chance of staying up in League One.

With Ethel and her daughters away at a wedding, I spend the rest of the day sat alone in the lounge in the darkness. There's a little bit of rocking back and forth to pass the time.

I wee myself when Ethel returns and tells me they had dinner at the wedding only to discover they were at the wrong wedding.

Sunday, April 29, 2018

I work all day for the MFC then haul my backpack five kilometres to Bulawayo train station. Guess where I am going? A regular now on the overnight Byo-VF train, I meet two young lads and three girls, doing a year's placement in Harare. They are very young but unusually good value. I take the lads to the bottle store for supplies for the train as they are intimidated by the darkness and the lads who hang out there. It is my third time in here so I am on *how's it* and fist punch terms with a couple of the blokes, which probably comes across a bit odd to my non-African friends. They must be pretty young because they have a chaperone on the train. The lads drink in my compartment. One of the girls is quite nice and flirty and asks if I'm staying in the same place as them in Vic Falls, appearing disappointed when I say no. At least that is what I tell myself. She tells me that up in Harare, the girls are expected to work in their placement homes by the men. The chaperone seems like a bit of a dick by Zim standards.

As we *choot choot* our way into the night, *we stop at every big tree* as my new friends joke. By 9, I give up being able to hang with them and crash in my rather filthy Rhodesian Railways compartment with three beers. The nuts must have been dirty as my stomach is like a chemical factory in the early hours.

Monday, April 30, 2018

It is the best sex I ever remember having. Petite, beautiful green-eyed brunette. Shunt. Wirr. Crunch. It is 5.40 and the last of my compartment mates is getting off at the last significant stop before Vic Falls.

The *Zambezi* leaves a rat's tail taste as I finally spot my first elephant out the window, far off in the distance; the railway track fenced off so the pathetically dwindling number of game can't cause an inadvertent derailment.

One of the train staff, a typically friendly and smiley African man, probably my age, shows me a photo of Harry Kane on his phone as he explains his love of Spurs and indeed England's Centre Forward. I tell him my team has just been relegated. And from that simple intro, we discuss more football before briefly delving beyond that into our own lives. The universal language of football creating friendships as ever, allowing strangers on a Zimbabwean train to briefly become friends, wishing each other well for the future with a handshake as I celebrate the sight of volcanic-like clouds spewing into an otherwise clear sky from Vic Falls. It was a similar conversation with another gentleman about Man City and Liverpool on here a couple of weeks ago.

A few minutes later, the former Rhodesian Railways train pulls into a now familiar Vic Falls station; huge flower pots decorate the platform. Feels like home. I pace off to Shearwaters having starved myself again and dreaming of the buffet by the pool.

Hope recognises me from my previous visit as does the guest manager, who is an absolute diamond. It is fantastic to be back in my bolthole with poached spinach eggs and black coffee.

When I last visited, I was blissfully phone- and internet-free but sadly, on this visit, I must power up and continue my work on the massive replica shirt contract. To put this in context, if we sell all 170 shirts, that brings in $8,000 but costs $4K. Get this right and it will guide us towards our final total. Get it wrong and, as always with merchandising, it will turn into a shit show, potentially damaging all reputations involved. Much of the incoming shirt money has already been used to pay for the team's visas so I see cashflow issues arising. In 3-4 weeks' time, we will have to pay the balance on our bill of $3,000. With many people only reserving and not paying, you can see the recipe for potential disaster. I realise that Busani, Nqo, etc. don't understand how complicated, stressful and potentially dangerous the whole exercise is. Only I do.

And so, 10.30 becomes 3. It's wrong really but, I have got my mum involved, pushing a payment through for me on behalf of the MFC. Meanwhile, another headache is that Replica Kit Jamie in Scotland and Paddy Power don't possess the away design as a file.

My eyes met over breakfast with a very sexy American girl. An exchange of smiles. Hope of a short-term relationship. Sat alone now by the pool in her bikini, this would be my chance to strike up a conversation but, instead, I am discussing XXL shirts with some punter from Croydon. And, when I do get to finally have a dip in the pool, said lady has been kidnapped by a slightly pudgy but friendly South African geezer. Part of me wishes I could just quit all this and return to my simple life of minimal responsibility. I certainly don't feel much like a football coach right now.

By 4pm, I have to give up hope of completing on the contract – another deadline missed – and head out for a stroll.

Down an overgrown pathway that I wouldn't walk alone in the UK – never mind most parts of Africa – a guide and two 50-something punters are nervously crouching behind bushes at the side of the road as two elephants cross the trail 100 yards beyond us. I am still thinking *wow* as I walk onto the restaurant deck of the nearby Look Out Cafe. But now it is *wow, fuck's sake!* as I set eyes upon the dramatic gorge below. This is a world-class sundowner venue and I have got it entirely to myself; clouds filtering in on a heavy breeze, threatening the full moon viewing later. Look at this view! The water makes unique patterns, below, with every collision of currents as it roars through the gorge and takes a 120-degree turn in the direction of Zambia. I linger and move to a bar stool when the restaurant begins filling up.

Oh my, moon rise! What a thing! The full moon, with an orangey-red hue, rising from close to the bridge with the majesty of a sunrise. I imagine the restaurant tipping like a boat as dozens flock to the balcony to film and observe the wonder. Just then, the two American girls walk in dressed elegantly and one second I am looking left to the wonder, then right to the wonders. Left, right, left, right, my head goes. I try to manoeuvre myself so they can spot me but the relationship gods keep throwing waiters and South Africans in my way. Gail, the manager, tells me it is too late to go to the lunar rainbow, *should have been there at 6*. I am gutted. This event only happens 30 odd days per year.

I am still unsuccessfully trying to catch the girls' attention as Gail returns "I have arranged a driver to take you up to the Park. Let's see if you can join a tour and, if not, he will bring you back here." What a legend.

I've got a whole bus to myself. You can't walk here at night because of wild animals. I can see a dozen rain-coated Japs by the entrance. I'm in.

I cannot stand tour groups, so plodding along with 100 people and just three guides through the darkness of a mini rainforest wouldn't be my thing if there were any other way of doing this. The moon is appearing and disappearing *Hammer House of Horror* stylie, insects noisily communicating across the trees and bushes. *Watch for snakes*, the guide warns us. *That's easy for you to say, mate.* Already soaked by the time we approach the first viewing-point, the moon and the falls are no longer visible. All my $40 is getting me is a wet dress shirt and jeans. *Biggest anti-climax ever, you twat.* I mutter to myself like I've got Gollum with me. *Why aren't you with the American girl?*

How spoilt am I? How high are my expectations?

Expectations - reality = happiness

Our group has split into the more-keen-to-see-something and the breakaway republic of photo-obsessed. The moon occasionally breaks free of the horror film clouds to reveal snippets of the falls by night. The noise is deafening. I am soaked to the bone. Majestic in the darkness, individual torrents of white water are crashing into the abyss.

The East Asians are going bonkers with their flash photography. For the love of God! This lot truly are the clowns of the tourism world. Finally free of them, the moon begins to free itself as it edges higher in the April sky, reflecting and refracting. Small arches of light appear in the darkness. Soon the arches are coloured. There is a strange energy to all of this. Primeval. Predictably 100 has become me and a Spanish backpacker lagging behind, mouths gaping at the bizarre spectacle. I'm soaked but grateful. That awe-inspiring night in Panama, swimming with the luminous plankton, flashes in my mind like the most wonderful dream.

I am the last to leave, and a soldier enquires as to whether I am Justin. The park is being closed up and he kindly guides me to my bus with us the only two remaining.

The girls are dancing as a singer performs Shania Twain. *Ladies! How are you?* Luckily, they react to me greeting them like I know them by greeting me like they know me. They are both lovely. One is celebrating her birthday. They helicoptered and bungee jumped their day. Now, they insist I dance with them.

I order a $16 dinner feeling it is the minimum I must spend after Gail organised those lifts to and from the national park for me. The girl I like beckons me back over to dance. She is lovely, fun. There is good banter. She is girlfriend material in a desert of female mediocrity. The transfer bus arrives. The girls are off. Shit, why did I order dinner?

Potato-butternut curry, table-for-one overlooking the gorge, the wondrous moon ever higher. I'm trying to eat as quickly as I can but I know I have screwed up. A young Japanese couple pull at their odd Western meal like a Swiss backpacking couple might pull at their colourful *bento* in Sapporo. The wait for the transfer bus is intolerable. Damn, this curry is good! I neck a Captain Morgan in case I need Dutch Courage shortly and share the lift home with two elderly ladies who, hahaha, go for a pee just as the bus is about to leave … and return at the pace of a couple of Mauritian tortoises. *Please drop Justin off first*, Gail asks the driver, winking at me. Gail drives in front of our bus but suddenly stops and reverses. Then reverses at pace. What is going on? I am half expecting another Mnangagwa cavalcade. We have reversed all the way to the entrance. We set off again. Stop, reverse. And, finally, as we fail for the sixth time, I see the problem. Of all the things I have seen in my life, this is something! A ginormous bull elephant, tusks the likes of which I have only ever seen in a documentary, is blocking the whole road vertically and horizontally. He is facing down Gail's car as she panickingly reverses. I am not exaggerating when I say this is the biggest elephant I have set eyes upon in my entire life. Fleetingly, my stomach drops and I fear he will run at Gail's car and crush it cartoon-style into a car wrecker's metal pulp before continuing its rampage by picking up our bus and hurling it into the bush. This is madness. Full moon madness. "We could be here three or four hours," the ladies comment. "I have only ever seen one or two bigger than that. We have got no chance with him."

I am thinking this is absolutely incredible, an absolute privilege to see but, agggggghhhh, it could be costing me a night with the American girl. Quite possibly one of the biggest Alpha males on earth is screwing up what little chance I might have had.

Gail suddenly accelerates, gesticulating out the window that Jumbo has disappeared off right somewhere. We surge off. No sign of the giant.

Back at Shearwaters, I jump out and unashamedly jog to the bar. Spurs v Watford. Two Spanish girls with a bottle of wine, are chaining by the pool as the staff close up. No American girls. Can you imagine, no shame, I run up the street to the local brew pub hoping they are there. I even resort to walking around the chalet paths hoping they are sat out enjoying a glass of something.

Finally, I sit on the steps by the pool like a lone wolf staring up at the full moon then place my head in my hands. What a magical evening.

Tuesday, May 1st, 2018

My word it is May. What is going on? Friday night blocked by Khanye and Busani. Sunday blocked by a chaperone. Last night blocked by elephants, curries and weeing grannies. I awaken at 3am and struggle to get back to sleep. I think I'm losing the plot a little bit.

I am up at 7, aware that I am under time pressure to sort the shirt bollocks, do the Zambia visa run, organise CNN, etc. I keep waiting for the girls to walk in, never considering that they won't actually appear because they have left Zimbabwe.

Jamie from White Label Solutions is losing it with me because I am still buggering around with the shirt order, haven't paid the deposit, and I have failed to provide adequate designs of the home and away shirts because, well, they don't exist. The winner of the Paddy Power shirt competition was the best drawing, not a ready-to-print shirt design for manufacture. This ongoing shit show means it is impossible for me to risk leaving today before this is sorted.

Unashamedly, once again, I enquire about the US girls at the reception. FFS, I don't know either of their names. How embarrassing. Ashley is one of their names, apparently, and they haven't checked out. Right, bugger it, I am checking back in. Busani is still not getting my messages. I need him to give me the green light to confirm the final shirt design for manufacture. And so, the coach of Matabeleland is going to miss training again today... and tomorrow. That is four sessions in a row. What a state of affairs.

CNN call me. They have landed in Harare. Thank God, I think to check whether they want to be included in the press conference which the MFC is rather assuming they are willing to attend. Mentioned, yes, but they won't be participating.

Oh, now, the WIFI is down for maintenance. Still no girls. I throw myself in the pool to cool off. This is an almighty headache. Despite selling market stall loads, we are not even at break even on the shirts yet. I've asked my friend John John to pay the shirt invoice. So many different people, with no connection to Zimbabwe, other than me or what they have read on social media, are keeping the good ship Matabeleland afloat at the moment.

On my way to the gorge, a bloke runs past and warns me there is an elephant to my left. In fact, there are two, one eyeing me in a way that makes my heart rate not so much spike as explode. I see my opportunity to escape and warn locals coming the other way of the impending danger. Once again, I remember that sense of this all being a game.

The gorge is wondrous. A Zambezi-fuelled photo session, I return back along the trail before sunset. Five elephants are strolling through the undergrowth together, munching, ears flapping. It is quite a sight, especially as I am on foot only yards away. *Choot Choot!* A blast of black, acrid smoke shoots into the azure sky as a steam train passes, a colonial beauty. This is a head spin. Elephants to the right, steam train to the left, local lads trying in vain to take selfies with the train.

It suddenly occurs to me that had anyone ever answered my emails in the affirmative about working with elephants, this lot would be my life now instead of a bunch of lads in Bulawayo.

Back in town, I must admit, to my shame (there is that word once again), to going all the way back to Shearwater to see if Ashley was there. And, would you believe it, as I stride in, if her minibus doesn't pull up and she steps out. Quite how underwhelmed she is to see me, makes me feel like a spotty 14-year-old with an absurd crush. They've spent the whole day at magnificent Chobe. I try to draw them on where we could meet later but they are clearly knackered and don't seem slightly interested. Tail between legs, I run off down the dirt road towards the lads asking *hey man you want marijuana.* God, I feel like a plonker.

Justin! I hear, as I stroll into the Vic Falls Hotel garden. Who in Satan's name could possibly know me here? Ah, haha, it is the nice students from the train. I am glad for their presence following the Ashley debacle; such good company for a young crew. Over drinks, we discuss the cultural absurdities that sometimes occur in a mysterious new home.

When they leave for their 8.30 curfew, I enjoy a second beer under candlelight watching the various characters come and go. The bloke with an Irish harp on his huge right calf is acting up with the waiters. I am actually amazed what a mess, in general, visitors and residents look. The Zims dress up but, the Yanks in particular, are often an embarrassing mess with their oversized and undersized shorts and caps.

I know this story is about my experiences as an international football manager but I still feel foolish about Ashley. How did I get that one so wrong, aged 47?!

Under the light of the full moon, I chat to an affable army guard and return to the hotel bar for Bayern v Real. It is the Champions League semi second leg, and I am relieved the girls aren't here.

Wednesday, May 2nd, 2018

When I see the girls at breakfast, I have made up my mind to be cool, so when Ashley strolls in wearing jogging gear, I just wave casually and return to my poached eggs and diary. If I'm going to be single, I have really got to sort my game out.

"You keep a diary?" Ashley enquires.

We chat for ten minutes, and she asks if she can join me for a coffee, the morning sun just beginning to intensify and the birds in full voice.

And so, you see, I do get to spend the half hour I so longed for with Ashley. And, no, I wasn't wrong about her; she is funny and smart and thoughtful. She is a nurse in the US. She'd like to travel more but does well by US standards with 5 weeks a year. Ashley asks me lots of questions about the project, living in Zim, my living out of a bag lifestyle. I realise I am now one of those foreigners living in the country you are visiting who get asked *how it really is*. Ashley invites me to her room to give me a load of stuff that would otherwise be discarded such as shampoos, bug sprays, and books. My heart is pounding, alone with her, those pretty green, mischievous eyes. Back in the day, I'd have chanced my luck but, I don't want to insult what is probably nothing more than thoughtfulness on her part.

I give both girls a goodbye hug by the pool before I head off for Zambia, forgetting myself as I pat my hands on Ashley's back, mid-hug. I am glad I was right about Ashley being a quality lass.

Striding down towards the border I feel good; the first time I have experienced such an emotion for a visa run. I am concerned that if the visa takes up a whole page, it will effectively take my passport out of action for Russia with just two clean pages left. I am absolutely roaring with laughter at the abandoned cars on the kilometre long road to the border. They are absolutely caked in orange dust and sand.

ZIMBABWE IS OPEN FOR BUSINESS is scrawled on them, taking the piss out of Mnangagwa's pledge at his inauguration, laughing at Zimbabwe in general.

What a sight below the bridge! Water churning, roaring, spraying. Mini waterfalls tumble down one side of the gorge; the main falls impossible to see for all the clouds of spray. A lorry crosses and the whole bridge shakes.

The Zambian side of the bridge is a mile of parked lorries. Some charlatan, offering lifts on the back of his bike, says *it is five miles to the border post*. I tell him *I know it is only one* but he says I am wrong and *good luck to me as I will be walking for hours*.

The Zambian border guard is very accommodating, agreeing to stick the Zambian visa on a dirty page. I walk to the park entrance. I was here in 2010 with Bjorn as we cycled, hitched, slept on the deck of ferries, and train rode our way to South Africa together from Kenya. But this time, I am keen to set a new record for the least amount of time I have ever spent in a country. I buy a cold drink, an aggressive baboon shows me his arse, and, 7 minutes after entering Zambia, I am gone.

Back to the bridge: photos, video, epic, roar, breathtaking, bungee jumpers.

"Welcome back! You are booked for a massage."

"No, I'm not, haha."

"Yes, a lady booked you a massage."

"Uh? Sorry, I think you are confusing me with the wrong person."

"Ashley says she really respects what you are doing and she has booked you a head and body massage."

I am in shock. That is so bloody nice. Women never do stuff like that. Never ever. Not the ones I know anyway.

"Do you mind me asking? Did you stay an extra day because of her?"

"Haha. Was it that obvious? Well, she was definitely a factor. I must admit to having a crush on her."

"I'm not surprised; she is a special girl."

Oh my word, that massage is good. My back is one big knot. I needed this big time. I needed all of this, truth be told: the lunar moon, elephant adventures, that gorge, 7 minutes in Zambia, red wine by the pool, Ashley.

I am buzzing with my cold Castle at the Vic Falls Hotel. That gesture. I can't tell you how good it has made me feel. I draw a heart in my diary. Yes, it is for her, but it is also for Vic Falls. This place has given me a special energy. I am ready to go back and face all that I need to face. The final chapter.

16: Frogger

Thursday, May 3, 2018

Turns out the old fella in my compartment is senile. He's been blanking me because he has reached the blank stage in his life. Poor lad. Travelling alone on an overnight train. In Europe, he'd be in a home with people looking out for him. He must have gone to the toilet 15 times last night and each time like a black comedy, pardon the pun, he couldn't remember how to unlatch the compartment door. I had to get up twice to torchlight him back in here.

We finally get in at 1.30pm, having departed last night at 7. I jump out on the rail side, and pace home, all too aware that I've got training after two hours and eight kilometres to cover. Mobile phone chargers, DVD films, car repairs, tomatoes and onions, bananas, microbuses, bad drivers aplenty; a game of Frogger. To be honest, this whole Zimbabwe experience is starting to feel like a never-ending game of Frogger.

The slim-fit tracksuits look class. We unveil them to the boys who are made up. They fit! Even the badge embroidery looks decent. It is 4-a-side under the lights. Bruce the Goalkeeper has got a right mood on him and takes out two of our lads. The lads walk tall in their tracksuits through the adjacent all-whites bar. I am proud of them. And I am proud they are proud of themselves.

Friday, May 4, 2018

I BEDDED ENTIRE VILLAGE - MAN CONFESSES.

I prepare an email begging letter and send it out individually to maybe 300 people I know. This whole process takes about five hours. By day end, Dan has dropped $200, Helen 100 quid, Ryan, who I briefly met at the CONIFA Euros, another 20. Navneeth, a mate from India, $250! Simbu, another 50. I also sell half a dozen shirts. Wow.

Strangely, I am not even slightly stressed by this evening's visit of CNN. I have organised a detailed and varied session. Jo and her team turn up right on time. Some of the lads aren't here, and there are only five balls, no ball pump, and no red bibs. I am absolutely fuming, and I let the lateshowers know it when they arrive. The trouble is, now I cannot snap out of my foul mood, and I am sure it will show on the cameras. I had drills planned using 10 balls; now I need to wing it.

The lads play like pants. I have never seen them so poor aside from the fat lawyers debacle. Ciro is absolutely dreadful. Sawusani is trying to showboat but is failing miserably. The players are not following my instructions. I jump into the dribbling and ball retention drill to try to encourage them to play with a bit more manliness. And, as we move on to my main drills, I turn to see CNN driving away before I get the chance to start my actual coaching session. I am massively disappointed, but I'm sure they'll cut the crap bits.

Hang on, CNN just came and filmed my training session! I made that happen! I made it happen by moving to Africa in the first place and by then sending them a speculative email one cold, snowy Sunday evening in Latvia! It is easy to forget these things in the haze of determination.

Saturday, May 5, 2018

The replica shirt designs are way off the mark. The shirt manufacturers have had to draw up designs out of their own pocket as I was unable to provide them with designs myself (as they don't exist). I'm not sure Jamie will ever speak to me again after all of this. But I owe it to everyone who has invested in a shirt that it is every bit as good as they thought it would be. I owe it to Matabeleland, and I owe it to myself.

Ethel and her daughter were up at 4am to queue at Western Union. I pass them at 9, en route to the CNN press conference at Carne Casa.

This restaurant is new and arguably the best in town. Not one Zimbabwean journalist has turned up on time for the start of the press conference. Can you imagine? Some apparently want $10 to attend. What a bunch of jokers. CNN are here for God's sake. It is pathetic. None of them consider that there might be greater benefits than seven quid for perhaps networking with CNN, or breaking an interesting news story, or just honestly doing their job! *Parasites*.

Busani wants to start without them. I don't blame him but, instead, I ask him to chase a couple.

There is bottled water on the table, branded with Matabeleland Football. Class. We are tweeting around the world because it is perceptions out there – beyond these borders – that matter more than they do inside Zimbabwe itself. Today, we announce and launch the tracksuit, warm-up tops, kits, the New Balance/Liverpool FC boots, Ray Newland and the J4K sponsorship, Graham Williams' sponsorship. There are lots of photos with the players and the kit-wearing mannequins.

We all feel brilliant; CNN are sat at the back. We are getting good at this. We look like the real deal. We are the real deal. Our day has come.

The Save Matabeleland Coalition tell me we are *doing a better job than ZIM PL clubs*. Truthfully, we are more professional at what we do than some national federations I have come into contact with over the years. *PL players are now following us. This project could be massive going forward: selling players, all of us making a living from this.* They talk of me being part of this but, from experience, I doubt it will happen. I bet I never make a penny out of Matabeleland, aside from perhaps a few quid from a book but that would be off my own back. But that is fine. I didn't do this for any financial reward. I'm doing it for the love and the art. Sometimes, helping others gives you more pleasure than helping yourself.

We all part company happy; especially the players.

I stay until 4, bringing in more cash, spreading today's positive social media message far and wide. I pass the long, snaking remittance queues on my way home.

Poor Ethel comes homes at 7pm! She queued from 5am. What a way to run a fucking country!

I feel so sorry for her and her daughter having to endure that. I think of the UK and how people love to moan. How would the so-called 'British reserve' hold up if we had to sit on the pavement, in 28 degrees of heat, for 12 hours, for some cash?

Sunday, May 6, 2018

CNN interview me on the pitch at the Crescent. We select five of the boys who are confident and speak good English to also be interviewed on camera. They do very well.

The pre-match warmup that Khanye and I organise is very good. And on this surface, it just looks better. The CNN drone flies overhead. The boys look great. This being Africa, the KO is 45 mins late as the ref hasn't shown up. And disappointingly, the crowd is a pathetic 20. Yeah, the local community isn't exactly embracing this team right now.

The lads play excellent football from the very first kick. Pele pulls off a turn of genius. I don't even know how he did it. Andy is absolutely bossing midfield. First-time touches, pass completion. Bruce sidewinders goal kicks into the channels like a top pro. Thabiso is dangerous every time he gets near the ball. We are spanking the league one team. Every time we lose the ball, it is won back immediately. This is the best we have ever played. Honestly, this is better football than English League One games I have watched this season. Only Charlton were superior to this. This is a standard good enough to pay to watch. This is better than Northampton Town. Thabiso goes around the keeper on a lightning-fast counter and is taken down. Penalty with a drone hovering above the taker's head! This is mad. Kiwa scores but Thabiso is injured. We need this boy in London. This boy could be a star. Andy is still winning the ball back like he is Gennaro Gattuso. Pele is at his brilliant best. But you know football! We have missed a lot of chances and go in 1-0 at the break.

"This is the best I have seen you play but you know what I am going to say. At 1-0 it means nothing."

For the second half, we make a lot of changes. The boys coming in are doing well.

CNN are filming the whole thing. The opposition manager is going mad with his players, but this game is down to how good we are and not how bad they might be. Our ex-player, Gary, shows flashes but it usually goes one of two ways when a class player returns to play against his old club. Unfortunately for Gary, our boys are determined to disappear him from the game and tell him *you are not good enough to join us!* Late on, our opponents should have a penalty. But it stays 1-0; a great win in front of the CNN cameras.

We say goodbye to the crew, and all go home happy. If all these boys get visas, stay fit, and remain on form, then we will definitely give others a game in London. I was proud of them today.

Monday, May 7, 2018

"Good work!" a toothless bloke smiles and exclaims with a thumbs up as I jog past him. Another lady selling stuff under a tree is laughing at my jogging style. On Mugabe Way, the driving is stupidly fast and the air stinks of diesel and burning rubbish. I'm pushing myself to the sounds of Above and Beyond. I cannot believe how fast I am running. 5.42, 5.26, 5.37, 5.28 and that last kilometre 4.58! That is my personal best! How we improve through repetition. Kicking a ball, writing a diary, sex.

Ethel is still exhausted from her 14 hours of street queuing. Poor lady. There is now $8k on my page and another grand from friends on other crowdfunders. Culture Trip interviews me. Another journo asks me about the support from my friends and family, and I tell him how humbled I have been by them all.

Tuesday, May 8, 2018

Wood pigeons, cool breeze, sunny of course, lots of birds chattering, the distant rumble of lorries, pot burning, smoke rising, dog strolling around, children's laughter, chicken bucking, Afrikaans music on the radio.

My brain is frazzled after a full day of being online; I don't know whether to laugh or cry as I watch several of our lads struggling to complete ten press ups. You could blow one or two of these boys over with a feather. Busani, Khanye, and I all stress how important it is that the lads work on their upper body but, at this late stage in the game, it won't make too much difference for London. My upper body strength is a joke, but I manage to keep up with most of them in a series of exercises. I have bought all the boys a banana each as I repeat myself for the umpteenth time about post-match eating. Most of these lads still think eating loads of meat every day makes you strong. I know they think I am mad when I talk about successful vegan athletes. Kiwa has seven of us on the back seat of his car as he kindly drops us into town. I guess that is one of the advantages of everyone being so damn thin.

Wednesday, May 9, 2018

I do a BBC Northampton interview, and Africa on the Ball have requested a podcast. The crowdfunder has hit $8,200. Up at the Crescent, on the adjacent pitch, an army team is playing against the lads we played at the weekend. Apparently, the army are asking who the hell I am. You don't want to get on the wrong side of the military in Zim.

It gets dark so early now that my sessions barely last 45 minutes before darkness engulfs all. Half in fear, more than anything, I clock 4:42 kilometre times on the sprint home.

Thursday, May 10, 2018

I am so damn tired. I have walked and run 80 kilometres in the past four days. Aside from the running around, my days now are spent entirely in a cafe using the internet and sitting on one cappuccino. Another 10 shirts sold overnight as the crowdfund page closes down today. I have brought in a great lad called Chris Dolman as our kit man, which takes a weight off my mind for London. Before I know it, it is 5pm, and I have had to miss fitness training.

I buy a bottle of rosé and sit in the yard with Ethel discussing her humanitarian work back in the day.

There are ants in my bed, and I can barely sleep with an all-consuming anxiety about everything there is left to do to get us to London.

Friday, May 11, 2018

We'd like to make you an offer for the shirt sponsorship. I am made up. Every day, I try to find sponsors to push us to our financial target. I call the interested party in the UK, and they conclude the call saying they *will be making a written bid to be the team's official sponsor.* I reckon this is going to be 1,500 quid minimum. While I am waiting for the email to arrive, I manage to sell 10 old used Matabeleland shirts for 300 quid. Maybe I should be a market trader instead of a coach. Meanwhile, Chris Dolman is already sending me graphics I can use for the team's social media. I can see that this lad is going to be a massive help.

Matt Perrella messages me to say he has booked his flights to London and will join us as one of our coaches. I don't know how much time Bruce Grobbelaar will actually be able to spend with us, but I know having Matt around for the whole tournament is going to be massive for the team.

Culture Trip have published a story about Matabeleland following our interview, and a couple of smaller blogs have gone to digital print today. I am also hard at work trying to organise a 3G pitch for us to train on in London.

There is also word on the visas; none have been rejected, but extra supporting documents are needed.

I realise, walking home at five o'clock, that I am desperate for the toilet having not got up from my cafe seat for six hours!

I am excited at the prospect of bringing in a shirt sponsor and, having netted over $500 today from various donors; I treat myself and Ethel to another bottle of rosé. I am buzzing – and a bit drunk – as day turns to night in that wonderful backyard, chatting to that wonderful lady, building castles in the sky about the CONIFA World Cup.

Saturday, May 12, 2018

Four hundred pounds! The sponsorship bid is a miserly 400 quid. Now, I don't mean any disrespect to the unnamed bidder; it is just that by the time I finished off the rosé last night and rolled into bed, the imaginary bid had hit four grand.

Twenty, yes 20 of us cram into a microbus. Busani is rather comically sat on my knee in the passenger's seat as we set off for Burke's Paradise, football management bringing us ever closer. I am hanging slightly out of the window, a window that is missing as it turns out. We have cashed out the $50 I raised from selling a replica shirt for cash in Bulawayo to hold a team day.

We begin by getting the team to arrange all the seats in the hall into a semi-circle as I ask "Why do you think we are here lads?" Silence. "I want you to go off to the gardens and pool and, when you come back, I want each of you to speak and say five sentences about yourself; reveal things to one another that we might not know." There is a look of complete horror on some faces.

I give them 20 minutes by which time, boys being boys, they are swimming and splashing excitedly around in the pool.

Kiwa starts and makes me laugh as he admits "I am a defender, but I like going up front near the goals." Something I keep scolding him for doing.

Some of the lads barely say anything because they are too embarrassed, nervous, shy, or perhaps scared to admit something that they feel might negatively harm their chances in the future. But, then, one or two of the lads start to tell stories of losing parents, brothers and sisters, at a young age. One lad sold peanuts on the streets. Some quit football until the MFC brought them back and restored their hopes and dreams. One lad, who won't feature in London and rarely gets game time, says the *MFC represents an amazing opportunity* for him. Pele is the one who decides to reveal the most. He played league one football and almost made it to the Premier League. Life took various turns, and he ended up in Botswana, fell on hard times, then quit football. Other stuff, I won't repeat now. The things Pele says, and his honesty, almost move me to tears.

Rather than describing my life to the boys, I tell them they must each ask me at least a couple of questions and there are no taboos over the subject matter. These being African footballers, I shouldn't be surprised that the questions are mostly about the beautiful game and not about my love life or such like. Who did you play pro for? (This is my favourite question) What is your preferred system? Man U or Barca? Do I have any kids?

Then Bruce asks about *dealing with players with bad discipline and whether I pick my favourites regardless of their form*. Our eccentric number two goalkeeper is clearly the most opinionated and outspoken of our players. Perhaps he is the most honest. It is a great question. I tell him that naturally there are players who I rate as better footballers and leaders, but if any player is out of form, he won't be starting in London. Nobody is in the starting line-up for London at this point. And that is simply the truth.

We take another break before addressing the issues of dress codes in London on and off the pitch, dealing with the media and fans, alcohol and fags, anxieties. This last one is difficult to prise open, but eventually one lad admits to being scared of flying; one of having stage fright.

"I still get scared before every match I play; scared every time I visit a new country even now," I tell them. I warn them of opponents, pinching, or maybe racially abusing them to try to provoke a red card reaction. I explain the consequences for them of us losing players. I feel I must say these things just in case some lads or opposition fans at the tournament turn on them.

Khanye does a drum-playing musical-chairs team-building exercise that the lads love but would never work in the UK with kids older than 11. And I love them for loving it. Then Khanye sets up a live video phone link with a UK-based auntie who explains to the lads the consequences of doing a runner while they are in Great Britain: every member of their family will never get UK visas again, and they personally could well end up destitute on the streets. We have to drill this stuff into them. They must understand the consequences for all of us involved if they were to abscond.

The boys enjoy a meat & sadze brai while I get my usual cup of sorry looking super noodles. They seem very happy, playing keepy ups with a dog-chewed tennis ball. Busani finds the Culture Trip story which states we don't have enough money for London and begins scolding me. He says *such a story will lead to us getting our visas rejected.* The paranoia.

Africa Time; our driver says he will be 5 minutes but underestimates by a factor of 18. Consequently, I am so late back to the North End bus pickup that there is no choice other than to get in a share car with a load of strangers at 10pm. Sardeened in the back, I don't pick up on the Ndebele question about drop-offs and subsequently miss my stop. Fortuitously, the driver is a very decent lad and reverses and drives back a kilometre to drop me off at the garage.

Sunday, May 13, 2018

I'm absolutely knackered. 9.30 is the latest I have ever been up in Zimbabwe. Time to start sorting a few things out like discarding things I no longer need, beginning my packing for the UK, and sweeping the room. It is Mother's Day here. Ethel is, of course, doing good deeds rather than having them being bestowed on her. I do at least get to share a bottle of wine with her by the crackling fire; she tells me the remarkable tale of one man who was tortured by the Rhodesian Army before escaping in bare feet after facing a firing squad.

Monday, May 14, 2018

I've got a cold and feel properly run down. I have had to cash out again, and changed my flights for the third time. Originally, I was due to fly home next week and meet the lads in Luton, for our training camp. That is now £380 I have spent, of my own money, changing flights to and from South Africa. My mate Michael says following the whole Matabeleland story is making him want to change his life and do something more meaningful. Living the Matabeleland story is making me want to change my life and do something less stressful.

Mondays are useless, to be honest. Social media is always dead, and shirt sales disappear. No one ever replies to my previous week's emails before at least 3pm. I call my mum who is sad that I won't be home for a week, as originally planned, before the WFC. It's another six hours online for me. It is grey today and it is strange how different it makes Bulawayo appear. I don't feel up to jogging and stroll home to find *gogo* with four kids, all of the parents taking the piss by turning up late to pick them up. I have a strange mood on me today. I almost feel like I have had enough and can't be bothered anymore. Of course, I want to finish this project and finish it on a high note for all involved, but things are beginning to catch up with me again. The disappointment of not getting the sponsorship does not help, and I go to bed with the blanket pulled up over my head.

Tuesday, May 15, 2018

For the first time since I returned, I awaken to hear it raining in the night. Soon all of this will be over, like some dream I had, hazier in the memory as the years go by. I won't miss the anxiety. I think I preferred last year's constant paranoia to the anxiety. I preferred it when it felt like a scary game instead of a massive burden.

I can't get up this morning. It gets colder every night now. Bugger it; I need a lie in. Sometimes you just need to hide. I haven't got it in me to run into town and digitise my brain all day. Sorry. Hope there are no emergencies. At the end of my tether. Anyway, I have got a backlog of five press stories that need writing.

Today's downpour is something of an event as it shouldn't really happen in May. It immediately brings a freshness, and my bare feet feel cold on the various surfaces outside. I am knackered. I can't believe I am putting on a sweater to go to the shop. One of today's tasks is making avocado sandwiches for the team. I manage 17 from one giant sized 50-center I picked up from a street seller. I know the boys aren't going to start making their own sandwiches, but the more I do this, the more it gets in their heads. And each recovery snack is at least something. It might only make them 0.005% better athletes, but better is better. I am putting together tonnes of drills that I want to work on; drills that cover game situations. I know I will never get to use a quarter of these now. We haven't had nearly enough technical sessions since I returned from Europe. It is meant well, but the Busanis think playing dozens of games and running the boys into the ground in the physicals is the answer. The lack of technicals will come back to bite us on the bum. With more time and resources, there is so much I would have achieved with this group.

Worryingly, at the office, Busani seems to be buggering around with the visa paperwork. It is fairly apparent that he (and Khanye) doesn't want me to be totally in the picture. Whatever it is, it is clear to me that we are still submitting documents – possibly on request from the embassy – just 16 days before the World Football Cup begins and less than two weeks before we fly. I understand how complicated it all is and I am happy to stay out of the process. However, keeping me out of the picture seems a bit foolhardy. There we go.

As a result, Busani is the one skipping training this time as he stays in the office and Khanye leads the lads up to Ascot. An orange cloud of toxic something spills out into the Bulawayo night sky beyond the abandoned finishing post. The wind and rain get inside my bones as I stand with only my head torch illuminating the darkness. Khanye is pushing the boys way beyond a place I think he should be taking them. On a damp, cold night like tonight, what Khanye is doing is madness to me. There's no telling him. We come from different worlds and, in his, pushing these footballers to the extreme like this is what you do. I'm sure it would have been the same in Brian Clough's day. Observing it, it is like something out of *Chariots of Fire*. I am amazed that none of the lads have torn their hamstrings as they do dozens of sets of extreme exercises on the steps. I am frustrated with Khanye, but I am not angry. Neither of us is qualified in sports science. I just know that this way of doing things brings more negatives than pluses.

I can see Kaka has pulled something and jump over to him, pulling him out of the next set. Khanye is only calling him back and, when I quietly tell him that we should end now with it being so cold and wet, he says the likes of Kaka are just faking being injured. Khanye is not being a bastard. He genuinely thinks that. I am aghast that we could lose first team players so late in the day because of overtraining. My fingers are going numb with the cold.

The lads make quick work of the avocado sandwiches I provided and are grateful as ever. I seem to have miscalculated, and two of them go without. Only a handful of them are still bringing water. I am blue in the face telling them to rehydrate. You'd hope the message would start to sink in after 7 months. Ah, if only Busani, Khanye, and the lads had taken me more seriously from day one about nutrition, rehydration, and their questionable upper bodies. We have made many advances but...

A member of our South African committee is visiting and kindly offers a lift back into town. Oh my God, his drive is a tiny Russian UAZ-style van with 18 lads crammed in the back and four of us in the front two seats. The windows are completely steamed up from the inclement weather. Bruce continually wipes them clean with an old musty towel. I'm so done with all this terribly dangerous minibus shit. At one point, the door flies open. If I'd still had my weight rested on it, as I had four minutes ago, I might now be out that door bouncing up and down on the Harare Road.

And then there is the wait for my lift home to North End. They are insisting on shoehorning 25 of us into this tiny death trap. I dread every single journey on the roads here. Thank God for the speed bumps on the road to Sauerstown. Just as we are about to hit warp speed, the drivers are forced to slow down.

I am modelling my Matabeleland tracksuit for Ethel and her family. They all think it looks great but as her daughter points out, put on half a kilo and this won't be fitting me. I am super excited at the prospect of wearing this in London... If we get to London...

Wednesday, May 16, 2018

I needed that. My best sleep in months. Relief, my RHR is back down to 59.

I ask if there is news about the visas and, again, you'd think I was asking Busani about his home life. I wonder if something is up; they are not sharing with me.

I am drowning in unfinished tasks. We simply don't have enough money, despite my best efforts. I feel desperately let down by the wider Zim community. I am working like a dog each and every day. I barely stop for a piss. I am not exaggerating. The scarves have not been sorted, and there just isn't time left. I am pulling the plug on them today.

I rush home at 4.30 after a day of frazzled brain, grab a peanut butter-avocado sandwich, and run down to Crescent for my session. And then I just stand there for 40 minutes because no one has thought to bring the balls, bibs, and cones. Half of the lads still haven't got shin pads or water. I eff and blind at them. They haven't seen me this mad. With only 30 minutes of light left when the equipment arrives, I abandon my plans and just do some shooting drills. I want to walk off and go home. They are like a bunch of school kids today.

"We have achieved nothing. We haven't even got visas, lads; never mind flights. The way you trained tonight, you will be eaten alive in London. If we get there."

Khanye and Busani call off the rest of training and let the boys go home to stew about what I said. We know football is played as much in the mind as on the pitch so, oh, how we need them thinking.

I pace around the bedroom until midnight tearing up notes, eliminating and discarding what I can no longer do here, reducing the final notes onto two pages of paper.

Thursday, May 17, 2018

Everyone is in jumpers and jackets. You probably don't imagine such a thing in Zimbabwe. A tiny, blue-breasted bird accompanies me for almost a quarter of the journey into town. I've got the tunes on, *good morning, how's it?* This will be gone soon. Forever. Becoming a chapter in your life that seems imagined at a later date.

It is super busy outside the vegetable market as usual. So much butternut at the moment. They have got 10-kilo bags of the stuff. Cabbage leaves are already scattered everywhere at this hour. Others sell coloured popcorn, tomatoes, bananas, and crisps. One bloke I usually see on the way home teases everyone by cutting open the most amazing avocado you have ever seen in your life. As ever, I look each way a dozen times before crossing the wide boulevards. No one ever slows down if you happen to cross at the wrong moment.

Rainbow and Carne Casa are my only two choices when it comes to decent internet. Isabel, at Carne Casa, is delighted that I choose her place and rewards me with the unlimited internet she has been promising to sort out for me. As an example of how my morning starts, I've got 32 emails, 7 Twitter messages, 28 Twitter notifications, 11 Facebook messages, and 3 friend requests related to Matabeleland. One shirt sold, four requested, no news on the visa. Cliff Moyo has found me on Twitter and is messaging me to tell me he *can't play for the Zimbabwe national team because he is leaving Halifax and needs to urgently find a new club. If he goes away on international duty in South Africa, he might struggle to find a club before the new season starts. He's asking if he can join us without a Zim passport.* I try calling him a dozen times. My heart is pounding. What a massive boost it would be if I could bring this lad in!

I message Grobbelaar and update him. I have regrettably abandoned plans to visit Mubane as I had wished. I wanted to see more of Zim before I leave so I could get my head together, in peace, for what lies ahead. But there is just too much to do. For starters, I need to work on set pieces during daylight hours.

Cliff says he has explained his situation to the Zim national team and would love to join us if there is no issue about the passport. I'm full on hard sell. Cliff agrees to join. I feel a bit like I do when I know a beautiful girl likes me. Can I tell CONIFA and announce this officially? He says *go ahead but, in the meantime, he wants to speak to his agent.* I desperately want to call Sascha and Busani to get this out. You know agents. He might start trying to change his mind for reasons unknown. Sascha says Matabeleland should put this out and then he will RT it. Busani and Khanye faff around for 10 minutes looking for the ideal photo to announce the good news. I keep checking my Twitter messages expecting Cliff to suddenly have a change of heart.

Finally, the tweet is ready.

And, oh no, Cliff has written: *Justin, will playing for you definitely not affect my future selection with Zimbabwe?* FFS, I want to press go. But I can't. I have to respect Cliff. I tell him we have players under ZIFA, such as our goalkeeper in league one. I also hint at Grobbelaar's potential future involvement in Zim footy … Twitter reply being written … *OK, Justin, really looking forward to joining you and the team.* I press go.

I have just signed an international footballer! Not my first – I signed a couple of national team ladies for Riga United – but my first men's FIFA national team player. Massive. I wanted at least one UK-based player for mindset, experience, etc. And, for our brand, this is also huge. Football people will stand up and look at this. In all honesty, though, I am expecting issues with ZIFA at some point. I don't think there will be problems for Cliff (or I wouldn't have agreed to his participation) but, perhaps, for us.

A lad called Louis Maughan, along with his mate Richard Lundie and the lads from Old Thorntonians FC, have been amazing and booked and paid Hendon FC for our May 30th training. CONIFA is providing half pitches for the World Cup teams, but I want us to do this professionally. I want us to have our own private behind-closed-doors-stadium, 3G pitch, etc. to work on. Prepare with the right state of mind. It is a huge bonus that these lads have taken on this cost for us.

Clubs have started looking at me on LinkedIn including Southampton. All of this will count for nothing if I can't get the team visas. I am hopeful some clubs will approach me at the end of all this.

The boys think they have got 4-a-side tonight but what they don't know is that we are punishing them for the debacle at training the other night. Instead, they are being taken out on a 10-kilometre road-run. That should sort them out.

Friday, May 18, 2018

The anxiety is kicking in. My stomach is playing up, and I wake up wanting to run to the toilet.

There is a message from Cliff. My heart is racing. Surely, he can't be pulling out.

Sorry Justin, we have got a predicament...Jamie Vardy Foundation have invited me...same time as the world cup...(I actually skip down to the bottom of the message at this point)...*I'm very sorry but I won't be able to play in London.*

I am just gutted. This is bad for the team and makes me look like an amateur announcing it and now having to 'unannounce' it. It is not like I can try to convince him to change his mind. He has left Halifax, doesn't have a club, and subsequently withdrew from the Zimbabwe national team because of this. He now has a massive opportunity to shine in front of the scouts at the Jamie Vardy Academy. I get it. He says he needs to do it for his family. Jamie Vardy is one of my favourite players. Fleetingly, I hate him. Vardy, I mean.

I speak to my mate Graham W about the predicament, and my mood soon changes from pissed off to simply being disappointed for the team.

Cliff's letter was long, considered, and polite. I have to respect that and, indeed, I do. Graham says spin it. Don't tell anyone Cliff is withdrawing for a few days but, when you do, announce that a Matabeleland player is withdrawing as he has been invited to the England legend's academy. That will actually reflect well on us, instead of negatively.

There is no visa news despite us now being two days past when we were expecting to hear back. We are the only CONIFA team left without visas. In fact, all the other teams have named their final squads.

I get to hear my BBC Northampton breakfast show interview. The National Student interview me. Forbes are in touch. I am trying to close down all the odds and ends now. Andrew Harding, the famous BBC journalist, says he is *on book leave and regrettably can't do anything with us this time*. The BBC Africa journalist is *too busy to come to Byo but is contacting London to pair us up*. CNN are going to film us before, during, and after the June 3rd Tuvalu match. I am telling them, off the record, that I believe the Tuvalu game will be our first ever World Cup victory. There is no way we will beat Padania's former Serie A lads, and Szekely requires everything to go our way if we are to get three points. I will be going into both of those games hoping to win, of course.

Paddy Power have finally released the documentary from their time in Zimbabwe. It is human nature but, my first thought is: I hope I don't look like a twat in it. I do laugh as they said they didn't want a travelogue and it is like a cool episode of *Globe Trekker* with Ian Wright. But it works well. It tells the story of the team, shows us training and dancing. Showcases the city of Bulawayo and the region, which I had hoped for. Shows how lovely the people are. My bald head, I am not so happy about, haha. They have barely used any of the material they shot with me. Good to see Busani and Khanye centre stage. They deserve it. Too much of the publicity has been about me. I have stolen the limelight and, subsequently, the 24/7 input of these two gents is relatively unknown. We share and RT it everywhere, of course.

Despite the release of the film and positive news from CNN, I trudge home feeling rather exhausted and dejected. No visas, no Cliff, money a mess; so many things left to do and I don't know how.

We are putting extra sessions on now. Busani does a very good fitness session, and then we work on set-piece free-kicks. My priority is the Northampton Town v Luton free kick. Check it out on YouTube. It is genius. I must laugh though, as our defenders case out what the strikers are doing the first time we try it, which is very good to see. They also don't like me telling them to allow the strikers to run free to complete the routine and comically screw it up several times before we finally perfect it.

We end the session playing a match, which I join in. Worryingly, I don't find it difficult playing against them. Yes, I know they are playing at 50%, but it is way too easy to find pockets of space. I break down the right wing, in acres of space, but as I attempt to cross the ball, it gets stuck in the long grass and my cross is shite. All the same, I should not, in a million years, be able to find that much space and have a full four seconds free of the fullback. The left-hand side of this team is giving me the fear. If an old bastard like me can cause problems playing right wing, then what will the Padania right winger do to us? Another observation is a recurring one. We have lots of skilful lads, but they are mostly inexperienced and way too nice. We don't have men in this team, and we will get found out against men. Goddy might be a lad who can front opponents. Andy as well, I guess. But I fear Padania will case us out and use their experience to beat us.

This time next week we are supposed to be playing in South Africa. And then flying to London...

But without visas, none of this will be possible. I am starting to fear this being an almighty disaster.

The royal wedding is being previewed on TV, and the ladies adore all this stuff. I am always slightly amazed at how many people from the former British Commonwealth still love many aspects of Great Britain instead of hating us for all the harm we did to them. I hear a story about a little boy with muscular dystrophy who knew he was going to die young. I also see a video of a Zim bus crash in South Africa, with people being pulled out of a burning bus. Horrific. All of this is a timely reminder of how fortunate some of us are in life. Count your blessings! It pulls me out of my bad mood and refocuses my mind.

Saturday, May 19, 2018

Training has been switched to a super early 8am session. I try to get up at six to plan my session, but I am just too done in... and it is cold. Anyway, I know what we need to do. A tracksuit and hat are definitely needed this May winter morning.

We practice free kicks, delivering crosses for two solid hours. I am copying a session I saw Brazil do in Tallinn in the lead-up to their match against Estonia. That was the time when Kaka (the Brazilian one) 'got lost' in Tallinn old town at 4am. I have got lost in Tallinn at 4 or 5 o'clock in the morning a few times myself, haha.

The priority here is defensive organisation at set pieces. We must be better organised, and I want our central defenders, in particular, to be animals about getting the ball out. I watched Dani Alves and co. pinging in balls for one-hour solid to the likes of Kaka, Robinho, Nilmar, and Fabiano and they scored a grand total of two goals, I think. That is how well organised your defence needs to be. We look shocking. There are three goals conceded in the first ten minutes. Some of the boys are wincing and closing their eyes when they go up for headers. Khanye goes mad. Busani bursts a blood vessel. I almost lose my voice shouting. As I always say, when you need to improve, sometimes you start from a very low position and work upwards. I'd say we are at 25% of what we need today. I intend to finish this session with us at least at 40%. 100% won't happen. 80% will need several sessions. Our first-choice keeper, Nonja, is present but injured. But it is useful to have him coaching the other keepers in defensive organisation; even coaching the backline. A small crowd has gathered to watch. Repetition brings results. *Repetition brings results.* It is 11 by the time we finish and, by the end, we've got Mica almost heading the ball to the halfway line and the whole backline screaming *Out!* We are now at 40%.

We do an analysis session on Padania, Tuvalu, and Szekely in the small room next to the pitch but the facilities limit what we can present. We also show the lads the Paddy Power documentary, CONIFA Euro highlights, and video compilations of great passes, teamwork and, of course, goals. It has been a great morning.

Szekely are asking for videos of our team so they can analyse us. Haha, good luck with that! Riga United Ladies are on TV for the second time this year. I am super proud. I created that!

Sunday, May 20, 2018

Look at the date! I just don't know how we are going to pull all this off. Panic, panic. This time next week I am flying home, regardless of how this all pans out. I need a morning in bed. I am shattered. Strange that I will soon leave this home from home.

MAN SLEEPS WITH HOOKER, DRINKS URINE

I meet the lads in town at 2pm. Except no one is there, and it is 3pm before three-quarters of us cram into a minibus to the Highlanders.

Matabeleland's finest are playing Caps United from Harare. The original idea was for the entire squad to show up and, shortly after kick-off, we all walk into a packed Barbourfields stadium in our Matabeleland tracksuits.

As ever, this has been far more complicated than you would wish. We asked the boys to chip in $3 each as we need every penny we have for London but, of course, some are struggling to find that kind of cash and others are having to resort to Ecocash as they possess no cash at all. Quite apart from most of the players being late, several are no shows. Now, as I have explained before, we run a tight ship. Khanye and Busani do not tolerate this kind of behaviour. We constantly strive to develop these boys as footballers. Mentality and maturity are key issues of this. Today's lateness and no-shows won't be tolerated and have consequences. If you can't attend, think you will be late, or are struggling to find the money, you communicate this to us. If you don't, it suggests you might not be mentally fit enough for London. We make it clear to the lads that letting us down today effects their chances of involvement in the WFC. We have to do this to them; we want our lads to be remembered as consummate professionals in England, not as some amateur African lads who just showed up. Myself, Khanye, and Busani expect our lads to behave and conduct themselves better than even the top pros do. We want them to be remembered for this.

We arrive outside Barbourfields to find it absolutely jammed with cars and microbuses. My heart is pounding as I know we are walking in as a team with 25,000 inside there. In all honesty, I'd call this fronting. As we gather outside, behind the home stand, some lads shout down from the top of the terrace. A couple of them are chucking lit cigarettes at us.

Seventeen of us march into the stadium. Highlanders are attacking the rammed home end. It's a wall of black and white Bosso tops. The crowd roars as Highlanders threaten to score. Vuvuzelas add to the cacophony. A lad, in what looks like a miner's hat, spots us and screams abuse. Many of these supporters will not know who we are and some, I am sure, will not take too well to a load of us showing up with tracksuits calling ourselves Matabeleland. To most, Highlanders are Matabeleland.

Turning up like this in the ultras end is fronting, despite the MFC not seeing it as such. A couple of plastic bottles are being chucked at us from one section of the crowd. Some lads, perhaps a dozen, are screaming abuse. I am actually fearful they will lob coins at us. My stomach sinks as we pass the edge of the six-yard box and the Caps United keeper glances back quizzically to see what is causing the commotion. Some boys boo.

There is genuine anger from a small section of the crowd.

As usual, much of this section of the ground are pissed up. I am wondering whether Khanye and Busani expected this or somehow thought they'd be clapping us. But we have made it across the main end without it going Pete Tong, and thousands have now seen the Matabeleland Football Confederacy tracksuits. That was better than I personally expected. The packed wing is not half as rough, or drunken, and we are more of an irritation blocking the line of sight of those sitting on the lower steps.

Nut kernels and discarded match tickets litter the ground. The sun is so strong and low that it looks like the seven or eight thousand on this side of the stadium are saluting in unison as left hands are used to block the sun.

The match is very poor. One take home is that most of the pros out there are significantly bigger and stronger than our lads. We definitely play sexier football than these two teams though and, honestly, honestly, we could give them a game now. Only the home 5 impresses me.

One drunk lad manhandles Kaka, and I have to stand up for him, half expecting this to cause a fight to erupt.

0-0, it is a shame there are no goals as I'd like to see how mental this place would go with 25,000 in here. The Harare team have filled the away end with I'd say 3,000. Monkey nuts, Subbuteo floodlights, riot police with shields, ice creams.

A few supporters come over and speak to us at the end; a few are quizzical about the project.

Monday, May 21, 2018

Originally, I was due to fly home today, the team a day or two behind me, for a pre-World Cup camp in Luton. Luckily, we abandoned that idea as, currently, we don't have a single visa to the team's name. Anxiety. I am up at 7 so I can get on with things earlier. I am so nervous. It is grey, cold, and drizzling; Ethel is wearing a woolly hat as she stokes the fire. I actually get back into bed with a coffee to try to warm up.

In town by 9, I discover that Yorkshire have been screwed over by Tibet, of all people, who have pulled out of a friendly match at the very last minute. Matabeleland is in Forbes.

From 9-3, I don't leave my seat. I am now checking for visa news from Busani every few minutes. But nothing from the embassy. I was certain we'd find out today. In Australia, 100 Africans have absconded from the Commonwealth Games. This cannot be helping us, especially with the majority of our boys never having stepped foot outside of this country.

There is some very bad news. Andy, our holding mid, has been involved in a car accident. I don't understand the exact details, but from what I am hearing, he was hit by a car as he walked around Bulawayo and is now in hospital. His World Cup is over. Right now, our biggest concern is whether he will be OK in general.

At training, we continue working on defending set pieces and defending opposition possession. We play on until it is pitch dark. Nonja doesn't look fit to me. He has only conceded three goals in six Zim League One games, but I reckon he is still carrying an injury.

I sprint from training to Ethel's daughter's birthday party. Jeez, they really do love their meat in Zim. Sausage, chicken, ribs. It looks disgusting to me. Tonight, I have the opportunity to take the ladies out and tell them how grateful I am for their kindness, hospitality, friendship, company, and home from home. I get the staff to come out with an ice cream and sing happy birthday to Linda, and she is well happy. We make a night of it, in the end, and I manage to take the ladies out for dinner, get tipsy, and get a taxi home for thirty quid.

Tuesday, May 22, 2018

3am, hangover, rat's tail mouth, anxiety, can hardly sleep.

Too Shy, Kajagoogoo, Bronski Beat's *Small Town Boy* and The Specials' *Ghost Town* sound amazing walking around Bulawayo. They just fit this place, somehow.

One of my ex-players, in Riga, has been shortlisted for the World Soccer United global award, so I chase RUFC and the LFF to publicise it. The Latvian FA also tell me, once again, I can't do the UEFA B, and I must do the LFF-C, having passed a higher qualification than that five years ago. International manager, five years coaching national league men's and women's football in Latvia... go and do the C badge (which isn't even recognised as UEFA C). I guess I have to give up on ever doing it in Latvia.

Metro call me for an interview, but the questions are mostly political to the point where I almost pull the interview. Grobbelaar says the boots are delivered and calls me *mate*, which I like. When I tell him we have no news about the visas, he suggests maybe he can help. Yes, there is still no news.

This is horrible. I feel sick the whole time. I just can't believe we still don't know. What on earth is the British embassy doing?

I am trying to get hold of some of our crowdfund money to pay bills, but Indiegogo are holding off giving us our $2,000.

I hear Andy is doing OK, but he is definitely out as the injury is to his leg. I feel so so sorry for the lad. We plan to get him to London even as a spectator.

I run home, change, eat a sandwich, then run 4km back to city hall. You know the drill.

Up at Ascot, Khanye and Busani work on the lads. I am roaring at big Goddy who, despite being a unit, has almost no arm muscles. We announce Kiwa is relieved of the captaincy. Praise is now club captain, and Kaka is vice-captain. Kiwa looks like he could cry. I warn the lads about disappearing in England, lack of discipline, and reliability. I make it clear *the management are properly pissed off about all the no-shows at the weekend and it won't be tolerated.*

Nonja gives us a lift back. Kiwa is acting up in the car, being the joker and pretending he's not hurt when clearly he is. I feel sorry for him. He's a top lad. But he's blown it, and I am sure Praise will make a better captain.

I am starting to get into Generations, the South African soap that is on in the house most evenings. I remember the same thing happening with EastEnders once. I realise that, in the same was as people get addicted to smoking, I have somehow become addicted to something I neither like nor approve of.

I also watch a disturbing programme about the poor men who worked in the South African gold mines and now have lung disease. *Slaves*, as Ethel says. The dog tried to come into the house with me. He now thinks we are best mates. My actual human mates are now joking with me about rooming with Grobbelaar and him keeping everyone awake snoring and drinking. *Perhaps he can do his leg wobble at the passport office to try to get the lads in,* someone quips.

I switch on the radio, and there is a story about a famous Zim bloke who has had his visit visa to the UK rejected. Then there is a story about Roman Abramovich also being turned down. With all the Commonwealth Game shenanigans, none of this adds to my optimism.

17: The President is not happy

Wednesday, May 23, 2018

"I'm sorry, mate. There is no easy way to tell you this. It seems like every single player and coach has had their visa rejected. It's over. Matabeleland can't come to the World Cup."

I am devastated for the lads. Devastated for myself. So sorry to all those hundreds of people who have helped and supported us. I guess we will never know the full truth of why but, clearly, based on the fact they kept all the passports for five whole weeks, requested extra supporting documents, and then rejected even Busani who had previously travelled to the US and all over Africa, sabotage is afoot. The excuse is the questionable financial status of the boys and the fear they will disappear in the UK as have dozens of athletes at the Commonwealth Games in Australia this week.

But the British High Commission in Pretoria is well aware that the unemployment rate in Zimbabwe is the highest in the world at 90 percent and that, in reality, many survive in the parallel unofficial economy. They know that the Zimbabwean banking system barely functions and it isn't possible to expect Zim citizens to adhere to the usual standards expected for visa applications of having thousands in the bank and regular salaries paid in. They also knew all of this when the Home Office officially declared a few months back that there was no problem with any of the CONIFA teams participating in London. They asked for extra supporting documents only one week ago. They also know we are due to drive to South Africa tomorrow from where we should fly to the UK on Monday.

Paul is the one who breaks the shocking news to me at 8pm after the visa agency working with us finally get some 'unofficial' news.

I hear his words but feel almost nothing. I just cannot believe what I am hearing. I expected some lads to get rejected but never this. I thought we might not raise the money, might be closed down or some of us even imprisoned; even some interference or collusion from the British government, but never this. Every single player and coach rejected. Unofficially. They have waited until the very last minute, so we have no time for contingencies. In fact, if we had not put so much massive pressure on them today, we wouldn't have heard anything today – official or unofficial. They'd have stretched this out until we had paid the thousands we owe for our Ethiopian Airlines flights, the hotel in London. This seems calculated in every sense to me.

I now have to phone Busani and tell him. He takes the news stoically, like the gentleman he is, "I see. That is OK. Thank you." But I know this has the potential to destroy him. It has the potential to destroy a lot of young men. I've had too much shit happen to me in my life for it to destroy me but we have built up these young men's hopes and dreams for a year. And it is as if those dreams are now being decapitated.

I decide that I must contact Grobbelaar and tell him. The Busanis don't want me to involve him directly in this way, but I feel I must tell him out of courtesy. And I feel I must tell him out of some vain hope that he can wave a magic wand and fix all this. He video calls me back almost immediately on Facebook. "I have just phoned President Mnangagwa. He says he is angry about this and there was no interference at all from the Zimbabwean side."

My head is spinning. Part of me thinks Mnangagwa is bullshitting Bruce. But the fact that the President is not using wishy-washy language makes me think otherwise.

"The President says they do not prevent sports people travelling for showcase sports events abroad. The decision has come from the British side."

Fuck me, the President of Zimbabwe is now involved, and I am trying to sort out this shit show via a spotty internet connection in a three-star Bulawayo hotel lobby bar with one of the biggest characters ever to come out of the game of football. Surreal doesn't even start to describe this.

"I'm in Canada and flying to the UK tonight."

"We have people going to the Home Office tomorrow to ask how it is possible they have rejected everyone, to explain that the negative PR from this when CNN, BBC, etc. get involved will be massive. On the plus side, this is all unofficial at the moment, so maybe we can turn it around."

"My flight arrives in London at 10.30, so you will need your guys to go in early. If this isn't sorted out by then, I will be calling the president when we speak tomorrow. Although it will be late in Zimbabwe, 1.30."

"No, there is only a one-hour time difference. It will be 11.30 here."

"The president says heads will roll. The team should not be prevented from travelling."

"Let me check with Paul what time they are going in. I will get back to you shortly."

Paul says their man is going into the Home Office at 9. I tell Grobbelaar and ask him what they should say. Bruce writes:

Yes, he must say Bruce Jungleman Grobbelaar. Make sure he says to them Jungle Man.

I double take. Triple take.

"Make sure you say Jungle Man," I tell Paul.

"I'm not sure I can actually ask our contact to say that in a meeting."

"Honestly, mate. Bruce emphasised that you must say Jungle Man when you meet the Home Office."

"Haha, OK. But seriously, the more I think about this, something isn't right. The Tibet team, some of them didn't have passports, never mind jobs. And they all got visas. It just doesn't make sense the whole team getting knocked back. Paddy Power are fuming. I think the Home Office needs to understand the shockingly bad PR that could be coming their way."

"I do believe that every single one of these lads will return home from the UK if they get visas."

"Sure. Let's not give up yet."

"Yeah, no way. Not after all we have been through. I will be online when your bloke gets out of the meeting and, hopefully, Bruce can get in contact."

Poor Ethel has been waiting for me for a couple of hours. 10 pm and we are at a garage forecourt trying to find a way home. The minibuses have stopped. I cram into the passenger seat of a Nissan Micra with a lady sat on my left knee, balancing her shopping, and me blocking the driver's gear stick with my right knee. I hate this shit. It is simply dangerous, and I find it very stressful. I couldn't live like this every single day. I think I'd go mad. It's too late to buy alcohol to numb my disappointment. To help me deal with the craziness.

At home, we eat, and I retire to bed. I try to stay positive but the disappointment keeps rushing in. We have probably got a 3% chance of pulling this off now. We are 25-0 down with half a day left to play. Instead of leading the team out at the World Football Cup, I imagine myself instead as a lone CONIFA stadium manager stepping in to help, looking on at the other teams at places like Sutton United and Bromley and wondering what if? I imagine the young lads of our team waking up the day after tomorrow realising their dreams are over. Will they ever allow themselves to dream again after we break the news to them tomorrow? Why would they allow themselves to? This whole project could now end up wrecking lives instead of making them. I feel like one of those false prophets that do the rounds here in Evangelical groups preying on naivety and hope.

I go to bed with the transistor radio on for company; the thick winter blanket pulled up over my head. I am dreading stirring tomorrow and that moment when reality comes flooding into my brain just after I wake up.

Thursday, May 24, 2018

Somehow, it was always too easy. I was never questioned, arrested, blocked, or detained. Like inconvenient politicians who conveniently die in car crashes, we were constantly monitored but allowed to get on with things knowing they would prevent us from travelling.

I go back to bed with the very last serving of the coffee I brought over, taking stock. I am not dejected because, I always assumed I, or we, or some of us, would never make it to London. And I have reached a point in life where very good news – stuff like Cliff Moyo joining us – can quickly turn to disappointment and bad news can become not-quite-so-bad-news. Meditating last night, I concluded: we don't let these wankers win. I don't know who the wankers are, but we don't.

They cannot stop us fielding a Matabeleland team at the tournament because I know CONIFA will let us field a pub team if we have to, with me, Matt, and Grobbelaar playing as well. I will get in touch with the lads from Luton Aces and ask them to play; Team Zim UK, Cliff Moyo's mates, the young Ndebele lad who plays for Burnley. Nqo can play if it means putting out eleven. Whatever. Whoever. All I have to do is convince Busani, and it will happen.

Talk of the devil… halfway through my second coffee, lingering underneath the security of the thick winter blanket, Busani calls.

"I have had time for the bad news to sink in and have come to terms with it. I think, whatever happens, we field a team that side. They can't stop you travelling. Let's put a team out mate!"

"Ah, I am so relieved you think that. I totally agree. We have to for the boys, for all the hard work and, of course, for Matabeleland. Even if Bruce has to play in goal. And don't give up yet Busani! I am hoping Paul and Bruce can pull rabbits out of hats this morning."

And with that, I jump out of bed and surge into town with my game face on. I pace so quickly that I trip on a bloody divot in the pavement and screw my groin.

PROPHET ACCUSED OF BEDDING MAN'S WIFE.

Only time will tell what I will miss from here aside from the friendships but, one thing is for sure… I will miss the daily newspaper headlines.

There is a missed call from Paul as I hit the noise of the city centre. I run to the hotel and call Paul back.

"Apparently, they were never gonna reject 25. They were gonna give four."

"Ah, so Busani was gonna get one. Still, four from twenty-five and Tibet got all theirs! Even pissing off the Chinese. We must be pissing off someone really important."

"Yeah, and they are offering three more."

"Really?"

"Yeah, but we said come on, you can't give us seven for a football team."

"Mate, if we get seven, we will make up the numbers and still put out a team. If Padania can bring in Stankevičius then we can play Matt Perella. I will find a couple of pros to play for us as well."

"Yeah, but listen, they have reviewed again, and they are saying nine of the twenty-seven can get in plus the original four."

"We've got thirteen?!"

"Yes, seems like it. The Home Office have taken the decision away from [the British High Commission in] Pretoria."

I am buzzing. If we can get 13, I am sure I can find five or six decent lads living in the UK. The press will be all over this, helping us. I am ashamed to say I have just added a 47-year-old has-been to the squad as well. Me. Can you believe I have done my groin on the morning I got called up to the Matabeleland World Cup squad!

Right on 10.30, Bruce video calls me as promised. He's smiling outside Heathrow Airport.

"Thirteen! Oh no, the president definitely said they should not be stopped from travelling. I am going to get on to him right now."

I message Busani and Khanye and ask them to meet me at Rainbow. I know this place is bugged, but the WIFI is stellar, haha. They are made up when I tell them the news although I warn them against getting their hopes up until we are one hundred percent certain. I don't mention Walley is in the Matabeleland twenty-three.

I am on and off the phone all day speaking to Bruce, Paul, and Sascha. Mister X, who has some connection to the president, is our contact there.

Bruce Jungleman Grobbelaar writes a letter to the Home Office saying he will guarantee the lads don't disappear in London. It's a brave move. The Home Office is softening at the eleventh hour, buckling. It sounds like we have definitely got the 13. But 12 cannot travel.

But, I say, "President Mnangagwa is unhappy. Surely they don't want to upset him over a bunch of visas?" "The Home Office want a letter from the president. If we get a letter, it seems possible that all the players will be granted visas. But we have two hours or the others will be rejected."

I suddenly imagine one of those bombs that countdown in films to 00:00 then BANG!! Although, of course, they usually cut the green wire at 00:03. I am going to have to front this; make sure we finish up cutting the wire at the very last moment.

I write, "It is 99% likely we will get a letter of approval from the President, but it won't be today as he's on official business and naturally we're not allowed to know where he is."

I have just made that up but, with two hours of game time left, I don't see that I have another card to play.

Time to message Bruce and ask him how likely it is we can get a letter.

I believe I can get a letter Justin, but it might not be until Monday.

"The Home Office is saying if you are going to get a letter from M then the visas will be granted."

Fuck, I should play poker.

Within minutes, Busani receives an email notification from Pretoria. He clicks on each of the 25 applications and each one states that a visa decision has been made. But not what the decision is.

Six hours have flashed by. What must people in the hotel be thinking when they can hear me shouting on Skype (like that *I'm in Belgium sketch* from Trigger Happy TV). *Got the letter from President Mnangagwa yet?*

It is all going off in London. There is talk that Busani might need to get his small arse to Harare and meet Mister X if the passports are delivered from Pretoria. I think my bluff has worked.

"Mate!!!!!!!!!!" Paul Watson messages me.

"I think we have just come back from 25-0 down!!!"

"If you can pull this off, you can definitely beat Padania!"

Yes, we can.

Suddenly, an email pops in from Ethiopian Airlines. They are cancelling our booking unless we pay the outstanding balance… today. Hell's bells. They have given us a couple of hours to find ten grand.

Twists and turns. *Banana Skin Republic*. Now, I happen to know that us finding ten thousand pounds in the next 100 minutes is impossible. I leave my phone call with Grobbelaar and manage to get through to the woman at Ethiopian. Payment today or we are done. The good news is the booking will stay on the system until midnight. *Please call me*, I tell her, so we can leave Rainbow and continue this madness from home into the night.

I get home, and there is a single missed call. I would have thought the situation demanded at least two hundred attempts to call me, not one. But there we go. There is no way of calling Ethiopian direct and they, it seems, have left the office.

We are now trying to find thousands from God knows where. Nqo is ready to transfer a load of the crowdfund money straight to Ethiopian.

"Shall we do it?" Busani asks me.

"Yes, the booking is until midnight. They won't be able to argue with that."

Nqo presses me on whether to go ahead or not. I have reached the delirious stage of tired. I wish I could put off this decision until after I have slept, but we are out of time. "Yes, do it!"

Despite all the good news today, myself, Khanye, and Busani are super snappy with one another. And who wouldn't be with the collective stress we are all under? I am pissed there is clearly no more money coming from South Africa. My mind wanders to all that stuff I heard back in September, about the community in South Africa being all over this. Yes, a load of lads have given us a few grand, and without them we couldn't

213

have paid the flight deposits. But the Ndebele expats thing, it was just a fantasy.

Fuck's sake, I have just had the sudden realisation that I am flying from South Africa on Sunday and I must leave for Joburg tomorrow at the latest. My attempt to buy a bus ticket fails as the horrible Greyhound website crashes. It is one of those where I don't know if I have actually bought a ticket or not.

I catch a late dinner with my host family. They are lovely and will be greatly missed. This lounge will be missed. Evening dinner together will be missed. Even the South African soap operas will be missed. I do my best to pack, but I am exhausted. Fucking exhausted.

Friday, May 25, 2018

My last wonderful Zim morning. Water boiled on the firewood giving it that roasted taste, washing down the world's greatest avocado. It is Africa Day! I am leaving on Africa Day! I love this continent and the many incredible people I have met here over the years.

The streets are deserted at 7.30, and so is the Greyhound office, which is closed. Fear upon fear upon fear. The lady manning the office turns up late, but I can forgive her; at least she has turned up. No ticket was booked and I need to drop an extra ten quid to physically book it here.

Grobbelaar video calls.

"You off to Kiev for the final?"

"No," he laughs and shows me his green top. "I'm off to Ireland to watch it."

"Hahaha. Fair play."

"Keep chasing our contact! Let's get all the boys to London!"

My last hours in Zim are spent online and under stress. We are being told that last night's bank transfer will take days to clear and cannot be used to pay our bill until it hits the bank account of Ethiopian Airlines. This is disastrous news and leaves us with new headaches we did not foresee. Our shirt manufacturer is also demanding three grand to release the product. They have every right to. We are in big financial shit.

After a pint of coffee, I am so desperate for a wee, but I am so busy on panicky calls that I have managed to piss myself for the first time in my adult life. No one sees this thankfully but, in the toilet wetting down my jeans, I find myself chatting to Roy Hodgson again.

Well Justin, you cwapped your bed in South Afwica so you should be weally pwoud you've followed that up by wetting yourself wight here in Zimbabwe.

I wanted to be home by one to finish packing and have a last lunch with lovely Ethel... but, 2pm panicking over money and getting stuff printed, I have an unsightly argument in the street with Khanye, who doesn't take well to me saying "The time for believing everything will work out has gone! We need to discuss contingencies one to ten." as he tells me *God and faith are going to ensure we prevail.*

I meet the players by the city hall. They don't have a clue about what is going on because we have told them nothing. They thought we would be in South Africa by now playing a famous first division team.

I have got two minutes. Some of them clearly think this is goodbye and there will be no London as they thank me for my time with them and wish me luck for the future.

"Thanks so much, coach."

"Come one, don't say that. See you in London I hope!"

"Goodbye coach!"

"No need for that! I will see you in four days!"

And then I run. Running is the only thing for it. Through those familiar Byo streets. My home from home.

Ethel has tea and sandwiches ready. I have a grand total of 20 minutes to pack all my stuff. I have had a few travel disasters over the years so, instinctively, I double and triple check my travel documents. May 27 the ticket reads. You have got to be having a laugh! The bird at the Greyhound office has only gone and issued me a coach ticket for the wrong bloody day!

Ethel's mum says, "You need to go home and see your mum!" Too right you lovely lady! Strong; eyes full of intelligence and experience. I see my own lovely grandmother in those African eyes, almost like a sign from heaven!

Ethel, being Ethel, insists she will see me off to the bus. Last look at the garden before I leave, saying goodbye to Buster, who is now my friend. It is funny how we do that look-at-things-the-last-time thing. Part of me is gutted to leave.

Our taxi drops Nan and Ethel off first at Byo Centre. With the driver paid, I jump out. The taxi drives off with my bags still in the back. I never

ever do this anywhere in the world as I fear the driver doing exactly this. Fear upon fear.

And, so, I lose all my belongings, including my passport.

Only joking.

I leap on the back of the moving car, my groin twinging and manage to pull up the boot as he drives off. He accelerates but stops as the flying boot creates a scene.

"Two things. I forgot you had your bags in the back and second…"

"Please stop. It's cool."

I want to believe him. My intuition tells me he was off with my stuff, but I am going to give him the benefit of the doubt. Everyone in Bulawayo has been wonderful since I came here. Let's leave it that way.

One of Ethel's close friends is on the bus. I am lucky because 1) like a complete eejit I have left my mobile on charge in the house and now have no phone or indeed numbers for Joburg. 2) My bank card has just been rejected at the supermarket. I now have 70 Rand left to my name – that is four quid – to survive on in South Africa.

Ethel and I hug.

"You are a legend and a brilliant friend."

"Oh, I didn't know that," she says humbly. "Please come back one day with your mum to visit." She smiles and leaves. What a wonderful lady.

We pull off from Bulawayo and take the shortest escape route via Ascot, meaning Byo is gone in less than ten minutes. The city hall and gardens look glorious. I hadn't noticed that all the red flowers are back in bloom on the top of the trees. I hadn't noticed when running for these past two weeks. Running, running, running. Bulawayo, I love you! Please take good care of yourself. Realise your full potential! It surely cannot be goodbye forever!

The countryside is resplendent. Those mystical strange-shaped hillocks, rondo houses, mini cowboy towns, rural, rural. The closing credits.

We are already at the border by 8pm and, proof that *Zimbabwe is open for business*, we are through in a record-breaking 20 minutes! I have actually left Zimbabwe without realising it.

South Africa is its usual mess, but we are done in an hour and a half. You might assume this is good news but, our record-breaking border-crossings mean that instead of getting in mid-morning, we now have a new ETA of

4am. Thank God Ethel's friend is around to call Thabiso for me and alert him to this fact. Stopping off at the now familiar service station near the border, the lovely lady grabs me and puts 50 Rand in my hand.

"Treat yourself to something vegetarian here before you leave."

I have my first chocolate bar in weeks and get news that Thabiso is coming for me.

The lady gets off at Pretoria. Another Zimbabwean superstar!

Almost delirious, I watch the oncoming traffic hurtling by us and, not for the first time, contemplate death. Don't die before you have lived. Read that again.

Saturday, May 26, 2018

It is a new concept: arriving several hours early, rather than half a dozen late. It is 4.30am. We have done it in 12 hours. Last Christmas it took nearly double that. Joburg looks suitably scary. Why wouldn't it?! In Park Station, everyone is huddled up like boatfulls of refugees on the hundreds of seats. I stick myself near the Greyhound check-in… and fall asleep in two seconds flat. If I do that one more time, there is a good chance I will wake up next time with my diary, money, and computer gone.

Am I pleased to see Thabiso!! He's parked about two blocks away from the station and, so, for the second time in two days, I almost wee myself, walking in the pitch dark to his car. This is a country where people pull guns at petrol station filling pumps in the daylight. Yesterday nine died in taxi shootings and riots in the Western Cape. Thabiso, what a star. Getting up at 4am to drive 30 minutes to collect me, having had an hour's sleep.

We go back to his, and I crash on his sofa in the foetal position, sweating tiredness through my smelly travel shirt. Delirious. People come and go in the tiny flat. Some of them must be imagined or dreams. Some of them are very small, like trolls.

Thabiso checks me into the same Kempton Park motel where the same hotel worker recognises me for the third or fourth time. You know when you reach that point where life has got so silly that having takeaway pizza and a bottle of wine for breakfast just seems like the thing to do? Well, that's me today. I mean why not?

Try as I might, I cannot reach the MFC. Messages are being delivered with ticks on various platforms, but they seem to be blanking me. Consequently, this means I cannot help with the flights. At this point, we have seven tickets issued. Someone, I won't name who, says Busani is fed up with me. Well, that is nice! But understandable to some degree. I am fed up with myself, to tell the truth. I feel like I have been dragging us all – kicking and screaming – backwards through a ten-kilometre wide bramble bush these past weeks, months.

Sascha calls me and says he has spoken to Lieutenant General Moyo about that missing piece of paper; the one I sort of white lied about the 99% certainty we'd be getting. With Busani and the lads now on the move without comms (in the direction of South Africa, we think), it is apparently down to me to close the deal about that piece of paper because, without it, we fear that visas or no visas, the airline might be told not to allow the lads to board.

And so, I take another big gulp of the red and realise that I have almost finished it. And now I need to phone the face of the peaceful Zimbabwe coup, the world's most famous Lieutenant colonel (now Lieutenant General, retired), the man who we all saw on the TV in his military fatigues announcing that *His Excellency, the President of the Republic of Zimbabwe, and Commander in Chief of the Zimbabwe Defence Forces, comrade RG Mugabe* had not been removed but had been removed from office.

What on earth am I going to say to him? The fact that I'm doing this on Skype makes this all the more silly. But perhaps not as silly as my phone still charging in Bulawayo. It is ringing. Five rings. I burst into laughter. Snot comes out of my nose. Abort! Abort! Pull yourself together! Perhaps you can call him for me, Roy? *I'm not sure that's a weally good idea Justin. Twy again!*

Ring ring. Ring ring.

Thank God he doesn't pick up. Even on my 12th attempt.

It is cold. 12 degrees. I announce to the world on Twitter that we don't have the money for all the lads to travel and the immediate response is humbling. Yet again. Ross from Leyburn Sports, the lad whose company very kindly donated Matabeleland its first ever kit, throws us 200 quid. Hundreds of euros, pounds, and francs come flooding in, buying at least one more seat on the plane. Just like that, from one 150-character tweet.

One of the countless plans that have never seen fruition was: come to Joburg, play a South African second division side, watch the Champions League final together in some posh Joburg lounge bar with a few press invited down, give the boys a sense of the big time. Instead, it is me alone in the motel entertainment 'barn'. I mean, how many places in the world could you get an entire bar or indeed entertainment barn to yourself for the Champions League final? It is like trying to book a table for New Year's Eve these days. Bale, that is unbelievable. Karius, oh, my word.

I try General Moyo again. I am halfway down my second bottle of wine. I know this sounds like I am an alcoholic, but I have drunk more today than I did during my first month in Zimbabwe. Moyo isn't picking up. Sascha is understandably concerned. I don't dare tell him I 'exaggerated' the likelihood of us getting that letter. I had to do it for the boys. They have to get to London after all this. I lay my drunken head down, giggling. Gone in 60 seconds.

Sunday, May 27, 2018

He doesn't know who he is or where he is. It comes to something when you not only struggle to remember where you are but, in fact, who you are. I guess after four or five seconds I finally remember I am Justin Walley, international football manager. It takes me quite a bit longer to remember I am in an Alan Partridge motel in South Africa. Again.

I start working on the merchandise orders at 7am. The shirt manufacturers have now got their money. The team hotel people are going to let me pay what we owe them in the next couple of days. Nqo is trying to book ten flight seats. I don't know what we would have done without this lad. Grobbelaar is not picking up. Possibly just going to bed in Ireland. I tweet again for help. Six complete strangers give us 90 quid in an hour.

Busani messages: *We are over the border!!! :)*

Nqo messages: *we now have 16 tickets :)*

Sascha messages: *the team could get deported upon arrival*

Bruce is up but not answering.

I am proudly wearing my Matabeleland World Football Cup tracksuit as I part company with my friend Thabiso at OR Tambo International... Check-in, tweets, fried breakfast, crowdfunding, interview... there are just 51 passengers on our Qatar Airways jumbo. I promised myself I would stop drinking before I get back to London but I am straight on the complimentary cognac. The South African bloke in front of me is off to Shanghai to learn Mandarin for two years, and I am off to a World Cup, actually two World Cups!

We fly over Mogadishu as it turns dark. The world is so small these days. My face is pushed up against the window, trying to peer down at Mogadishu; my mind turns to the lads. Will they make it to London or are greater forces at play? Will Harakat al-Shabaab al-Mujahideen try to shoot down our plane?

18: We will conquer! The 2018 CONIFA World Football Cup

Monday, May 28, 2018

I am getting some intrigued and sometimes bemused glances and stares as I pace up and down in my yellow and black Matabeleland Football Team tracksuit outside Birmingham International Airport, waiting for my lift home to Leicestershire. I feel very proud wearing this. Representing the Matabele people; representing my team and Zimbabwe.

I have got 24 hours at home to see my family, get my head and stuff in order, try to deal with any jet lag I might have, unpack, repack, find the missing money we still need for the team, and then travel down to London tomorrow.

Tuesday, May 29, 2018

We are two grand short of the money we need to pay all our bills, including some last-minute flights for the boys, and our hotel bill for the two nights CONIFA isn't covering.

It is more a cash-flow issue than anything as we are confident of making up the shortfall through replica shirts, late sponsors, matchday cash collections for the team, etc. But bills must be paid immediately otherwise the team won't have a roof over their heads tonight. Did I mention how wonderful my mum is? Well, there are now a few Ndebele people who think the same as she has loaned the Matabeleland Football Confederacy the missing £2,000 it needs. Meanwhile, the lads are on their way to London on two separate flights. I am a little vague as to what has gone on in Joburg, but with the usual 24/7 never-say-die commitment from Busani, Khanye, Nqo and others in SA, ZIM, the UK and beyond, who are supporting the team, they somehow sorted the final details with accommodation, transport, and flights. Ethiopian Airlines have been extremely accommodating throughout all of the chaos of the past few days.

Right Said Fred have released the catchy tournament anthem "Bring the House Down" today and I am roaring with laughter as I spot myself in this. 2018, aged 47, the year I featured in two pop videos.

My World Football Cup build-up starts here in the Railway Tavern, Nuneaton, with a pint of Hobgoblin and Elvis on the jukebox. Some quiet contemplation before the madness begins. Strangely, I don't feel very nervous about it all. I guess it has just been so full on that all the extremes become a new normal each day. 48 matches (6 of those ours), 16 teams, 10 stadiums, 5 continents represented. Best get myself on that train to London and get this party started.

The Confederation of Independent Football Associations is hosting its teams at the Stay Club in Colindale. One or two of the richer members, along with the UK-based teams, are staying elsewhere but this is essentially the CONIFA World Football Cup HQ for the teams, match officials, volunteers, and the WFC management team.

Almost the first people I spot are Bruce Grobbelaar and Tony Morton. They are here to greet the team and to kit the three goalkeepers out. I have only met Tony now a couple of times, but I am already a big fan of his. Another person I am a big fan of is Nqo, who has spent today with Xolani picking up players from Heathrow and transporting them all the way across London in its usual stupidly heavy traffic, before turning around and going back for more.

And let me also sing the praises of Mari-Anne Chiromo, another legend or, perhaps, I might call her 'an angel sent from heaven'. She first got in touch with me just seven or eight days ago, saying that through her project, *Positive Afritude*, she supports deserving initiatives in Africa, especially those from her homeland, Zimbabwe, and that she would like to help the MFC in as many ways as possible. She's been trying to bring in last-minute sponsors, player mascots, etc. etc.

When things seem too good to be true, they usually are. Remember the paranoia about the omnipresent *Thing?* I will be honest; Busani, Nqo and I have all been extremely skeptical of this lady's intentions. It is the timing more than anything; an angel appearing as she has at the very last moment to help guide us over the finishing line. All three of us suspected that her promise of a last-minute sponsor, covering two of the Matabeleland delegation's flights, was a delaying tactic, so those lads never ended up travelling; sabotage from Mugabe's people or some other shadowy group of people who don't approve of us. You see, this is what living in Zimbabwe does to you. After a while, you don't even trust the people closest to you, never mind strangers.

Well, not only has Mari-Anne launched campaigns on various social media platforms in support of the team but she has also been good on her word and brought in ZimPay as a last-minute sponsor, covering the cost of Busani and Khanye's flights. Like captains staying on a sinking ship, they both insisted that all the lads get tickets to London before them. If I understand events correctly in South Africa, my fellow coaches were the last two members of the MFC delegation to have their flight tickets bought. Talk about leading by example.

The Matabele team begins arriving at the hotel. They look tired and a little overwhelmed by everything but overjoyed, of course, to be here. Grobbelaar greets each of them individually and makes sure he gets every one of their names right the first time. I could learn a thing or two from him in that regard. I am shocking with remembering names. I always have been. With our lads having nicknames, first names, impossible-to-pronounce click names, as well as surnames that are sometimes used in diminutive and elongated forms, it has been something of a porridge in my head since day one, particularly as I never fill out match protocols and never see their names written down. Praise, for example, is also 'Uncle', 'Malume', 'Ndlovu' ... 'Captain'.

The best moment of this entire experience follows as the phone rings, and I am informed that all of our players and coaches have got through customs and immigration. What an absolute relief. They're in!

By late evening, the team delegation, including the coaches, have arrived at the hotel. For some reason though, our vice-captain Kaka didn't get on either of the flights, and it's a bit vague to me how that failed to happen. Busani is all teeth and embraces. You can tell he is absolutely buzzing to be here. Khanye, of course, not known for his smiling, is keeping most of his emotions inside but, it is clear when I speak to him that he is absolutely made up to finally be here . *We've done it!* I tell them. *We're here!*

As of tomorrow, CONIFA provides three meals per day for the MFC but with us getting the team here a day early to allow enough time to fight the jetlag, no accommodation or food is provided this evening. We are so tight on money that not only could we not afford to pay for a bus to pick the MFC squad up from Heathrow but there is also no budget for an evening meal. Nqo has sorted the transfers and some food out of his own pocket, and now Mari-Anne calls me to say she has ordered several party buckets of food from KFC, for all the lads, so they can sit down as a team together in the lobby of the hotel and share an evening meal. All dressed immaculately in their Matabeleland tracksuits, we are creating a very positive first impression of ourselves; Grobs, meanwhile, is in the corner kitting out Nonja and the other pair of Bruces with two or three pairs of J4K goalkeeper gloves each. The Warrior Birds have landed in London.

Wednesday, May 30, 2018

Matabeleland has taken over the reception area of the hotel. The ringleader is a guy called Bruce Grobbelaar, who has got 30 boxes of New Balance football boots lined up like a pop-up shoe shop, ready for our players to get fitted up for the World Football Cup. All the teams are starting to arrive now, flying in from the four corners of the world; the Stay Club lobby a hive of international football team activity. The North Cyprus captain kindly hands over 28 Matabeleland polo tops for the team on behalf of Orcun and the rest of their federation. A very kind gesture. It is an amazing feeling being part of all this, leading the Matabeleland team at this major tournament. I feel so proud and honoured.

We have Louis Maughan, Richard Lundie, and the lads from Old Thorntonians FC to thank for financing our first ever MFC training session on English soil. I wanted a behind-closed-doors session at a professional stadium, within five miles of our team HQ, and that's what we have got at Hendon FC. Robert Morris and Tom Stockman from the football club have also been a terrific help and pay for, and organize, a couple of taxis for the players, while the remainder of the boys squeeze into the back of Bruce Grobbelaar's Toyota Hilux pickup truck. It is a surreal sight watching a baseball-capped Bruce sardine tin them all in his boot with the ball bags. It almost feels like we are back in Bulawayo.

We are warmly welcomed at Hendon as I set up the balls, cones, and bibs for our morning session. This needs to be fairly light with us playing tomorrow, but we have also got quite a bit to cover. My main emphasis is simply getting used to the alien surface. I even have them doing slow jogs and turns for several minutes without the ball to allow their brains to form new connections; to feel and remember how the artificial pitch is. Naturally, some of the lads are struggling with their new boots and, more generally, some of the boys look sharp whilst others look like they are still on the plane over. Once Khanye and I have gone through our first drills, we send the goalkeepers over to Grobs, who begins his session with them. What a joy to watch the former Liverpool man pinging balls at our three keepers. Who could have imagined such a thing six months ago?

We are spending much of today's morning session practicing defending as a unit. After half an hour of attacking and defending set pieces, I have to laugh as Grobbelaar who, unprompted by me, talks the lads through the Northampton Town v Luton Town free kick we practiced in Bulawayo. Clearly, the Cobblers are not the only team who have used this brilliant routine or Bruce is a closet Chris Wilder fan.

Predictably, the session goes on a bit longer than I had intended but I think the players have had a good opportunity to get used to the surface and I am sure training with Grobbelaar, at this beautiful facility this morning, has the boys believing more in themselves.

After training, Tom and Robert bring in a big group of local kids to meet the team. Photos and banter, many of the excitable children want the Matabeleland players to sign pieces of paper, shirts, and even their football boots. It is a lovely moment for all involved.

Hendon FC (and of course Louis and his mates) have been brilliant. They've welcomed us with open arms today, provided drinks, allowed us to overrun by 30 minutes, and Tom also ends up giving a carload of us a lift back to Colindale. I'm sure none of the other CONIFA teams have had anything like as positive a day of preparation as us.

Back at the Stay Club, I realise I accidentally stole the CONIFA match balls for training. I thought they were a bit bloody good for training balls!

With the tournament kicking off tomorrow, this afternoon is 'Press Day'. A couple of hundred are crammed inside the auditorium; journalists from all over the world here to attend this festival of punk football. The tournament programme is unveiled. Originally, I was going to work on that with Matt Guy, but it just wasn't feasible for me after Christmas. Matt, along with CONIFA Press Secretary Kieran Pender, Cassie Whittell and Pat McGuinness, have done a fantastic job, and they should all be really proud of themselves. After the tournament launch press conference, it's time to meet the journalists in the mixed zone. There's literally a line of people wanting to interview Busani, Praise (our captain), and myself. It feels like an out-of-body experience speaking to the likes of NHK Japan, while half a dozen other journalists wait patiently and not so patiently to speak to me. Amazing. I believe we might probably have done more for the awareness and positive image of Matabeleland than any project in the region's recent history. You might even want to extend that more generally to Zimbabwe.

Starting this evening, the teams enjoy three buffet meals per day in the top floor restaurant, another of the many things provided by CONIFA out of its relatively tiny budget. While FIFA literally needs billions to host a tournament and clubs spend hundreds of thousands to play one solitary European cup match, CONIFA is running this entire 48-match tournament on a total budget of £175,000.

Again, it is a wonderful feeling seeing our lads in their tracksuits, mixing with the likes of Tibet and the United Koreans, as they joke and enjoy their first evening meal together.

Kaka has flown in and joined up with his teammates. His brilliant attitude during my two stints in Bulawayo earned him the vice-captain's armband. But, as well as being completely knackered from his extended journey, he doesn't seem quite right to me. I am not sure what went on with him not flying out with the rest of the team, but something feels amiss.

I tell Praise that I want the lads settling down by 11 in their rooms and trust them to be sensible after another of my long – no-doubt-boring – speeches about *the importance of sleep on the mind and body*. Do as I say, not as I do; work continues in the coaches' room until 2am.

Thursday, May 31, 2018

The day has arrived. Today, Matabeleland Football Confederacy makes its World Football Cup debut. It is fair to say this is one of the biggest days of our collective lives.

After a chilly early morning stretch in the park, a leisurely team breakfast and a tactics meeting – Grobs, Tony, and Chris set off ahead of us to south London to pimp up the changing room. That's after they first go off in search of a captain's armband from a sports shop.

Gone are the days of shoe-horning 25 of us into two cars to travel to an away game. Today, we have our own 50-seater luxury coach, driven by a lovely lady driver who goes by the name Julie.

Zabayaba ya, Sizonqoba

Zabayaba ya, Sizonqoba

Zabayaba ya, Sizonqoba

We, we, we will conquer

The boys are in fine voice as we set off for Gander Green. London, oh, London. It is barely 20 miles from Colindale to Sutton, but with traffic considerations, we need to head out west onto the M25 and circumnavigate the capital. Stuck in heavy traffic, it ends up being a two-hour journey, the highlight of which, aside from the singing, dancing, and wonderful inner joy of travelling to our debut World Cup match, is seeing the lads' reaction to a topless English bloke walking down the high street somewhere in south London with his huge belly hanging out. The boys literally cannot comprehend how and why he should be doing such a thing.

My mum phones to say she is stood outside the nearest pub to the stadium, waiting to wave to the team as we pass, but we complete our journey down a different road and pull in at Gander Green, singing. We continue to do that as we get off the bus so that we can announce our arrival to every single supporter, player, and match official inside the stadium (involved in the early kick-off between Isle of Man and Cascadia).

Grobbelaar pops out wearing a beaming smile and, soon, Bruce and the lads are dancing a Ndebele jig in the car park. Another person smiling a lot is Caroline Barker who is waiting to interview me for BBC Sports Hour about how I feel, now that the team is actually here, ready to make our debut after all that went before. In all honesty, there is still a sense of shock that we are here at all. Exactly one week ago, today, all of us were waking up in Bulawayo to the horrible, creeping realisation that we appeared to have no visas and our World Cup dream was over!

Bruce, Tony, and Chris have done a super job with the changing room. It really does look a picture! The shirts are out on coat hangers in numerical order, each of the lads has individual towels, their shorts and socks are folded, and a litre of coconut water sits aside each neat pile. Bruce told me way back in March, when we met at the M6 services, that he wanted to do this today. And that he planned to get here early and 'accidentally' nab the home changing room off Padania to get inside their heads. Apparently, Bruce succeeded because I am hearing from one unnamed CONIFA official that Padania are properly upset that they have ended up in the away changing room instead of the home one. Bruce does an interview with *Talksport* in the changing room and then it's time for the lads to walk in and let the endorphins circulate as they see what Tony, Chris, and Bruce have prepared for them.

The team pretty much picks itself although I reckon Kaka should not start. He is still clearly suffering from jetlag, having only arrived a few hours ago and aside from that, as I mentioned previously, he just doesn't seem right to me. There is also a debate about our formation. As ever, Khanye and Busani want to go 4-4-2 but, I am tempted to use some form of 4-5-1 until we case out our experienced opponents. I think how a team sets up not only has to be determined by the players you have day to day, but by the players you have on that *particular* day, the conditions, the surface, the calibre of the opposition... even the weather.

I have never really understood coaches who say: *we always play 4-4-2 or 4-3-3*. I don't understand how, unless it is a team like Pep Guardiola's Man City, they have that luxury or certainty and, indeed, the individual quality in their players for systems to be so rigid. And I don't think it would be smart for us to set up the same way against the European Champions as we will against Tuvalu, for example. But, 4-4-2 is the way we usually play, the system we have been mostly working on, and this is pretty much our best eleven, so I am not going to throw my toys out of the pram. Truth be told though, in football management, you shouldn't agree to what you don't agree with.

With all the myriad of distractions that come with such a day, the warmup is decent but not as polished as I would wish. A bit rushed frankly. There's a final tête-à-tête with one or two individuals in the changing room. Khanye, Bruce, Busani and myself all make short *Braveheart*-type speeches before we head off to the tunnel.

As well as my mum, a load of my good friends have come down to support. Some of their kids are player mascots today, earning the crowdfund a few hundred more much-needed pounds, and the kids hopefully an experience they will never forget. From coaching in Latvia, I know how these things can go wrong, so I wait for the players to walk out of the tunnel and then make sure that Toby, James, Josh, Olivia and James get to walk out onto the pitch with Praise and the lads before I take up my pew in the away dugout.

Bruce has his hand on his heart for the Zimbabwean national anthem. The very fact that we chose to play the nation's anthem – rather than a song celebrating Matabeleland's individuality – should, I hope, show everyone that this project is not about creating division but unity instead. What a proud, proud moment to be stood in front of the dugouts as the two teams sing their respective anthems.

We go for the fastest goal in history as Goddy shoots tamely wide from the kick-off, causing a few chuckles and groans to erupt in the crowd. That certainly wasn't my idea, but I guess it will make our early stats on the betting sites look encouraging.

It's neither a particularly good or bad start from us. Until that is, after ten minutes, their right winger beats our fullback for fun and delivers an excellent cross into the six-yard box for Innocenti to steal in, and head past our keeper. It is a carbon copy of the kind of crosses and finish I was working on at the Crescent. 0-1 to Padania.

We win a free kick 30 yards out, and Goddy forces the keeper into a comfortable save.

We are finding it tough out there. The lads are not completing their passes as I would normally expect. Our four coaches are spending a lot of energy PlayStationing the Warrior Birds.

I take a deep breath knowing we have made it to 30 minutes at 0-1 and are still in the game but... disaster strikes. They get behind us, and despite a great save from Dube, Grumellese's Piantoni hammers the ball into the net. 0-2

The third goal shows their class. Starting with a throw out from their keeper to their left back, five passes later and the sixth touch is fired into the net from a brilliant five-man move. 0-3.

The fourth goal though is just too easy; going long down the right channel and working the ball to the back post. 0-4.

We've gone from being very much still in the game at 0-1 after 39 minutes to being thrashed 0-4, seven minutes later. That is hard to take.

I was expecting great things from Pele today, but our most talented footballer is missing. Playing with just the two of them in central mid, the gap between Goddy and Pele is huge, and Goddy is overwhelmed. Kaka is not at the races. The left-hand side of our team is too high and easily exposed. I feel deflated as I jog into the tunnel at halftime but I am certainly not going to allow us to roll over and die.

Halftime is all about damage limitation. I switch us to 4-5-1. I honestly believe this will suit us better in London as the lads are so fit and fast that we will easily get players up in support of the one. *Play your game. We do not let them hammer us. We don't give up. Some of these Padania lads are old men. Be patient. Keep the ball, move into space. Do what we did in those passing and possession drills at the Crescent.*

We begin the second half much improved. We are definitely back in the game. But, as often happens in football, we suffer another temporary relapse and concede two goals in one minute; the second a shocker as our keeper goes walkabout and one of their players heads into an unguarded net from a quick corner as he sprints back to his goal. 0-5.

0-6.

We are 6-0 down after just 61 minutes, five of those conceded in just 22 minutes. Unless we sort our heads out, this is a double-figure humiliation.

But this team has a special spirit. Thank God, the lads recover from that horrible 60 seconds and continue doing what they have been doing since halftime, namely simple passes and movement, keep the ball… move into space. It is basically the rondos I went mad on for the last month in Bulawayo training. Now, all of a sudden, we are too quick for the old pros. There are some fantastic passages of play. We cut the Padania defence to pieces a couple of times. A four-man move down our left wing completely undoes the Padania defence, but Sawusani fails to convert with a header from just 5 yards out.

However, the talented young forward soon makes amends. It is a quick corner routine over on the right-hand side. Sawusani takes the corner then gets the ball back, cutting through two defenders just inside the right-hand side of the box. Pez and the lads behind that goal are singing ooh, *Mata Mata, Mata Mata Matabeleland* as Sawusani delivers a perfect cross to the back of the six-yard box where Thabiso Ndlela comes flying in and uses the pace on the ball to head home. The stadium seems to erupt with noise. Goooooooal Matabeleland!!!!!! 1-6.

The lads behind the goal are going mad. The goalscorer runs over to the bench. I'm off my feet jumping about celebrating, as are Busani and Khanye; the three of us congratulating the goal scorer. We have scored our first ever World Cup goal! What a moment! What a goal!

It might sound churlish to claim a team winning 6-1 is spent, but we now break 3 v 2. Thabiso dribbles around the last defender; six yards out, he tries to square it for the unmarked Shylock to tap in but the Padania keeper forces a corner. I reckon if we could play another 30 minutes, we'd pull back three or four. We have finally arrived at the world football cup.

Final score: Padania 6 Matabeleland 1 (Ndlela 78')

At the final whistle, I love the fact that every single player kept going, and played with a smile on their face. I told the lads before we came to London to get up close and personal to the fans. Make them understand you appreciate them. What is that thing with the England national team where they clap the fans from the halfway line, instead of being bothered to walk all the way over to the away end and applaud the travelling supporters from ten yards away? So, I tell the lads to go over to the supporters after the match but what happens next, I did not ask them to do. Not only do they venture to that final five yards but they venture another five more, and they are soon shaking hands with every single supporter behind the goal, near the corner flag, in the main stand… in the stadium. It is one of the most beautiful things I have ever witnessed in football.

After walking around the entire ground, shaking hands and applauding those present, we gather over the far side in our usual circle, holding hands to pray and give thanks. Bruce suddenly leaves the circle and crouches down in the middle, so all the lads' heads are high above his. You can see the humble meaning in what he is trying to convey.

Be proud! You did yourselves proud out there! I am very proud of you, the way you kept going. Especially the football you played at the end. It is another wonderful, wonderful moment.

In the midst of all of this, I have got several journalists trying to grab me on the pitch for my post-match comments. I'm even having to apologise and ask Deutsche Welle to wait as I console one or two of the lads and do a follow-up interview with Caroline Barker. In those minutes, it all becomes a haze.

The lads are obviously disappointed, but I make it clear that I am super proud of how they picked themselves up and played in the final half hour. The likes of Sawusani made some of those Serie C, D, and ex Serie A boys look average at the end; a team that included the likes of former Lazio player Marius Stankevičius.

Chris makes sure we leave the Sutton changing room looking exactly how we found it when he, Tony, and Bruce arrived several hours ago. And we make sure Arsenal's and Sutton's fans get to see images on social media showing the difference between how the Premier League boys and the African lads left it.

I grab a quick beer in the SUFC bar with my mates Dav and Graham Foster; Graham, of course, having been one-half of the Chuckle Brothers when we filmed here back in March. There's even time to proudly introduce my mum to Bruce… and Bruce to my mum.

No sleep for the wicked, we are straight off to the CONIFA WFC Opening Ceremony at Bromley…

It is fair to say, the atmosphere at Bromley's fantastic stadium is a bit tame. Wet. Funeral-like. The competing teams are quietly parading around the side of the pitch while CONIFA President Per and Commercial Manager Paul address the crowd on the microphone. It's time to get this party started. The Matabeleland squad sings and dances its way into the stadium and, instantly, the atmosphere changes. I believe in the power of positive energy and you can feel those good vibes bouncing off the terraces, off the various national team players, off the fans. *We will conquer!*

Padania's old pros suddenly seem to perk up and enjoy themselves more as they see how much we are enjoying ourselves after that 6-1 defeat. They begin to smile and dance. Journalists mob the team, taking photos and recording sound bites. Matabeleland is absolutely bossing the 2018 CONIFA World Football Cup Opening Ceremony. It is another beautiful and unforgettable moment in a day overflowing with them.

The lads don't seem to want to depart the pitch, so I leave them to their never-ending dancing and parading to speak to some of my CONIFA Exco friends, coaches, and FA presidents, as well as the fans. Literally dozens of people are coming up to me wanting to say nice things about the Matabeleland team, some offering me a pint in the bar. Many introduce themselves as *such and such from Twitter whom I have been chatting to.* It is so so nice how so so many people have embraced our team. I feel truly humbled. Our cultural ambassador, Sisa Senkosi, has also stolen the show, off the pitch for Matabeleland; she looks resplendent in her beautiful eye-catching Ndebele dress and jewellery. We watch the opening few minutes of the Barawa v Tamil Eelam game before we are forced to leave with Julie, our coach driver, close to going over her permitted hours for the day.

Matt Perrella has flown in from the States. I am absolutely delighted this lad has joined us both as a coach and role model for the players. And there's an added plus for me, as I now have a good friend to hang out with.

With the players tucked up in their beds, I am lain on my bunk bed trying to catch up with emails and social media. Chris comes and takes away the dirty kit to be washed, dried, and ironed before he drives all the way home to his family in the Midlands and then back again tomorrow. I wonder what would have happened if I hadn't brought Chris in to do this. Was the kit going to wash itself? I suspect we would have ended up sticking the dirty kit back on to play, to be honest.

I am also reflecting on today's game. I kicked up very little fuss with my management team about our formation and Kaka's initial inclusion, so I cannot complain afterwards, to be honest. But I am saying to my fellow coaches that I believe we need to be a bit more savvy when it comes to team formations and selection going forward.

My mate John Whitmore messages me, saying he watched today's game live, via the internet, and jokes that he *thinks we would have won if there'd been a third period.* Apparently, several thousand people watched Padania v Matabeleland online around the planet. What a day!

19: The strangest crowd ever?

Friday, June 1, 2018

Big up to Hendon FC who have invited us back in to train free-of-charge. It is a super club. Only this week, they have offered free tickets to anyone "suffering from depression or loneliness or anything similar".

It's fantastic to have Matt added to our coaching staff. We are spending much of today's mid-afternoon session with the keepers, firing off those rapid sidewinder goal kicks I love, to set up quick attacks. Our forwards, meanwhile, are being encouraged to be super mobile, pulling the defenders this way and that. Bruce S and Nonja are two of the best kickers you could ever wish to see. I know we can hurt teams with their kicking. And if the likes of Shylock, Thabiso, and Sawusani can be quick, clever and mobile tomorrow, then we can cause the Hungarians problems.

Turkish international news channel TRT are down filming today, with Hannah O'Neill interviewing, so Busani, Praise, and I nip off at various times to the main stand to speak to her. It is raining cats and dogs. Matt does some great work with the keepers and then, back in the changing room, the boys sing and film the *We Will Conquer* song for social media. BBC 6's legendary Stuart Maconie has declared his support for the team live on air a few times this week and we want to send him an MP3 he can play to his listeners, as well as a shirt to wear as a token of our appreciation for spreading the love.

With no transport organised, I have got Matt sorting us out Ubers before he leaves to help Panjab with their session as I agreed with their boss, Harpreet, that it was OK for Matt to give them a hand. Busani is upset with me that I didn't approve this with him first. I see his point, but with Matt volunteering for us, and coughing up hundreds of dollars of his own money to come here, it seems unreasonable not to let Matt make his own mind up, frankly. Anyway, to keep the peace, I have asked Matt to make it a one off. And, yes, I know I have been guilty of making decisions on far too many occasions without consulting the MFC president and the technical director, so, I stand corrected.

I realise when the final taxi comes that there is space for everyone bar one of us… which is obviously going to be muggins. Luckily for me, after a complete soaking sorting the lads' taxis out, and half an hour pacing around the stadium on my phone trying to deal with various MFC matters, Hendon FC's Tom very kindly gives me a lift back to Colindale.

Praise is off in a taxi to make his debut on a TV chat programme. His head must be spinning.

I have had Ka Chun, James Kay, Daniel Fatomide and Karl-Erik Laid doing lots of brilliant data analysis on our opponents for me, and Karl Erik very kindly travels all the way to the hotel to go through the analysis for the Szekely game. Our backroom team now not only includes the four students, but I have also got Jasmin Eveleigh, Jack Curry, Dominic Stevenson and Nathaniel Holland doing social media, and Jim Shepherd, Nqo, and Chris very kindly helping with replicas and merchandise. Chris is actually doing a million-and-one different things. And then I have also got physio Jermain Joseph-Franklyn and masseur Georgia Lambe hard at work, Georgia delivering more than half a dozen massages, back to back, in a room we set up for her downstairs in the Stay Club basement. Indeed, Georgia has very quickly become a friend and her, Matt, and I escape the intensity of the hotel to the nearby Beaufort Pub for a pint later in the evening.

With all that needs doing, Khanye, Busani, and I don't get to sleep before at least 1 or 2 every night. Our room is becoming a chaotic mess; full of replica shirts, first team kits, balls, cones, general merchandising, discarded lunch packs, and smelly coaching gear. The mess is unavoidable, but I don't like sleeping amongst it all as it gives off a bad energy of chaos.

Busani, meanwhile, is watching the video of our first goal and the wild celebration from Pez and the group of fans behind the goal, over and over again. And then over and over again. What must this be like for Busani? This is the man who created the MFC out of absolutely nothing just two years ago. What an achievement it is by this smart young man, especially in the tough environment of Zimbabwe. Just getting this thing off the ground, and the team into CONIFA, was a massive achievement, never mind the MFC being here at a global tournament followed by the world's leading media. He is another one whose head must be absolutely spinning. No wonder he has watched that first ever World Cup goal video 387 times.

Saturday, June 2, 2018

Game Day Two. Defeat today against Szekely will mean we cannot advance to the quarter-finals. I wake very early to hear the sound of Pez celebrating Matabeleland's first ever World Cup goal emanating from Busani's phone.

We are down at the ground early; Chris Dolman is doing an absolutely fantastic job of setting up the changing rooms to look like something you might expect in the Championship or above. Bruce won't be joining us today, as he has a prior arrangement, but that is no disaster with us having Matt joining the fray as goalkeeper coach.

It is good to get to Haringey in bags of time. I don't want any of this rushed. I want the lads to take it all in. And I want time to prepare properly. I have a chuckle to myself when I remember us turning up nine minutes before kick-off at the Highlanders.

With everything running smoothly, I meet my sister and her daughters outside. My mates Paul Sweetman and Jaime Morris are also there. I have got to laugh because, when I originally asked Bernadette to attend the tournament, she expressed concern about bringing the girls to a hostile football environment with the threat of football hooliganism. *Come on! This is the CONIFA world cup!* I told her. *The ground will be half empty and there's more chance of hell freezing over than there being trouble.* Just as I stroll out into the car park to meet her, there is the noise of drums and what sounds like a small, menacing army approaching, as Szekely Land's band of rough-looking black T-shirt wearing ultras comes marching around the corner, en route to the stadium. They've genuinely got a few lads.

Jaime's son *Hulk* – as I call him – is holding Nonja's hand as the two of them lead out the team to the sounds of Right Said Fred, my lovely nieces Alisha and Leah following on behind in their brand new Matabeleland home and away replicas. How good is it seeing my own nieces, as well as Jaime's lad in his Leicester City top, as player escorts out there on that pitch!

Red, blue, and white smoke spills onto the pitch from the terrace. The central Europeans bang their drums, the southern Africans bang theirs louder. This atmosphere is unreal. Some of their fans are wired, many with their tops off and bellies out. After seeing that English lad parading down a south London high street a couple of days ago, the Matabele players must really wonder what the hell is going on.

When I said *let's go at Szekely Land straight from the kick-off*, I didn't quite expect a four-man move from the centre spot, which ends with Sawusani being sent free, with a final pass from Shylock that Iniesta would be pleased with, inside the penalty area with only the keeper to beat. A player of his talent should do better – he was scoring goals for fun in Bulawayo before the team flew over – but, sadly for all of us, nerves get the better of him, and he blasts high over the bar with just 13 seconds on the clock. 13 seconds.

I turn and look at the opposition coach who looks visibly shocked by how easily we opened his team up from the kick-off without them having a single touch.

Within a few minutes, Thabiso wriggles free of his marker inside the box, but he shoots tamely at the keeper when I think he probably should have scored. This is fantastic stuff. Szekely look like they don't know what has hit them.

They go long, as we knew they would, to try and catch us pushing high. Nonja is quick off his line and, good with his distribution as always, he clears quickly and long over the top of their now high line and sends Sawusani clear again on goal. On the rock-hard pitches off Bulawayo, I reckon young Sawusani would use the heavy, fast bounce to shoot directly on goal but the slower pace and shallower bounce of the 3G means he only has time to lift it over the onrushing goalkeeper. The crowd gasps as the ball threatens to bounce into the net. But a covering defender is there to clear it to safety from 8 yards out. *This is fucking good* I think I say to Khanye and Busani, now feeling wired myself. Moments later, I find myself walking, half strutting, over towards the Szekely lads to my left, who have got flares and smoke going. I nod my head in their direction to show I'm happy with how we are playing but stop myself at the last moment from trying to wind them up. That might seem clever now, but it could turn the atmosphere.

We could have put this out of sight by now. We are doing a really good job of pressing the ball. We are too fast for them. One such press leads to our number 4 pressuring two Hungarians before he easily sprints past the second and finds himself clear, 25 yards out. He could probably use his momentum to advance another ten metres but instead shoots, forcing the Szekely keeper into a full-length save.

Football matches, like life, can change in a moment. With us completely on top, and knocking on the door of the quarter-finals, they play another one of those speculative long balls into the channel. We are pressing so high that we are inviting this, to be honest. A Szekely striker breaks free and immediately Nonja comes hurtling out of his goal. Magyari, still 30 yards from goal, spots our keeper advancing and lobs the ball over him. I might be wrong, but it looks to me like our two covering defenders might beat the striker to the bounce of the ball. But, oh no, hell's bells, Nonja has only gone and karate kicked him!

What's a referee to do? It is one thing to take a man out thirty yards from goal – frankly, he might have got away with CONIFA's first-ever green card – but it's another to do a Bruce Lee on him right in front of a couple of hundred angry Hungarian football lads. Of course, he's going to get a red!

With us down to ten men, suddenly there are more smoke flares, the drums are louder, and some lads you might consider skinheads know the balance is shifting their way.

But we keep going, playing the same way. Thabiso makes a fool of their right back, dribbles to the sideline and pulls the ball across the face of the goal. He can't do more than that. His cross is crying out for an easy tap-in from three yards out but, reminiscent of Gazza in the Euro 96 semi, our two incoming players have left it fractionally too late to attack the ball and fail to get a decisive touch, leaving hundreds of people with their heads in their hands. That is five clear-cut chances in the first 30 minutes. You just know what is coming next.

Again, they dissect our defence, but substitute keeper Bruce is quick off his line and looks likely to block their striker. But, oh, woe! Mica has given their lad a little tug, and it's a penalty! Bruce almost gets to the spot kick, away high to his right, but it's 0-1.

They are bossing it now. They've won a long-range free-kick. You might argue that Bruce should get to it, but that's a hell of a nasty dip and bounce. 0-2.

And treble woe! For the third time, they've got behind us down our right channel. A long ball pumped upfield is headed on by one of their giant lads in the centre of the pitch to the left winger, who coolly squares across the box for Magyari to tap in 0-3. We have done another Padania! About to go in at the break, 1-0 down, we have conceded two just before halftime in the 40th and 42nd minutes. It should be 3-1, minutes later, as one of our players – I am not sure who – gets played in behind them but blasts over from 8 yards out when he could have side-footed past the onrushing keeper.

How on earth are we 0-3 down? Well, apart from failing to stick away any of our six very decent first-half chances, our defensive line is horrible. I am screaming at the lads to drop the line back, towards our own goal, but the problem is the discipline has gone. Mica, or Praise, or Kiwa, is always playing the opposition onside.

It is always hard to pick yourself up, and a team, when you concede goals just before the break knowing those goals have likely killed the game for you, but we must try to sort the boys out. Quite apart from dealing with the walking wounded, we need to talk to that backline and make sure they play as a unit, not as a bunch of headless chickens. I had this experience once in club football when we went in 0-5 at halftime, and it should have been ten from the backline going to pieces. We put it right, and they never scored again against us.

Into the second half, and we are doing alright. I can't help but get distracted by the crowd and turn to my left, right, and behind me a few times to observe it all; to suck it all in. I might never experience an atmosphere like this ever again as a football manager. We are all here to succeed, but we are all ultimately here for the experience. When the football has long gone, memories like this will stay with you. It is the strong emotions that forge the memories as far as I am concerned. Maybe I am biased, but I reckon the Matabele supporters, who have completely filled the main stand, have begun to out-sing the Szekely ultras. It is a bizarre spectacle. While their fans are very 1980s passionate, mean and moody, with their dozens of flags and flares, ours are happy-clappy gospel choir meets non-league groundhopper; some are dressed in Ndebele tribal clothes and animal hides, many wearing our replica shirts which they kindly bought to support the team. Hungarian ultras vs. Zimbabwean tribal dancers: the strangest crowd ever? *We will conquer.* Sadly, not the tournament, but certainly the hearts and minds of the neutrals.

Bruce pulls off a couple of good saves to keep the score as it is. But then there is a cross from the right wing, Praise miscontrols and they punish us with a fourth goal. 0-4. Game over.

Szekely obviously know they have done enough now and I think we have finally sorted out that back line. The teams we play from hereon in will be nowhere near as good as today's opponents or indeed, Padania. So, steep learning curve, I believe all our defenders will be better for the lessons they have been taught. Bruce is playing really well. And like the Padania game, we are growing instead of falling apart. Again, this could have gone to 8-0 but instead we are dominating passages of play and threatening to score. It is just very frustrating that we switch off in search of a consolation goal and gift them a fifth in injury time. 0-5.

Final score: Matabeleland 0 Szekely Land 5

After our post-match circle for prayer, all of our players and coaches once again shake hands with every member of the crowd that wants to shake hands.

The Szekely Land FA President, Kristóf Wenczel, rushes over to me to tell me he was amazed by how well we started the game and believes *we will be one of the best teams in CONIFA after 1-2 years!* It is a lovely gesture from Kristof who was one of the hundreds of people who donated to our team to get us here to face his players today. Best of all, I can see from his excited reaction that he means it. We scared the hell out of them in that opening 20-30 minutes.

It is perhaps rather strange to be feeling happy when you have just been thrashed for the second game running. But I am happy. The lads were fantastic today. They tore Szekely apart in the first 30 minutes and had Nonja not turned into Bruce Lee, then who knows what would have happened. Not that I am making him the scapegoat! I said that if we got a couple of early goals, I felt we'd beat them. And we almost did. And we should have. The thing is, the lads have given 100% in both matches and they have never given up, even when things suddenly went very wrong. They have earned everyone's respect – mutual respect – for how they have conducted themselves on the pitch. And as for off the pitch, well… observe the sight of some very manly Hungarian ultras dancing and trying to sing Ndebele with our young Matabele players in the Haringey Borough Football Club car park. It is surreal, brilliant and one of the strangest sights I have ever witnessed in football. The Guardian photojournalist covering the match, Tom, tells me has never experienced a match and atmosphere quite like it in all his years. One day, none of this will seem real. Actually, it doesn't seem real now.

Back at the hotel, I discover that another Matabele lad turning heads today was our very own referee Raymond Mashamba, who becomes the first ref in CONIFA and FIFA World Cup history to issue a green when Stefano Baldan is ordered to leave the pitch in Padania's 8-0 win over tomorrow's opponents Tuvalu.

20: We just beat a country!

Sunday, June 3, 2018

Georgia is treating players on her mobile massage table in the narrow eighth-floor corridor of our hotel. If the sight of the ultras and the Ndebele dancing together was something to always remember then this comes a close second.

A couple of hours later, Matt and I are leading a coaching session about defensive shape in the basement of our London hotel. Truth be told, Matabeleland now has five head coaches. It might be the first time in international football history that such a thing has happened. Regardless, this is needed. With the lack of pitch markings in amateur Zimbabwe football, playing a strict defensive line is, and always will be, a headache to get right. The halfway line at the Crescent wasn't so much a straight line as a meandering curve. And, on many pitches in Zim, there was no halfway line at all.

Matt has got the lads' full attention. You can see that they pretty much all respect him early doors. I glance anxiously at Busani and Khanye to see whether they are reacting negatively to one more cook – and want me to cut Matt short – but clearly, they can see that this session is going well.

Estonian Karl Erik has very kindly travelled to the hotel again to update me about how Tuvalu set up and played yesterday. We definitely should be able to score goals against them, but if we don't respect them enough, they will use their front men's pace to get behind us.

Back at Coles Park, I am on my back at how painfully slow the Isle of Man v Barawa game is. In the hot weather, the Isle of Man look spent. Not realising the changing rooms would be taken by the two teams playing in the early kickoff, we have actually arrived here way too early. But it's not a bad thing; the lads get to watch some of the other CONIFA teams play, with all the different football styles and cultures that are on show in London. Matabeleland will hope to be challenging for the 2020 World Football Cup, so the more that can be learned, the better. Also, today is the day that the lovely Rachel is down to film us for CNN and complete the documentary about ourselves, Barawa and Kabylia. There are interviews with Bruce G, Busani, some of the players, and myself. Quite apart from all this, I am also pleased that our players get the opportunity before the game to meet some of our new fans, chat to them, and take photos together. These are special moments that should be enjoyed and remembered.

I must say that Bruce Grobbelaar seems absolutely wired today. And I don't blame him, to be honest. He could be making his return to international football, 20 years after he last pulled on a national team shirt for Zimbabwe. Him, Chris and Nqo are busy ironing a number 96 onto his goalkeeper top in the Haringey Borough supporters' bar.

I don't want to overload the lads pre-match, today, and I barely speak. We've worked on the defending, and told them we want them to play their natural game. Haringey's away changing room is like something I have often frequented playing Latvian League Two football. It is stupidly cramped and claustrophobic in here. It makes you just want to get out there and get on with it!

As was the case against Szekely, we threaten to score very early on as one of our strikers runs clear on goal, one-on-one, only for their keeper to palm it wide. Our stand-in keeper, Bruce, has gone down with an injury inside the first five minutes and I turn to my left to see a more famous Bruce giggling and raising his eyebrows to me as he pulls off the top he's wearing and sticks on the Matabeleland 96. With Nonja suspended and our third-choice Bruce injured and out of the tournament, Grobbelaar starts warming up. If our keeper's injury is serious, Mister B. Grobbelaar might need to come on and play almost the whole game for us. You might say be careful what you wish for, but I am confident this seasoned old pro will come in and do a good job for us if needed at some point today.

We miss another two decent chances but then, to the relief of the bench, Shylock puts us 1-0 up inside the half-hour mark; the coaches, physios, and subs jump about celebrating. That goal was straight off the Crescent training ground: quick pass out to the winger in space, looks up, and cross passes it into our striker, who takes a touch and buries it. Gooooal Matabeleland!!

But, as often happens, we don't settle down properly after scoring and within 100 seconds, 100-metre sprinter Timuani equalises, their coach jumping around and turning to show our supporters that he knows they are back in the game. 1-1.

Me and Grobs are now jumping around in the technical area like a couple of Italian police officers directing traffic, the third official warning us both about the abuse of the technical area. Suddenly, we counter fast again, and Shylock is released inside the centre of the penalty area to almost toe-poke the ball into the roof of the net. There is an almighty roar from the crowd. Gooooal Matabeleland!!!! 2-1. The third official turns and asks me who scored as I think he got rather distracted by our goal celebration.

And still in the first half, we have been presented with the opportunity to open up a two-goal cushion as we have been awarded a penalty. Normally, Kiwa would take these but Shylock is confident he will complete a 20-minute hat-trick. I have seen much worse penalties, but the Tuvalu keeper Katepu Ousua hasn't bought Shylock's shimmy and saves comfortably down to his right. We go in at the break leading 2-1.

It is quite an atmosphere again in the main stand, which is almost completely full with Zim and non-Zim fans singing and dancing for the boys. Into the second half, and Tuvalu's lads are trying to use their physical advantage to bully us. The game has really opened up now and they miss two really decent chances to equalise from headers, one of them a sitter.

With the clock ticking down, the tension is unbearable. I turn and see my mates Andy H and Graham willing the lads on and forget myself for a moment or two at the madness of all this.

A long ball from us, for once, sees Ciro inside the penalty box get clumsily bundled over by their last man. Penalty! It's our regular penalty taker, Kiwa stepping up; the man who thrashed everyone on the crossbar challenge in my first ever technical session with the team last October, and by far and away our best dead ball man. He steps up, tries to give the keeper the eyes, but the keeper has gone the right way. No matter though, because Kiwa has stuck the ball into the right-hand corner of the net and is running off to the corner flag to begin the celebrations with his teammates. Gooooal Matabeleland!!!! 3-1.

Scoring what is certainly the winner in the last minute only adds to the tension and the emotional release, and we are all jumping about hugging each other on the sideline. Pele is suddenly taken out horribly though. I only see the incident out of the corner of my eye. That looked nasty, and he has to be helped off the pitch by Georgia and Jermain.

Clément Auclair blows the final whistle. Oh my God, we have just beaten a country. What an unbelievable feeling. After shaking hands with our opponents, all of our players, coaches, and staff embrace. We clap the crowd then, holding hands in a line, the lads run to the main stand in celebration. Hundreds are singing and dancing above us. I want to hug Mica, and our blonde-haired keeper, and not let go. We walk from the corner flag to the halfway line shaking hands with everyone by the sideline. Joel Rookwood is nearby, recording everything for his documentary film about our wonderful team and its never-say-die spirit. Then, of course, we gather in a circle to say thanks, pray, and congratulate one another.

Sisa is leading the dancing in the car park. I'm pleased to see that lots more Zimbabweans came down today to support their fellow countrymen. I know many of them are Shona and I take off my hat to them for their support!

The tide of emotion has swept me to the Haringey supporters bar where, still wearing my football boots, supporters are buying me pints in the bar and asking to have selfies with me. Incredible. Outside, a brai is being prepared for the players. I am hearing hundreds of pounds has been raised in a bucket collection! There is also time to grab a beer with my close friends Graham and Andy H; Andy the first person to ever give me a position of responsibility in football when, as the first team player-manager of Bournemouth University in 1989, he asked me to be player-manager of the Bournemouth Second Team. And I am feeling super proud, of course, that my mum is here today to witness all this; to see her son lead Matabeleland to beating a country.

Leaving what seems like two hours late, a shifty-looking old guy has apparently been speaking to a couple of our players, trying to find out where we are staying, and asking for their phone numbers. He is allegedly Zimbabwean. Busani is going bananas as he thinks the lad in question is up to no good. I miss half of the incident, but it ends with Busani being kept apart from the bloke, who is then escorted away from our bus, shouting. I must admit something seemed a bit odd about all that, as if the bloke had been sent to cause problems. I wonder if he works for the *Thing*?

I told myself before the tournament I'd have a maximum of one beer all week. But by the Sunday night – three games in four days, going loopy sleeping in a corridor littered with replica kits, dirty match kits, boots, leftover lunches, balls, cones, smelly bibs, three men's dirty underpants and socks, and having just beaten a country – I have got to get out of here. It is physically impossible, and frankly counter-productive, for us to train tomorrow, so our management team has agreed to make Monday a rest day for all involved.

Matt and I head out with Georgia on a Sunday night clubbing mission. England is so utterly shite compared to a great many countries. Despite this being London, 'the world capital', there is almost nothing open at such an hour on such a night in this part of the city. We end up at a random club with a live band, five quid in on the door, only about 20 people inside and rough around the edges. It is good fun though, and the three of us roll in sometime in the early hours. That was needed.

Monday, June 4, 2018

There is a knock at the door at the crack of dawn. Praise comes in, apologising for waking us, and explains that Pele is in a bad way. He was apparently crying in pain from his injury during the night. I help organise a taxi and Busani, and a couple of the lads, head off with him to A&E.

Thank God for Nqo and Chris helping me with the merchandising. I just cannot cope with it anymore. A few days ago, an Exeter City supporter called Jim Shepherd also kindly offered to step in and help us with it all. More than a hundred people won't be in London to pick up their shirts and other stuff, and it all needs coordinating and mailing out. Once this is all over, I am pretty much headed straight to Russia, so I am extremely grateful that Jim and Nqo have agreed to take on the whole job from here on in.

The shirts have probably ended up raising three grand in pure profit towards our fundraising target, but every single penny of that money has been hard-earned from the initial discussions with Paddy Power about them sponsoring us, through the design and manufacture stage with The White Label Solution, to the non-stop social media campaign to sell them. It took weeks before we got to the break-even point on sales, but now we are handing them out and supporters are wearing them in the stadiums; many of them declaring the Matabeleland home and away shirts to be quite the most beautiful football tops they have ever seen.

Quite apart from the shirts and the million-and-one other tasks required to help manage the Matabeleland team, my presence is also needed this week in CONIFA Executive Committee meetings and also in daily WFC technical meetings. I won't be attending any more of the latter though as I think our Technical Director should be the man responsible for representing us at them.

There is trouble at mill for CONIFA. The likes of Jay, Kieran, Sascha, and Paul – already at their wits' end – look absolutely drained as we sit down for another discussion about the Isle of Man situation. Basically,

Ellan Vannin (the Manx name for the Isle of Man) are threatening to pull out of the tournament after questioning the eligibility of a Barawa player, who they say should not have been allowed to register after the tournament had started. There is also a question mark about his nationality although the CONIFA rules governing individual players are not watertight, or strict, so that cannot be a reason for chucking the hosts, Barawa, out of the tournament.

I am in the room voting on behalf of Matabeleland. The vote is held and the Isle of Man's challenge is rejected. I won't say how Matabeleland cast their decision; the only thing that matters is the final vote and that Ellan Vannin lost their appeal. Everyone in the room is aware that the subsequent withdrawal of the Manx team is very bad news for the tournament, and CONIFA's reputation, but the members present must cast their votes on the basis of what they all think is the right decision. This could yet impact Matabeleland because, with the Isle of Man in the 'placement matches' end of the draw, we might end up losing one of our fixtures.

Pele is back from the hospital with a pair of crutches. He is out of the tournament. I feel dreadfully sorry for him.

I am so damn tired. It has just been non-stop full-on now for weeks. I escape for a couple of coffees with Irish journalist Pat McGuinness, who has been one of the big characters for me around the tournament, and then have dinner with Matt in the pizzeria across the road.

Tuesday, June 5, 2018

I hope he doesn't mind me telling people this, but CONIFA's Global Business Director Jason Heaton sheds tears on the bus when he sees our boys singing and dancing. These lovely boys have that effect on people. They are so damn natural and good-hearted. Every single group of referees and officials who share our matchday journeys end up having their hearts melted by it all.

With us failing to reach the quarter-finals, today's game against Kabylia, from modern-day Algeria, will determine whether we finish this tournament in the 9th-12th place bracket or 13th-16th – or 15th in fact – with the Isle of Man withdrawing.

The Queen Elizabeth II Stadium is a long way out from the centre of London. It's a cold, gloomy Tuesday afternoon and with most people at work, the crowd is a fraction of what it has been for our other games. This feels flat, like our WFC is truly over now.

Grobs only just makes it in time as he started driving to the other Enfield before he realised, from text messages to me, that we are, in fact, playing at Enfield Town. The former Liverpool man seems more boss-like today. As does everyone else aside from me, to tell the truth. I don't think any of us really ever understood how this three coaches/managers thing really worked and now there are five of us… haha. We all have days when we are a bit off form, and this feels like one of those for me. Perhaps I can be forgiven after all the weeks and months of madness.

The game starts off quite poorly. Kabylia are physically stronger than us. And I think, having got used to the 3G, we are finding it difficult back on the grass. Lots of our lads are also carrying injuries and are operating at 50%. Truthfully, at least three of them shouldn't really be out there, based upon the advice of our physios.

Bruce is having another decent game in goal. Prof is also playing well and scores only for it to be adjudged offside. Overall, there isn't much in this. Overall, it is quite boring, to be honest.

As we often do, after a half-time chat, we have begun the second half better. We go close through Kiwa, I think.

Kabylia look like they've won it, but again it is ruled offside.

This is a game of brawn v brain and in, the end, the two styles have pretty much cancelled each other out. Both sides look tired. I can relate to that.

Final score: Kabylia 0 Matabeleland 0

There is no extra time at the CONIFA World Cup, so we are straight into penalties...

Captain Praise goes first and scores.

It is 2-1 to us after three, and we are looking good.

But next it is 3-3 after five and, when Musah misses our sixth, Enzo Mezaib steps up and scores to give Kabylia a 3-4 victory.

The thing about penalties is that when you win with them, you feel like you won the game outright; fair and square. When you lose, you feel cheated by the lottery of penalties. I don't resent my friend Lyes and his Kabylia team beating us, but I feel hard done by at the fact that a couple of spot kicks means we will finish the tournament no higher than 13th instead of potentially 9th, which would be a more accurate reflection of our quality for me.

Case in point, I am learning that Padania and Szekely Land are both in the semi-finals. They both thrashed us in the end, but we had five clear-cut chances against Szekely before we went down to ten men and they finally took the lead. We have played some of the slickest, most entertaining football at this tournament, and I am disappointed we will finish no higher than 13th. We are much, much better than that number suggests. As other teams will discover at the next World Football Cup.

With game four done and dusted, and with the Doc and the injured Andy flying in from Zimbabwe to join the team, I vacate my bed for the Doc, and move into Matt's room. What a relief. I am now cut off from the entire coaching staff and squad by two floors and finally have my own personal space. It was a mostly enjoyable experience rooming with my fellow coaches and residing on the same floor as the team but, understandably, there were constant comings and goings in our room; my bed by the front door was in a corridor-sized space. And that mess in there from all that stuff! Clearly as well, Busani, Khanye, and I have been in each other's hair now since early April. The pressure on the three of us has been intolerable at times, especially in those final days in Zimbabwe when it looked like there would be no visas. As the management of 'the national team', in an ideal world, we'd have had our own rooms in London, for some privacy and time away from one another, rather than sharing bunk beds in the same room. Matt's room is an oasis of calm. There are only the two of us in here while every other room now has four people sharing.

With the Isle of Man withdrawing from the tournament, we now have no game until Saturday as we should have been playing the loser of their match with Tibet. Tibet have been awarded that game by default, so there is no loser to play. And after four matches and two training sessions in just seven days, and with seven players suffering from injuries, there will also be no training tomorrow. If I had a car, I might drive home to see my mum, sis, and nieces for the night and come back tomorrow lunchtime. But I haven't. Regardless, I need to completely escape this madhouse for a few hours. I haven't had a proper, proper night out in months. Camden is calling.

Matt and I put on our best clubbing gear and head for the Underground, roaring at the names of stations such as Chalk Farm and Belsize Park that we pass on our route south.

I haven't been out in Camden since I last briefly lived in London, back in 1997, temping at the time for a business in the mind-numbing task of separating invoices and receipts all day long and adding up the two counter figures to check they tallied. I was very kindly being allowed to stay rent-free at my mates, Andy H and Neil J, at the time as I saved up money to leave England and set off on a year around the world, backpacking. The finest year of my life as it turned out.

I certainly don't remember it being this downtrodden here, 20 years ago. Not only are there homeless people every few yards but the streets are filthy and there are some very odd people knocking about. *I fancy both of you and I'm not even gay!* one bloke declares as he urinates up against a shop window. And it certainly wasn't six quid something a pint in the pubs back in the day! Are they having a laugh?!

It is great to be away from all the chaos of team HQ, but disappointingly the pubs are mostly bereft of punters. We've heard that a certain bar – don't remember the name – is guaranteed to be a top night out but this is actually the worst karaoke night I have witnessed since one shockingly depressing night in a private karaoke room with a load of English TEFL teachers and our Japanese teaching assistants in Kofu, Japan in 2003. Actually, this is so bad that it is good. A couple of the singers sound suicidal. Matt and I are both roaring aloud with laughter at the spectacle as well as the comical prices of their beer.

Into the third minute of added on time, about to cut our losses and head home, we have managed to blag our way onto a pub & club crawl. Now, instead of it being just the two of us and some *Britain's Got Talent* wannabees on the mic, we have three dozen new friends and are ushered into a warehouse pub and club complex. This place is brilliant, friendly vibe, decent tunes, and eye candy, and full of foreign tourists and backpackers. I have met an Italian female ambulance driver who seems impressed by me being an international football manager and, well, to cut a long story short, next thing it is 3am and I am on my way back to the Stay Club with her.

Oh, the great satisfaction of kicking out my significantly younger and better-looking roommate to sleep in the hotel corridor for an hour!

Wednesday, June 6, 2018

I am kissing goodbye and putting the Italian on a 6am Underground train as the first of the suits flood into Colindale tube station. Twenty years ago, that was me rushing off to work. It is almost like an out-of-body experience observing them all, with their Oyster cards, free copies of

Metro, and briefcases, the last of the night's six quid pints still in my system.

I half tiptoe back into the Stay Club hoping nobody will spot me but the first of the players, refs, and officials are up and about. Some of them, I imagine, might be thinking: *respect to the Matabeleland manager, up early for a stroll and coffee, preparing his mind for their next match.*

Good morning! I say brightly, trying to keep up the facade.

Unintended consequences. I have just found out that CONIFA have organised a replacement match after the Isle of Man's withdrawal and we are now playing the Chagos Islands tomorrow.

I am not saying I wouldn't have gone out if I'd known this, but I'd have certainly toned down the evening somewhat.

Our squad is in pieces with injuries and muscle strains. We could really do without this game, to be honest. The cancellation of the placement game had been a blessing in disguise in some senses, giving us a few days for some of the lads to recover. We had discussed the coaches playing in one of our two pre-WFC friendly matches in South Africa so as not to overburden some of our lads. Now I am thinking that Sibindi, Khanye, Grobbelaar, Perrella, and Walley should all have a place in tomorrow's squad along with, of course, the three or four lads who've so far played no part in the tournament for us. And call it the lingering effect of the alcohol but I have had this brainwave that we auction a squad place in the team to raise much-needed funds for the MFC. I want us to take the lads into London to experience its sights. They cannot come all this way and just see the four walls of the hotel and half a dozen football stadiums.

The Busanis agree with my entire proposal. This is very good news. Yes, I must admit, that Walley being called up for international duty is clouding my already hazy thoughts, but this all makes sense to me. I reckon we start Grobs. Why not? I promised to give him minutes in the tournament although it was always likely to be the final five minutes of a placement or knockout match. Better still, why not start him and make him captain as he returns from retirement to play for the place where he spent his formative years and even fought in a Bush War. Matabeleland.

I nervously call Bruce.

How do you feel about starting tomorrow?

He's roaring with laughter.

It's a friendly match so I want to play all the coaches and the reserve team lads. You could play half an hour perhaps. I am going to use Matt in goal as well. I just need your approval so I can officially announce it.

Bruce is in. My mojo is on fire today.

I grab the affable Dutch lads from FC Afkicken at the teams' buffet and ask them if they want to break the story. They are delighted. A few hours after leaving Colindale tube, and still a bit wired, I stare into FC Afkicken's TV camera – my eyes looking like I am on Speed – and announce that Bruce David Grobbelaar is returning to international football and will start for Matabeleland against the Chagos Islands tomorrow.

Ever dreamed of playing international football?

Here's your chance!! MFC is auctioning 1 place in our squad for tomorrow's match vs Chagos Islands!!! Highest bidder gets 15 mins of international football! Funds raised will help pay off our outstanding bills. Bruce Grobbelaar also starts for us tomorrow. Your chance to say you played in the same team as the legendary Liverpool man!

It is a shame this match is such short notice and at lunchtime on a weekday otherwise, I suspect, the bids could be astronomical. Sky Sports, Talksport, and the BBC are immediately in touch, all over the Grobbelaar announcement. Five Live want to get Grobbelaar surprising Mark Lawrenson by calling him live on the programme to break the news and give him some banter about returning to international football duty. Sky Sports are coming down tomorrow to film the whole thing! Bids are flying in for the auctioned place, but the amounts are a little disappointing. When you consider how much people drop for a weekend away, you'd think some punters might be willing to drop three of four hundred for the chance to play international football, even for just 15 minutes.

I return to the peace of my room and work from bed, social media exploding, then I snooze for a couple of hours as I realise I need to get my shit back together for my own international debut tomorrow. I cannot believe I have got a hangover 24 hours ahead of international duty, haha.

Like an all-inclusive holiday in Turkey, the three meals per day are starting to come around quickly now. The CONIFA officials look more knackered than me. I don't know how on earth the likes of Sascha, Paul, Jay, Kieran, Jens, and Per have pulled all this off but they have. It is an incredible achievement. And I feel sorry for Joscha Berger who has organised an entire film festival based around the culture and history of all the participating teams. By the time the teams get back from their matches and eat, nobody much is in the mood for watching anything.

I have to close the bids for the auctioned squad place. Sam Bodmer has won with a bid of 220 pounds. Liverpool fan Ross Hagan, meanwhile, was bidding all day long and, feeling sorry for him missing out; I offer him the chance to come down and grab five minutes for a few quid tomorrow. He bites my hand off at the chance.

My latest social media post says it all:

When you manage a team in a major global tournament, there is an endless list of tasks that need to be done. 22:45 just took the washed home kit and put it in the dryer. Need to return there before midnight and bring it up to the room and start folding it ready for tomorrow's game. Thanks to Matt Perrella (helping in the video), who is also our assistant goalkeeper coach and current kit man. And a very special thank you to Christopher Dolman who was washing and drying all the kits as our kit man for all of our group games, sometimes in the middle of the night! Time now to plan stuff for tomorrow's game before bed and then up at 6.30 for morning stretches, team breakfast, team talk, match day prep, 8.30am bus to the match...

Thursday, June 7, 2018

This is the morning I have been dreaming of since I was a little boy aged six. The morning I wake up and the first thought that floods into my head is: I am making my international football debut today. Now, don't get me wrong, this isn't what today is about. I am the manager of Matabeleland, and my main focus is on us getting everything right today and recording our second international win... but... every few minutes, the excitement of expectation comes rushing back in... I just cannot believe it really.

We are playing in Essex at Isthmian League side AFC Aveley's brand new multi-million-pound Parkside Stadium. It is one of the best 3G surfaces I've come across.

Our players, sat in the main stand, all cheer and clap as a local kid scores an unbelievable goal in a junior match. The Italian match officials all mob Grobs asking for hugs and selfies. He's chuckling to himself at that one.

There is dancing in the changing room before the game. Grobbelaar gets a clap going as the lads all sway from side to side singing their hearts out. With everyone sorted out, I put on the number 19 shirt for my debut knowing that if the game goes a certain way, I likely won't get any minutes. Whatever happens, clearly, as the person managing the team, I will be getting the fewest minutes of match time.

I was going to give Sam a few minutes mid-match, but Busani thinks that as he's paid for the experience, he should start. Fair enough. Sam, understandably, cannot believe his luck when I tell him he is starting in holding mid and he's suddenly nervous that he won't be up to the job.

This is Bruce David Grobbelaar's comeback game and almost certainly his last ever competitive match. In saying that, you just never know with this guy! Bruce is handed the captain's armband, and I agree with him that Matt, Nonja, and he will all play 30 each, although if Bruce feels he's struggling, he will give me the sign.

There is dancing in the tunnel as Bruce and the lads prepare to take to the pitch. What scenes!

Grobs is way off his line as one of their lads tries to lob him from 40 yards out in the early exchanges. Bruce seems to shrug his shoulders and chuckle as it flies wide. They are trying to play their forwards in over the top hoping, naturally, that our 60-year-old former European cup winner, six-time English League champion, three-time League Cup and winner of the FA Cup on three occasions goalkeeper will be too slow off his line. But Grobs is out 'quickly' and even has time for a bit of ball juggling. He might not be a spring chicken but he has still got the presence. That never leaves you.

We are missing chance after chance after chance. Grobbelaar comes out again for the ball after a failed attempt to catch him out but seems to pull up in pain. Moments later, he is giving me the signal to substitute him and bring former Newcastle United Reserve team goalkeeper Matt Perrella into the game. Grobbelaar has kept a clean sheet on his return to international football, aged 60.

We are playing rolling subs as injuries and general tiredness continue to mount up. Some lads, including the impressive Sam, come on for a second time. Mister Bodmer has slotted in very nicely, playing the link passes for the team. Matt makes a brilliant double save. Ross looks like he could explode from happiness when it is his time to take to the pitch and almost has a hand in a goal for us.

Jeez, there is no way I can bring myself on while it is 0-0. But, wait, a fantastic free kick is delivered deep from the right wing and Musah has risen high and headed us into the lead! Gooooal Matabeleland!!! 1-0. This lad has been a great addition to the MFC squad on and off the pitch. I have been tremendously impressed by him as an individual, particularly coming in as the only outsider and UK-based player in the squad. It has suited us much more having him and Goddy 'sitting in' in matches, and one of our two forwards functioning as the attacking midfielder.

81 minutes. It is time Walley made his international debut! Even Bruce Goalkeeper, injured and unable to play in London, is having a stint as one of our forwards. And with Ross having had some decent minutes, I am the very last man to get a game. The manager has given me nine minutes. It doesn't matter really; even 30 seconds would be good. To say I played an international cap for Matabeleland against the Chagos Islands!

I come on up top.

I don't expect to get much of the ball, so my main tactic is to make a nuisance of myself and move their backline around for the other lads. There is actually more space out here than I am used to playing, against the better teams in the Latvian Second League.

Suddenly, they are horribly high, and we've picked up possession outside our penalty area. At times like this, I like to make an arching run back into my own half to play myself onside and then sprint forward into the channel. All kinds of things are going through my head: *I am about to run clear of their backline? Is any of this real? And come on you slow bastard! Arch your run as far as you can and pump those old little legs as fast as you can so you can do their backline!* My run isn't so much a two-yard drop back into my own half as resembling the elliptical orbit of a planet, my legs pumping like I am running for the departing last train home on a Friday night.

Run, Forrest, Run! Grobbelaar shouts from the sidelines, to the great amusement of Matt. The long pass is short, and one of their backline heads to safety.

We are still missing chance after chance and, a bit like a park game, our defence has gone walkabout leaving us completely open to counterattacks.

With a couple of minutes left on the clock, I am on the left-hand side of the penalty area with Sibindi on the touchline. If Busani pulls it back to me here, unmarked and in acres of space, I am conscious of the fact that I can take a touch and cross shot to the far, right-hand corner. He seems to take an eternity weighing up his options and then, alas, passes to one of our players running late into the box who fails to even keep the ball. That was that moment right there; in a parallel universe I just curled the ball into the top right-hand corner and scored my first ever international goal.

The Italian referee blows the final whistle. It is a second win in three matches for Matabeleland. Sibindi, Khanye, Hagan, Bodmer, Perrella, and Walley have all started and ended their international playing careers with a victory. Grobbelaar has played his 34th international match in 41 years, having now played for Rhodesia, Zimbabwe, and Matabeleland. This all feels like a crazy, bonkers dream.

There are, understandably, lots of smiles, laughs, hugs, and banter after the match in the changing room from all involved. Every single one of the lads who got on the May 27 flights from South Africa has now played in London. *I reckon Busani Sibindi did enough today to warrant a full callup to the Matabeleland squad!* I make sure I get a photo of me wearing my number 19 Matabeleland shirt for posterity. *See! I told you I'd play international football one day!* I joke to a couple of my mates, who have come down again to support me and the lads. Supporters wait outside the players' tunnel asking me to get the whole Matabeleland team to sign their matchday programmes. Naturally, the queue of people wanting selfies with our famous goalkeeper is also growing by the minute.

Not surprisingly, I am hearing that video of Grobs dancing with the team in the tunnel before today's game has gone viral, mainly thanks to Copa90. Grobs, meanwhile, is refusing to go on camera with Sky who are down filming our game and want to put the story out on their six o'clock news bulletin. There's history between him and Sky's Rupert Murdoch, so they must have suspected Bruce wasn't about to do anything to help their channel.

You have to have dreams in life. I've dreamed all my life of playing international football, as absurd as that idea has been. I fleetingly even considered moving to the South Pacific to chase that dream more than 20 years ago. For a much shorter period of time, I have fantasised about being an international football manager. Never give up on your dreams because you just never know how they might end up coming true!

England are playing Costa Rica tonight. Originally, when I assumed this match was at Wembley, I was going to make sure we took all the lads up the road in their Matabeleland tracksuits to the national stadium to watch the game but sadly the match is being played in Leeds. Plan B is to take the Matabeleland squad to a local pub and, for the first time since they have been here, get them away from the hotel to do something other than playing football. You just cannot believe how smart and cool most of them look, ready to head off to the Chandos Arms. Some of them could be fashion models or rich playboys; you certainly couldn't imagine that these are poor lads from Bulawayo.

I run ahead to the pub, reserve four tables, jog back to the hotel, then return again with the players. But rather than looking pleased when we walk in, a handful of them look aghast. I cannot believe it. This lot are usually embarrassingly grateful for anything. An unnamed player shuffles over to me and immediately the penny drops. *Where are the ladies?* he asks. Oh, no, they all thought by pub I meant a room full of locals, 50 percent of them no doubt girls. They certainly didn't imagine this deserted old man's pub with its couple of tiny TVs, faded tartan carpet, beer mats and pints of real ale on draft. The next thing is a couple of them are suggesting I get the round in … for everyone. And another unnamed player is asking me if he is going to get paid for the games he has participated in, in London. WTF?!

To be fair, most of the young lads are happy with their orange juices and Costa Rica match, but we have one table of miserable sods who are lowering the tone. I have a quiet word with Busani and Khanye and, strict as ever when it comes to discipline and attitude, they are soon hauling the guilty party out into the back garden for a talking to. Earlier today, a couple of the lads were spotted hanging around near the tube station and we had a fear they were planning a runner. They say they were kicking a ball about in the street and it ended up on Colindale tube station roof. We realise this is probably true but it also needs fully investigating, which is playing into all of this. Truthfully, one or two of the lads are now sick and tired of the *you are going to do a runner* chat and are giving us backchat. I don't blame them, to be honest, and I genuinely feel terrible and embarrassed for the insinuation but the repercussions for all involved, if it happened, would be rather severe. Not only has Grobbelaar put his name down as a guarantor but we did get that letter from General Moyo. So, if the shit hit the fan, we'd have the office of the President of Zimbabwe on our case, as well as the British Home Office.

And, by the way, I completely get the lads' disappointment at the absence of women. Boys will be boys.

After dropping all the lads back at the team HQ, Matt and I are back in Camden, buzzing after beginning and ending our international playing careers this very day. First bar:

What do you do?

Oh, we are international footballers.

Oh, wow! Really? That is sooo cool.

Yes, we played today against the Chagos Islands. Won 1-0. How about you, what do you do?

Love it.

Friday, June 8, 2018

I check up on Grobs who tells me he tore something in yesterday's game and has got his knee in a brace. *I think it is time to leave the playing to the young men*, he says. What a way to end your playing career! Clean sheet aged 60 in an international match! It is befitting of the true legend that Bruce is.

In many senses, the tournament is winding down now with the final tomorrow, and many teams departing immediately afterwards. Many new friendships have been forged between players, referees, volunteers, press, and CONIFA officials. There is a unique brotherhood in CONIFA. We all respect one another and are grateful for being a part of all this.

The Padania players have been real gents to myself and the Matabeleland lads these past days. They won our respect for the way they thrashed us and that special aura they have as experienced old pros; and we, I can see, have won their mutual respect for the way we have continued to conduct ourselves with smiles on our faces, and a song and a dance. I hang around with Marius Stankevičius and a few of their other lads – their bosses chain-smoking, as always, out in the street – and I have to suddenly remind myself that one or two like Marius, a player I have now managed against, used to play for some of the biggest football clubs in Europe. Abkhazia are another group of players that stand out for me; rough around the edges but very real and genuine. Personally speaking, I expected Panjab to win the tournament. They narrowly lost 1-2 to England C last year and have a very talented squad along with a very determined larger-than-life boss in Harpreet. But they have massively underperformed and I can tell by how strangely quiet and reserved Harpreet is, that he's about to give his head coach the bullet.

Today is all about our trip into central London. I am so pleased that we are doing this; thanks again to a great number of kind people who have donated cash to enable the Matabele lads to enjoy a day out in the big smoke as well as the money raised from the squad place auction.

It is 28 of us on the tube from Colindale to Leicester Square, where our guides – Robin Millard from AFP and Georgia – are awaiting us. It is a glorious day and central London is at its absolute sunny best. Robin is a very sound, positive man. He says, for him, the Matabeleland story is one of the best feel-good stories of the year. He photographs the boys walking the streets, sitting in parks, entering the tube station, chatting to passers-by; soaking up the vibe of London on a gorgeous June day.

There's a street performer doing keepy ups, offering the chance to join him to any of our lads brave enough to match his performance. I saw Pele do 100 keepy ups the other day on his right foot with a tennis ball, his supporting leg out of action after the horrible injury he sustained against Tuvalu. I'm half-hoping Pele will hobble out and put on a right-footed show. On to Chinatown and Soho we go, Goddy grabbing a photo with a stunning blonde woman coming out of a posh five-star hotel. Mica drops back to chat to me at one point saying all of this is the best experience of his life. He just loves it all. Mica is one of those I have seen grow the most during this incredible experience.

Trafalgar Square gets a visit. From time to time, intrigued individuals come over to ask the boys who they are or to take selfies with them. We finish kicking a ball about outside Buckingham Palace; Busani and myself play keepy ups in front of some clicking Chinese tourists imagining the Queen is peering out the window from behind her curtains wondering what all the fuss is about. A photo of the squad stood by the front gates of Buckingham Palace feels especially apt: a declaration of we came, we saw and, as the song says, *we conquered!*

Saturday, June 9, 2018

On June 21, 2010, I was in the Cape Town Stadium in South Africa watching An Yong-Hak and his North Korean teammates playing Cristiano Ronaldo's Portugal. Eight years later, I find myself having breakfast with the very affable Korean legend as a fellow manager at the 2018 CONIFA World Football Cup. How completely mad is that?! The Korean team is super nice and charming, hardly surprising really when they are led by the most charming coach at the tournament. And I love that name, that statement: United Koreans.

This being the UK, we should all be seat-belted up, of course, but every few minutes one of the lads gets up, starts a song, and half the team is dancing in the aisle of our team bus. The refs travelling with us to the game look blown away, humbled, and most film the lads with their phones. If the singing and dancing stops, Khanye, Praise, Bruce S, Busani or myself get them started again. We are on our way to our final match. My favourite part is always when the injured Pele sings. Oh, my word, the bit where he sings about London – it makes me smile inside and out every time. I am so gutted for the lad that he has barely played in this tournament due to injury, and the world never got to see what a brilliantly-talented footballer he is.

We are down to bare bones and carrying passengers now. Three of our remaining lads shouldn't be here at all based on their ability. But they do deserve to be here based on their commitment. In my humble opinion, had we had the services of Percy, Gary, Cliff, the injured Andy, and two more non-league lads, we'd have made the quarters. Possibly even gone further. But anyone can say if.

This is the 13/14th place final. This is our final, this year.

Thabiso, our best striker, has an ankle twice the size it should be. I got the Padania physio to look at it last night, and he suspects there might even be a broken bone in there. Of course, I want him to play but there is no way he should go out on that pitch. Despite the pain and the analysis from Padania's professional medic, Thabiso still wants to play. The Busanis wants him to play. I am outvoted 1-2. Thabiso plays.

Into the game and we are a far superior footballing side to Tamil Eelam. I'm sure they are missing key lads but if we had a full team out fit, and on form, I reckon we'd do them for about six or seven. But, once again, we are not putting the game to bed. Chance after chance goes begging. They even threaten, briefly, to steal it as frustration builds that we cannot break the deadlock.

When we do finally score, right at the end, I find myself sprinting onto the pitch and celebrating with the players in the penalty area. I don't intentionally plan to do it; I just suddenly find myself running. It is just one final release of emotion. 1-0 Goooooooal Matabeleland! Shylock has put away the winner! We have won our final game at the tournament. I have won my final game in charge. We end on a high.

Zabayaba ya

Sizonqoba…

We, we, we will conquer

Over by the main stand, the lads and fans are celebrating in style. It's one last post-match rendition of the songs and dances, a celebration of our time here in London. Suddenly one or two of the boys grab me and I am being hurled up and down in the air, being given the bumps. Up and down in the air I go, giggling aloud, as the boys sing their Ndebele songs. I see

Busani get chucked in the air next. Anyone would think we'd won the tournament.

It is also a last team bus song and dance session en route to the CONIFA World Cup Final and closing ceremony at Enfield Town. All the teams and officials will share the coaches back later this evening so, as goes our World Cup, this is where the story begins to end.

Plonked in my seat, I am reflecting upon the fact that our final four matches have ended: 3-1, 0-0, 1-0, 1-0. We have not conceded a goal in five and a half hours since Tuvalu's Timunai scored 333 minutes prior. I think that is bloody amazing in itself.

There are more than 2,500 spectators crammed into Enfield Town for today's World Football Cup final between Karpatalja and Northern Cyprus. As Robert O'Conner of Al Jazeera so rightly says: this is "International football gone rogue, a thrilling, subversive defiance of the status quo."

Indeed, the atmosphere is unique in itself. Noisy Karpatalja fans are only a metre or two away from the goal nets with their flares burning; smoke spills out onto the pitch and completely obscures that stand for some minutes. All kinds of fans are here. The groundhoppers, the curious, those colourful Hungarian and Turkish fans, and, of course, the non-league fans; those very often from the margins of football, supporting their local club teams, week in week out, in every kind of weather, no matter whether the crowd is 7 or 777. The real football fans.

The Tuvalu team are sat atop a builder's skip they are using as an improvised stand of sorts, the Abkhazians are on the roof of the main building waving their very distinctive flags, and hundreds of fans have taken a higher vantage point on the grass verges at the rear of the stadium. TV crews are here from all over the world. The elderly North Cyprus kit man has had his hair dyed, shaved, and styled and now looks like the geezer out of the Prodigy; there certainly appears to be no shortage of *firestarters* behind the goal to our left. Mark Clattenburg, also something of a *firestarter* in the refereeing world, is in charge of the final. This ain't Saudi Arabia. This is punk football.

General Secretary Sascha Düerkop sums it up best: "CONIFA aims to build bridges between people, where others have built walls. We aim to give a voice to the voiceless and unheard. We want to make international football and grassroots support a natural fit – not a contradiction."

I have brought the replica shirts box down, splitting at the sides, and I am handing them out even now to anyone who purchased them and who is attending the final. I must receive 30 requests to buy the shirt on the day but, as tempting as it is, it wouldn't be the correct thing for me to sell shirts that others are patiently waiting to receive.

I am also getting a handful of requests to do TV and radio interviews; an Iranian channel interviews me pitchside during the final. Famous for 15 minutes – although famous is somewhat of an exaggeration – this time tomorrow I will be pretty much forgotten by everyone. I certainly hope the same doesn't apply to the Matabeleland Football Team's 2018 odyssey.

Like so many finals, this is a disappointing game not helped by the rain. There are thrills and spills, but 0-0 pretty much reflects the reality. Karpatalja, from the Ukrainian Carpathian Mountains, who weren't even meant to be at this tournament (coming in at the last moment as a replacement team) win the cup on penalties, 3-2.

With Clattenburg having left the building and no dead bodies at the bottom of Karpatalja's huge celebratory pile of players and coaches, the medals ceremony begins. There are trophies and 'winners medals' to every participating team and its players. This is a beautiful thing. Everyone gets to applaud and cheer each of the 15 remaining participants. We are up on the roof ready to be crowned World Football Cup 13th Place Winners. 13, unlucky for some, not for us. Yes, I believe we are much better than that number suggests but we are here, up on this rostrum, being cheered by hundreds, photographed by dozens, filmed by CNN and VICE to be shown to millions. There was no luck involved in us getting here. Just months and months – years in the case of Khanye and Busani – of hard work. We might not have won this tournament but to many, I believe, Matabeleland will be remembered as the true winners of the 2018 CONIFA World Football Cup. And, personally speaking, being up on this roof with this group of wonderful young men is a truly fantastic feeling. In that moment, when we each receive our World Football Cup medal, it feels like we have actually won the tournament, there are so many people cheering.

With the teams beginning to depart on the coaches, I cannot track down a single member of the Matabeleland team. That's because they are dancing and singing in the park, enjoying a brai fired up by Nqo and a load of our supporters. I spot Jermain and Georgia posing for photos, proudly holding our 13th-place trophy aloft. It has been a pleasure working with these two. As well as being very good at what they do, they possess a lovely combination of beyond-their-years maturity and good fun. I must mention Chris Dolman again too. His efforts for the team, driving backwards and forwards from the West Midlands throughout the tournament will never be forgotten. Some supporters from the match also snap photos, this time with the team in the rain. *Your team is just amazing. How the lads are. Just look at them having a barbeque in the park!*

Back at CONIFA HQ, it is the 2018 WFC After-Party. Copious amounts of copious things are being consumed by the CONIFA officials, refs, volunteers, players, and coaches; much of this taking place in the Stay Club lift, which some of us seem to have spent hours travelling up and down in these past two weeks. Per, the President, looks like he could do with a few after getting through all of this.

It is a fantastic evening. I am not sure I could describe it too much and do it justice, so I won't try. It is simply a celebration of what has gone before here in London, not so much even the football but the camaraderie, the new friendships.

By the early hours of the morning, several teams are already leaving for the airport, while the majority remaining crash into bed, worse for wear. The Tuvalu lads are the ones with the greatest staying power and take their beatbox and some of the remaining booze out into Colindale Park. They are a super bunch of human beings. They are different. You can tell they come from the edge of the world. But I mean that in a complimentary way. I don't know why but the thought suddenly fills my head that I will coach these lads from the world's fourth-smallest country one day in the South Pacific. I'm not sure why I have that thought. It's possibly bullshit like when you think you have fallen in love with someone new, but a week later the very idea is absurd.

Sunday, June 10, 2018

Packing my things alone in my hotel room in London as the CONIFA World Football Cup ends, I have just found myself breaking into tears at the beauty of all that has gone before these past two weeks. It is not just one little tear; it is a sudden waterfall of them. And, ten minutes later, another quick deluge. These are tears of joy from the heart.

As Sky Sports said: *As for Walley's players, whose main purpose this month was just to make it to London and compete, it's the promise of so much more — a chance for the game to flourish in their homeland, to one day have a pitch that's at least flat and free of sharp stones, and to find a place in the world through football. With their stylish new shirts turning heads even before a ball has been kicked at London 2018, Matabeleland are proving that even when the odds are stacked against you, in football, you can always depend on the kindness of strangers.*

It has been all of this, and much much more.

Matt departed a few minutes ago for the USA. What an inspired and inspiring individual that lad is. A person who constantly offers positivity, competence, accountability, and friendship.

It is no wonder that Grobbelaar is talking about the possibility of taking Matt to southern Africa to work with him in the future as a coach and as a talented goalkeeper.

The rest of the MFC are down in the basement, where the London Zim community have come together and donated clothes and money to our lads to take back to their families in Plumtree and Bulawayo. Mari-Anne meanwhile, has organised a final day out for the team in London before they fly home tomorrow…

Mari-Anne drops 150 quid to get us all on the tube as we start our day off on the Embankment. It is another resplendent June day, the lads enjoying a game of street football, sunbathing in the park, flirting with girls, a few requests for selfies and autographs (one holding a baby), while Busani and Khanye are treated to a trip on the London Eye.

Afterwards, it is a Thames River trip for everyone. I've never even done this myself and treat myself to a bottle of IPA as I sit at the front of the boat alone taking it all in, observing the lads. Praise is chatted up by an attractive young lady.

We alight at the Tower of London and pose for team photos outside its centuries-old walls.

And then, the strangest thing happens. A load of black lads are outside a nearby lounge bar. A couple of them even claim to be Zimbabwean. They are drinking champagne and hanging out with some provocatively dressed girls. Not only are they a bit in our face but they are trying very hard, right from the first moment, to get the lads to pose with a champagne bottle and to cuddle up with the girls. It all feels completely contrived, as if they are bad actors who knew we were coming and they want the lads to misbehave – or appear to do so – on camera. I am not even talking about the old Zimbabwe paranoia, about the omnipresent *Thing*. It is my intuition telling me someone is trying to set us up. And, let me tell you, my intuition is pretty honed after a quarter of a century of backpacking, meeting every kind of chancer, spiv, and charlatan you can imagine.

Sensitive to our public image as always, the three MFC managers grab the champagne bottle and politely ask them to refrain from taking any more photos. The ringleader almost looks like he might start fighting with Khanye. Our lads though, super nice as always, have not been provoked by them.

There's then time for a London red double-decker bus ride stopping off to gawp at St Paul's Cathedral, before we end up at Nando's for dinner. Outside, I spot two blokes, one of whom is wearing a Celtic top, muttering to each and taking an interest in us from afar. They don't come over to speak to us though, and something about all this registers in my brain.

Enjoying their chicken and chips dinners, the lads are taking the piss out of me. Every few minutes they break into a loud chorus of *Why?* I shouted this a lot in Zim – not when someone made a mistake as such, but when they partook of unnecessary showboating, shooting from 60 yards, the goalkeeper dribbling past three, and got too close to public transport minibuses zooming by at 80 miles per hour.

I think my *Why* shouts and my Joburg knife drill – where I went around stabbing players in the back with a twig during training matches to get across the idea that you must permanently look around you when you play football, and have eyes in the back of your head like you would do walking alone through the streets of the South African city – are the two things about my coaching that stick in the memory for most for them.

Goddy is going a bit overboard with the *why*; I am not sure, but I think there is a touch of humbug to it. I don't mind because Goddy has been one of our standout players at this tournament. There is a little bit of naughtiness to him sometimes and, oh, how this team has needed that from him in our matches. He has shown the world that he deserves to play at a higher level.

As Mari-Anne pays up for our huge feast and we make our way to the bus stop opposite, those two blokes I saw earlier suddenly stroll by and then make a beeline over to us, acting like they have just seen us for the first time. They are South African and are asking about the team, and more specifically (and almost immediately) about the project. They are giving me the willies.

I definitely saw these two characters more than an hour ago, in the same spot.

They have got that air of police officers or immigration officials about them, and I suspect they are spooks. Actually, there is something unpleasant about them; a negative vibe. They are rough as fuck in a formal way, if that makes sense – the sort that big muscly types underestimate in a pub fight and end up getting pummelled by. Busani and I have a quiet word in the shadows, and he's of the same opinion. These lads are trouble. We grab the team away from them, jump on the next bus, and set off on our way to the Emirates.

Neither of those two incidents add up for me. Call it intuition, but I feel like these are tests, attempts to provoke us and/or case us out. And the champagne African lads and the football shirt-wearing southern African whites briefly entered our universe what must have been less than an hour apart.

Outside the Emirates, the lads are going mad with the poses and photos. You sense they love this more than they enjoyed central London. Football is their world so nobody should be surprised at such a thing. We were actually meant to do a real stadium tour but, frustratingly, there was a mix up with the booking. Not that we are going to tell them that. They are all super grateful we are here at all, outside one of the world's most famous football arenas. Plus, a number of the boys are actually Arsenal supporters.

We are in danger of missing the last tube, and I've still got the willies. Busani, Khanye, and I agree we should cut the Emirates thing short and get everyone back to the Stay Club; we cannot risk missing the last tube and creating a giant mess before the team flies out tomorrow. We all say a big thank you to Mari-Anne. She's dropped hundreds today with all of this. Unbelievable. Nando's alone must have run to 400 quid. This lovely, positive lady has really helped make our London adventure about so much more than just the football.

That was a really pleasurable day and night out but I am totally convinced that dark forces – or black and white in this case – were at play trying to provoke dramas. The drunk party crew outside the bar and the football supporters outside Nando's were all fake as far as I am concerned. I will be glad when I am in Russia with no responsibility, no management, no coaching, no media, and no paranoia to contend with.

It is weird saying goodbye like this. It's 2am in the morning, knocking on doors, even having to wake one or two lads. Hugs. A million different handshakes. *Thanks for everything you have done coach!* Many of the players humble me even now in my last moments with them. I make sure I give Busani and Khanye the biggest hugs of all. I am sad that the stresses and strains of all this, much of it the blame of *the omnipresent Thing*, have caused damage to our relationships at times. How many people could have endured what we have and largely kept it all together? They are brilliant lads and, for all of our individual shortcomings, what we have achieved with the Matabeleland Football Team is nothing short of a miracle. Actually, let's be honest, it is a miracle!

In that room though, with smelly kits and footballs, knee-deep in second-hand clothes as some of the boys try to bag it up (not having realised that flying this free donated stuff to Africa will cost more than the clothes are worth), in all that clutter and chaos, I feel absolute relief that my job has been successfully completed and my time with these boys is done.

We say goodbye, good luck; all of us aware, I think, that it could well be goodbye forever.

I set out with a dream to become an international football manager, and that dream has been realised. Matabeleland is a national team of sorts, and for a few months of 2017 and 2018, I joined John Herdman (Canada), Stephen Constantine (India), Gary White (Taiwan), Trevor Morgan (Bhutan) Daniel Neville (British Virgin Islands), Jamie Day (Bangladesh) and Gareth Southgate as one of just eight Englishmen head of men's senior national teams in the world.

Let me also steal a couple of quotes from the Guardian newspaper's wonderful photo essay about the team:

"This journey started as a dream," says captain Praise Ndlovu. "No one ever believed we would make it to London, but we made it. I'd like to say thank you to everyone. We have discovered there are a lot of people who love us out there."

"Everyone's in love with Matabeleland. It's mad, it's amazing," says Matabeleland's British coach, Justin Walley. "None of these boys have ever been outside of Africa. I said just come over and enjoy it, you're in the shop window. Life is short, come here and say 'I played in a World Cup in England'."

[1] Field of Dreams: Crescent Training Ground, Bulawayo.

[2] 17 players in a pickup as we travel to an away game in the rural areas.

[3] Khanye prepares the lads ahead of my first ever away friendly match (Turk Mine) with the Matabeleland team.

[4] My first team photo with the lads, November 2017, Zimbabwe.

[5] Left. Zimbabweans celebrate in Bulawayo after the military takes over from Robert Mugabe. [6] Right. Robert Mugabe has finally resigned after 37 years of rule. Tens of thousands take to the streets of Bulawayo to celebrate!

[7] Coaching on the sidelines at Barbourfields Stadium, Bulawayo, as Matabeleland took on the mighty Highlanders Football Club.

[8] Left. Liverpool legend Bruce Grobbelaar agrees to join Matabeleland at Hilton Park Service Station on the M6 motorway, England. [9] Right. A million and one plans sit on the table in Riga, Latvia as I begin work on the seemingly impossible task of raising $20,000 for Matabeleland.

[10] Riga United FC's players donate to the Matabeleland cause during winter training.

272

[11] A corner flag in the rural areas.

[12] The world's biggest penalty spot? Matabeleland are out in the rural areas with Paddy Power for a tournament and some filming.

[13] Press Conference in Bulawayo to unveil the new
Matabeleland tracksuit and plans for the World Football Cup.

[14] The MFC coaches enjoying a Zimbabwe Premier League match
at Barbourfields (Busani Khanye, centre; Busani Sibindi, right).

[15] The Matabeleland lads dreaming of the big time as they watch the Highlanders playing in the Zimbabwe Premier League.

[16] Ethel (centre) and friends/relatives see me off on my bus to South Africa.

[17] Left. My friend Thabiso sees me off at Johannesburg Airport as I leave southern Africa at the end of my two stints. [18] Right. Worth its weight in gold - the letter from Lieutenant General (retired) Moyo requesting assistance for the team travelling to the UK to play at the World Football Cup.

[19] The Matabeleland team bossing the
World Football Cup opening ceremony.

[20] The busy Matabeleland changing room ahead of a game.

[21] The teams line up. Matabeleland v Szekely Land.

[22] My nieces Leah (left) and Alisha dressed in the Matabeleland home and away kits with the players.

[23] The Matabeleland players dance in the Haringey Borough car park.

[24] Mica arriving for a match. This wonderfully positive lad wore a smile on his face on and off the pitch all tournament!

[25] Matabeleland physios Jermain and Georgia help the injured Pele off the pitch during our match against Tuvalu.

[26] Celebrating victory over Tuvalu.

[27] On the Aveley FC pitch pre-match with Sawusani, one of the stars of the 2018 World Football Cup for Matabeleland!

player #8

Player #9	Sarrusqmi Mudimba
Player #10	Mdudyzi Money
Player #11	Oscar George
Player #12	Romeo Sibanda
Player #13	Sipho Mlalyi
Player #14	Bruce Sithole
Player #15	Ndlovu Praise
Player #16	Mthulisi Dube
Player #17	Musa Sthumbun
Player #18	Thomas Nkomo
Player #19	Shyloek Ndhlovu
Player #20	Thabiso Ndlela
Player #21	Dumoenkasini Ndlovu
Player #22	Professor Tshuma
Player #23	Bruce Grobbelaar

ench. They must be named and their role must be mentioned.
...t the number and write the correct one. Mark Goalkeepers with (GK)

[28] Bruce Grobbelaar's name on the match day team sheet for Matabeleland.

[29] Pictured during my international football debut for
Matabeleland against the Chagos Island.

[30] The Matabeleland Football team enjoys the first of our
two days out in London.

[31] Myself and Busani enjoying a game of keepy ups
outside Buckingham Palace.

[32] Breakfast with Korean legend An Yong-Hak, who played for
North Korea at the 2010 FIFA World Cup and was player
manager of the United Koreans team at the 2018 WFC.
Also pictured, Irish journalist Pat McGuinness.

[33] The Matabeleland team prepares for their final match
at the CONIFA World Cup.

[34] Shylock scores the winner against Tamil Eelam.

[35] The players throw Busani in the air after our final match of the CONIFA World Football Cup.

[36] The Matabeleland players in fine spirits.

[37] Joyous as we await our 13th place trophy on the
final day of the World Football Cup.

[38] Nqo and Bruce.

[39] Goalkeeper coach Matt Perrella and me unwinding after the football.

[40] Kit man Chris Dolman with Bruce.

[41] Enjoying our day out in London with Mari-Anne Chiromo.

EPILOGUE: From Russia with love

Becoming a Football Fan (again)...
my time at the 2018 World Cup
in Russia

Monday, June 11, 2018 | England

I am up at 5am to travel back to Leicestershire. It feels strange to be departing the Stay Club; so many emotions have been created inside these four walls.

There is literally nobody around as I wrestle my bag onto my shoulder and make for Colindale underground station. As goes Matabeleland and me, in an ideal world, I'd like to quit now. My mission is completed and, with the team flying back to Africa today, this would be the perfect time to say thank you and good luck. However, my contract runs until June 30, and I know there are lots of loose ends that will need tying up in the next few weeks: media enquiries, interest in players, completing all our crowdfunding responsibilities. I believe in finishing a job, and so I will continue as the Matabeleland manager until at least June 30. Plus, I want to leave my options open, frankly. Part of me would like to help them from afar in a development capacity. But they'd have to ask me, rather than me suggesting it.

Surprise, surprise, the train out of London is completely rammed with nowhere left to sit. I look at everyone going about their daily routine: reading their morning newspapers, drinking their takeaway coffee. What I have just experienced these past nine months is the absolute antithesis.

Daily Mail: *Matabeleland Football Odyssey Wins Hearts Ahead of Russia 2018.* Wow.

Talk about crashing back down to earth… I am having my tooth removed in a dozen pieces. As suspected, part of it shattered when I was on that train to Bulawayo, and now it needs to be removed bit by bit. It is one of the least pleasurable experiences of my recent years.

Tuesday, June 12, 2018

A lie-in. Joy. So good to be back at my mum's, be it just for a couple of nights. Of course, I wake up panicking that I should be doing something for the Matabeleland team, taking me a few seconds to compute that that is all over now.

Actually, it's not because Nqo is in touch. Apparently, the lads' connecting flight got cancelled, and they were marooned all night in Paris. Initially, they were told to sleep in the airport and offered no food, but with Mari-Anne hearing about it, she got on the case with Nqo, and I think the airline has finally pulled their finger out and sorted it. They are still in Paris as we speak. Shocking treatment of the lads from the airline.

Text message from Bruce Grobbelaar saying *thank you for asking me to help with the Matabeleland team...* that is has been an honour and he has really enjoyed it... and suggesting that he'd like to *be involved again next time.*

How fantastic it was having Bruce involved. Not only did he get us over the line with the visas but his involvement earned us recognition, respect, and admiration from the outside world. Bruce has a wonderful no-nonsense spirit about him that rubs off on all around him. You can tell he is a Matabeleland son because spirit is something that group of young men does better than almost any team I have come across. That special fighting spirit you find in the people of Bulawayo.

When Bruce first agreed to come in, I knew it was brilliant news for the team but privately I thought it would end up undermining me as a coach because of my obvious lack of experience compared to Bruce's lifetime full of it, and big, big personality. I was happy, though, to take that risk in the interests of the team. But I needn't have worried. Despite his decades of experience as a world-famous player and coach, he was just another member of our management team, taking a leading role when it was needed (using his priceless experience), and taking a back seat at other times. I (and all the Matabeleland players and coaches) will be forever grateful to Bruce Grobbelaar.

Wednesday, June 13, 2018

My World Cup medal is now displayed proudly on my bedroom wall. I pop into Hinckley to package up and mail Stuart Maconie his shirt. He has mentioned us again on BBC 6 today.

Chris Dolman drives over in the evening from Tamworth for a pint with me, Paul, and Dav as we proudly reminisce, laugh, and smile at what just went before at the CONIFA World Football Cup.

Thursday, June 14, 2018

I could have done with a few more days at home just doing nothing, but I need to start moving myself to get to Russia. Flights to Kazan were super-expensive a couple of months ago, so I am taking the far cheaper route via Riga, staying overnight at my friend Kelvin's, and then onto Kazan via Moscow.

Going through the usual tedious security check at East Midlands Airport, my clumsy hands have dropped my camera and passport onto the airport floor as I empty my pockets. I am gutted as I have managed to smash my camera and put it out of action. As I don't own a smartphone, I now have no way of taking photos at the World Cup. Gutted.

LATVIA

It is the opening ceremony of the 2018 World Cup, and Robbie Williams has just flicked his middle finger to the TV camera. I get the feeling this tournament is going to be 'different'. I watch the 2018 World Cup opener with my mates Austin and Graham; Aus and myself sporting the Matabeleland home and away kits in the pubs of Riga Old Town. Russia look brilliant and tear Saudi Arabia to pieces. There is a really good energy about their team and indeed their coach, Stanislav Cherchesov.

Graham – the man who sponsored the Matabeleland tracksuits – is now very kindly donating to me as he presents me with a very decent smartphone so I can take photos in Russia. I can't tell you how many times Graham has helped me out in one way or another over the years. He chuckles and points out that *someone giving me a smartphone is the only likelihood of me ever starting to use one*. So, yes, I finally have my first-ever smartphone, only beaten to it by 2.5 billion other people on planet earth.

Friday, June 15, 2018

I am sat with my Basque friend Josu, who is now the fourth person in Riga wearing his new Matabeleland shirt, the two of us surrounded by Iranians in a Mexican-themed Latvian bar. They go bonkers as Iran grabs a last-minute winner against Morocco, guaranteeing added spice for the Iran v Spain game I will be attending in Kazan in less than a week.

I grab my backpack, bid farewell to Josu, Victor, and some other Spanish friends, who have gathered for their World Cup opener, and make for the international bus station.

It cost 40 quid to fly to Riga, and now my overnight Ecolines Express to Moscow is 43 Euros.

It is a typically gorgeous Baltic summer's evening as we set off for the Russian border; it won't get dark until 11pm, and the passing forests are full of life and positive energy. This is luxury. I have got superfast Wifi, more legroom than a first-class airline, complimentary hot drinks, and I have managed to live stream what is turning into an epic encounter between Portugal and Spain.

Estonia

We reach the Estonian-Russian border after midnight. The Russian immigration officials ask anyone with a Fan ID to get off the bus first, which means me and a handful of South Americans. The Russians are being super-thorough in checking and double-checking all our documents. It is hassle free but, clearly, it is useful I speak some Russian. They've given me a stay until a couple of days after the World Cup ends. I expect to be back in Latvia long before then.

Saturday, June 16, 2018 | Russia

This is my fourth time in Russia, my first trip here in 1997 saw me travel from the Finnish border to Mongolia by train. I have also travelled extensively all over the former USSR including the likes of Tajikistan, Armenia, and Ukraine. Together with my time spent in the Baltics, this part of the world has been a pretty constant part of my life for the past 20 years. I'm not scared to come here, but with the absurd propaganda war of the past few years, I'm more than aware that British-Russian relations are shite, to say the very least.

I tell you what I think, so it's out there before this tale even begins: Political correctness, outrage-culture, and identity politics are destroying debate and intelligent conversation in the UK. If you criticize the often atrocious behaviour of, for example, the state of Israel, you are branded anti-Semitic. If you think obese models parading around in swimming costumes saying *fat is good* is wrong, then you are a sexist, fattist, chauvinistic pig. If you question the idea that *peoplekind* needs a couple of dozen gender pronouns, when you believe only male and female exist as sexes, then you are a something (I'm not quite sure what the correct word is). But, despite all these limits on what you can or cannot say, if you suggest Russians are evil, smelly, vodka-drinking, wife-beating, war-mongering, rude-bastards, who are planning to take over the world and turn it into a communist paradise under the supreme leadership of Vladimir Putin, well, that you can say, print, and shout from the rooftops as far as the mainstream British media and political establishment are concerned. I have never seen so much negative bullshit propaganda against a single nation in my entire life. It is the worst media circus since the lies in the lead-up to the invasion of Iraq.

If you say anything remotely complimentary about Russia or Russians, you will be trolled, called a *Putin bot*. The Russians are waiting for the English. They are going to capture us all and burn us at the stake. The British Foreign Office is warning our nationals that we could face "racist or homophobic intimidation, hooligan violence, and anti-British hostility". We are not completely stupid. We know they have lads. And for God's sake, it's not as if our lads didn't run around terrorising towns and cities across the European continent for a couple of decades.

I won't be too surprised if there are only a half dozen of us who haven't been scared off from traveling here by all the hype and hatred though. The first rule of travel: don't go out of your way to insult your new host. This very day, the British media will be fixating over printing and saying as many horrible things as they possibly can about Russia and the Russians hosting this tournament. Almost all of those journalists will never have set foot inside this vast, multicultural country in their entire lives. You cannot vilify an entire nation. That is just plain wrong.

And Boris Johnson really takes the biscuit as he compares the 2018 Russia World Cup to the 1936 Olympics held in Nazi Germany. What a complete and utter arsehole. Quite apart from the great sacrifice the people of my nation, its commonwealth, and our allies made fighting fascism, without 14 million dead Russians, Hitler's Nazis would have won that war and Johnson would now be speaking German. There are lots of things wrong with Russia, but there are many things wrong with the UK and some of our more questionable friends such as Saudi Arabia. In this context, I arrive in Russia feeling embarrassed to mention to anyone I am British.

The Russian countryside is quite a picture. We pass vast forests, serene and devoid of the signs of human life.

Having arrived in Moscow around breakfast time, I catch the underground to the city centre. As the British media so prophetically warned, I am met by a mob of Russians as I reach the centre of the city; a mob of dancing, chanting Hare Krishna. They are so happy, I find it almost threatening. The weather is gorgeous and I am able to dine outside near Red Square. I have not been back to Moscow since December '97 when a pint was almost five quid. Twenty years later, my prime location breakfast, in a rather posh establishment, costs quite a bit less than that pint two decades ago.

I have a whole day to kill in Moscow, but I simply was not prepared for the amazingly positive carnival taking place on the sunny, pristine streets. The spectacular Kremlin is mobbed with football fans from all over the world, and thousands and thousands of young, super-friendly volunteers are on every street corner helping out linguistically-challenged travellers. World Cup games are being beamed live on video screens inside the underground trains!

Thanks to Graham, I am now able to snap lots of photos capturing the atmosphere and am posting them to social media, where many of those who followed Matabeleland and myself are now keeping an eye on my Russian adventure. It is a great feeling, knowing that I have not been instantly forgotten and I am also enjoying the communication and banter of sharing this adventure with those people.

Having hauled my backpack around all day, I find an upmarket hotel near Kazansky Vokzal ahead of my night train. They are happy for me to grab a beer in here and watch the match between Peru and Denmark. There are FIFA officials everywhere. I seem to have inadvertently stumbled across the World Cup referees-HQ for Moscow.

If you have a fan ID, and a ticket to a World Cup match in the end destination, then you qualify for free train travel, care of the Russian state. Comically, they have called it FREE RIDE. As I have a ticket for the Spain-Iran match in Kazan in four days' time, I qualify for this and booked up FREE RIDE on tonight's overnight train a few weeks back.

I certainly didn't expect this though; the double-decker train is brand new and my private sleeping compartment is air-conditioned and comes with fresh linen. Each carriage has its own security staff, and smartly-uniformed ladies working through the night who provide hot drinks and snacks if you want to purchase them. There is even a restaurant & bar on-board. Honestly, it is better than some three-star hotels I have stayed in over the years and, best of all, I have got an entire compartment to myself, which I lock, get undressed in and have the best night's sleep I can remember in weeks.

Sunday, June 17, 2018

I booked the Geography Hostel in Kazan, way back in October, for about ten quid per night. It is a short stroll from Kazan's beautifully ornate central station, and is located next to the Bolaq Canal, just a couple of hundred yards away from where all the main action is on Bauman Street. I can see why this place has earned rave reviews on TripAdvisor because Karima, Aigul, and Aidar are absolutely lovely and it's spotlessly clean and really comfortable. Having tweeted about my positive experiences in Moscow yesterday and about last night's luxurious overnight train, my Twitter account is going mad. I am getting hundreds of likes and retweets.

There is an amazing happy buzz on the main pedestrian street, football fans of every creed and race everywhere, and so so many pretty girls! I spend the whole day sucking in the vibe, feeling incredibly free after all of my commitments of the past weeks and months. That sense that you need to experience unfreedom to truly appreciate freedom. I end the day watching Brazil v Switzerland from the street. It is in the mid-twenties, and the atmosphere is just too amazing to go and spend my evening sat in one bar.

Monday, June 18, 2018

I watch England's opener versus Tunisia in Volgograd from a huge place called Twin Peaks, where the attractive waitresses all wear short, tight jean shorts. Yes, I know. But I like it, so who cares? England look absolutely brilliant in the first few minutes and could score half a dozen, instead of Harry Kane's solitary goal. But just like Matabeleland on many occasions, if you don't put a game to bed when you are dominating it, then you only have yourself to blame. It is a tense second half, but a last-minute winner from Kane sets us up nicely in our efforts to reach the second round.

I followed England 'away' at Euro 92 in Sweden. I was soon going to most of the qualifying games and international away friendlies. France 98, Belgium 00, Japan 02, Portugal 04, Germany 06, South Africa 10... even Ukraine 2012 with *Woy's Bwave Two Thousand*. But, eventually, I grew tired of the expense and constant disappointment. The England team became boring and one-dimensional, seemingly in almost terminal decline for years. As I got older, I also lost my capacity to hang around with some of the lads following the team who made you constantly on edge that trouble could kick off at any moment. By the time England played Estonia, away in Tallinn in October 2014, I knew I'd had enough. I have something of a connection to Estonia and with the game poised at 0-0 in the second half, I actually found myself wishing Estonia would win to teach England a lesson! When England finally grabbed a winner through Rooney's free kick, I didn't even feel inclined to jump up. *Why aren't you celebrating?* my mate Paul Featherstone asked me. *Because I don't care anymore. I think I'm done with this*, I told him.

That was me done after I'd say 70 England home matches over the years and I'd estimate 40 away matches. 100+ caps for my country.

No Brazil 2014, no France 2016. This time, too, I doubt I will watch England play live. I am no longer a *Travel Club Member* so, even if tickets become available, the English FA won't let non-members access them. They say it is because of the threat of hooliganism (which it was, at one point, back in the day), but the truth is it is because they make a fortune from annual membership fees. The FIFA website, meanwhile, seems like an almighty waste of time. If England do get to the quarter-finals, then I intend to travel to wherever that is, and attempt to support them either inside or outside the stadium but, I am here in Russia first and foremost to relax and enjoy the party. God bless Matabeleland, but I really need a holiday.

Tuesday, June 19, 2018

I love the local fast-food concept in Kazan: Tatarstan dishes rather than some contrived American nonsense. *Tubatay* offers traditional Tatar dishes such as *Echpochmak* (a triangular pastry) and *Kystyby* (stuffed flatbread). How refreshing to see a chain restaurant offering local dishes made from locally-sourced ingredients. What a brilliant way to promote your unique cultural identity abroad also! I hope they open a chain in the UK

I am down at the riverside Kazan fanzone for Poland v Senegal. I was half-fearing it would be boozy and rough, but it is quite the opposite. There must be 15,000 inside here, and I'd honestly say I've seen four idiots all day. Russia are up next, and again they are on fire! Dzyuba makes it 3-0 against Egypt, and this place absolutely erupts. The hosts, I am pleased to say, are into the second round. Already hundreds have left the huge viewing screens to queue for more beer as the party begins.

By the time I depart, with it close to midnight, the fanzone looks like and has the feel of an Armin van Buuren concert rather than a load of people celebrating winning a football match.

The party goes on all night in Kazan. There is even the sight of pretty lipstick-wearing Iranian women drinking, smoking, and wearing very feminine clothes as they join the party. No one will stop them from attending football matches here! It's already been light for a couple of hours by the time I reach my dormitory bed.

Wednesday, June 20, 2018

The first thing that happens every morning when I wake up is I still experience a moment or two of relative trepidation, trying to remember what I must do this day for Matabeleland. The tournament ended 11 days ago, so I am wondering how long these morning panic attacks will continue for.

Today is the day of my only ticket for the World Cup, purchased online in Ethel's spare bedroom in Bulawayo, back in October. I love the vibe of Kazan and tweet a jokey message to emphasise how much I am enjoying it...

Is there any chance I can stay in Kazan after the World Cup and get a job in the city's tourism department? Please

Actually, my Twitter account is on fire. I am getting crazy traffic from my tweet about Tatar food yesterday, including – rather amusingly – kickback from some Americans who are upset at me seeming to mock their fast food culture; the fast food culture that has helped spread obesity to the four corners of the planet.

Russian journalists have started contacting me, asking whether I am available for comment about my tweets and my time in Russia.

It is easy to say nice things about Kazan. I was blown away by the city the minute I got here. It is a spectacular metropolis. The picture-perfect Kremlin overlooks the River Volga. Kazan is full of stunning architecture, brilliant bars, and restaurants and, as the capital of Tatarstan, has its own unique culture, including that unique, tasty cuisine I was trying out. And then there are those visions of beauty, promenading.

With a nasty hailstorm having passed, it is free transport from just below Kazan's absolutely remarkable Kremlin mosque to Kazan Arena. I just cannot believe quite how lovely and charming all the young volunteers are, working here, trying to ensure that our experience of the World Cup runs smoothly. Any nation that can produce so many fine young people deserves credit. The vibe is so damn positive in the streets. You will laugh but, after taking a dig at American fast food culture, I am in McDonald's, near the stadium, buying some French Fries to quell my beer-induced hunger. They have got the dance tunes on – *Freed from Desire* – and I can honestly say I have been to many nightclubs around the world that haven't got a thing on this place!

Outside the arena, a DJ adds to the vibe with dance tunes as smiling volunteers with giant foam pointy hands ask for high fives off everyone who passes.

The security getting inside Kazan Arena is full scope airport security: scanners, X-ray machines, body searches. This country has been at the front line of terrorist bombings for decades, and it is reassuring knowing that the stadiums at this tournament – which ones assumes will be targeted – are as safe as they can possibly be to enter.

Inside, I hit a wall of noise as I reach the level where my seat is. Goosebumps have erupted on my arms. I am not a big fan of modern arenas. I find most of them lacking in personality and genuine atmosphere. But immediately, I can say that Kazan Arena is up there with the best of modern stadia, along with Cardiff's Millennium Stadium and Durban's Moses Mabhida.

It is large but compact at 40,000, with brilliant sightlines close to the pitch. There are obviously a lot of Russians here, but there are significantly more Iranians. It seems like tens of thousands of them. The noise is deafening. I have been extremely lucky to attend 6 World Cups, 6 Euros, and 2 Copa Americas but in all those stadiums, all over the world, I have rarely heard the noise generated at the Kazan stadium tonight. You'd think there were 100,000 in here, not 40,000. The game is decent. No point me writing much of a commentary on the match, but I am roaring at Diego Costa acting up throughout, although it is him who nets an extremely fortuitous winner for the Spaniards. The Iranians should grab a late equaliser from a header close to where I am sitting. I cannot imagine the noise in here if that had gone in. It is so loud from the vuvuzelas, Persian horns, and chanting that I can barely hear what the bloke next to me says when he asks me to take a photo of him.

Thursday, June 21, 2018

Graham's smartphone is beeping so much I think it might explode. My Twitter account notifications are almost in treble figures. I am finding this all very amusing and entertaining, *like a game*. Russia 24 are in touch, and a few minutes later I am doing a 20-minute Skype video interview with them about my experiences thus far in Russia. I have only just finished that when Feruza contacts me and asks whether I'd be happy to meet to do some filming. Remembering my *Jim Carrey Yes Man* attitude to the press in the lead up to the CONIFA WFC, my intuition says just run with it here as well. Within an hour, I am back in Tubatay Restaurant where I am being introduced to the founder of the chain.

We are being filmed for Tatarstan TV and the next thing I know I am being sat down at a table overflowing with a cornucopia of tasty local delicacies, desserts, and tea. It is like I am on a Russian cookery programme as I try various dishes on camera and give my feedback about the taste. My favourite question of the day is: *Would you stay in Kazan if you got the Rubin Kazan job?* The tears are almost rolling down my cheeks at that one. With the owner and the film crew filming outside while I tuck into the remains of my feast, I find myself messaging Graham: *You won't believe the trouble your bloody smartphone is getting me into. I am on a Russian cooking programme because of you,* I joke, sending him a photo of the TV cameraman filming me eating some *chakchak.*

One hour later...

Hi, Justin! It's so nice to hear that you are so interesting about Kazan. State Committee on tourism of The Republic of Tatarstan happy to invite you to us to talk about it! We always have a lot of work for the curious and hardworking people.

This is mad.

Argentina look like a Welsh pub team against Croatia, who themselves look class when they get going. I am spending most of my non-football hours exploring beautiful Kazan, particularly the area in and around its unbelievable Kremlin, which looks like something out of a fairy tale. Then there is six hours per day watching the three World Cup matches, drinking in Kazan's cool bars, and meeting friendly local Russians and football fans from all over the world. What more, frankly, could you ask for in life?

Back at the hostel around 3am, there is a lovely Iranian bloke whose name, I think, is Alizibar, chatting to the even lovelier Karima on the front desk. He is asking foreign football fans to sign Iranian football shirts so he can keep them as mementos of his time spent in Russia. I sign on behalf of England and feel humbled by his attitude to life. The Iranians, they're another lot who are often vilified as an entire nation by the media. Leave them the hell alone you presstitute jokers!

Friday, June 22, 2018

I have been invited onto *Good Morning Russia.* I think this is the equivalent of being interviewed by Susanna Reid and Piers Morgan.

Next, it is Matt Perrella messaging me to say the boss of Panjab – Harpreet – has only gone and offered Matt and me the Panjab national team job! In the midst of all the craziness going on, I just have to laugh at the breaking news.

That is madness!

Yeah, great news mate. He is saying though that we will need to share a flat in the centre of Birmingham.

Yikes, that doesn't sound too appealing.

Actually, Matt has succeeded in winding me up. But it is a useful exercise realising I wouldn't want the Panjab job if I was offered it, and I had to live in the centre of Birmingham, with or without Matt as my wingman and fellow national team head coach.

Katya has arrived from Tolyatti. I haven't seen her since the end of February. She looks gorgeous, and we are getting on super-well from the first moment. A couple, who are friends with her mother, have invited us to stay with them near the epic-looking Farmers' Palace. What a result. I am absolutely exhausted so I am more than happy to spend the evening away from the 24-hour-football-party at her friend's flat. Although, Russians forever the perfect hosts, the man of the house has brought me in a tray with four bottles of beer, two giant bags of crisps, and a huge bar of chocolate as he sticks Serbia v Switzerland on for me on the plasma.

I am getting a lot of messages now from various strangers on *Twatter*, a number of them increasingly weird. Someone claiming to be an 18-year-old girl from Moscow, for example, says she *likes walks in the park and would like to meet me*. Another wants to meet and discuss Matabeleland. The following message has also just arrived on Twitter messenger from a character calling themselves the rather oddly sounding @XSovietNews:

I write about Russian influence and propaganda for the website Stop Fake. Would you be willing to answer some questions about CONIFA and your visit to Russia?

I honestly cannot be bothered to tell the truth. That opening line sounds rather aggressive to me but, as I mentioned, I am doing a *Jim Carrey Yes Man*, so I reply:

Hello. Thanks for contacting me. Please let me know what you have in mind. I'm just here on holiday. Cheers. Justin

Ping. A reply. *You're on holiday but you've been featured in TASS, are a CONIFA coach and worked in Latvia. Did you pay for your trip to Russia yourself? Did you get a CONIFA team while in Latvia, via Russians? Also, why are you in Kazan?*

Oh, wow. Who *exactly* is this? My word, they have got thousands of followers. It is intriguing though. I love the insinuation that the Russian government might be paying for my trip and steering my football career as I lie on the sofa-bed of Katya's mum's friends' retro spare room munching some cheese crisps, swigging *Three Bears*, and watching Shaqiri acting like a twat as he scores the winner in the last minute. He should be kicked out of the tournament for that political bollocks.

Didn't know I had been featured in Tass. Please send me the link. Of course, I paid for the trip to Russia myself haha. I work voluntary for Conifa. My Conifa team is in Zimbabwe. Don't see the Russian connection. I don't really understand where you are coming from on all this. I have worked nine months for free and I am staying in 1000 ruble per night hostel dormitories.

Recent Conifa wfc in London was completely run by volunteers. Revenue was from main sponsor and ticket sales. Main sponsor was Paddy Power. Conifa is not funded by governments. I am in Kazan because I had a ticket to Spain v Iran. And because it is an amazing city. Anything else you would like to know?

I bet this person feels silly now. But no….

It's in TASS also. What makes you want to live in Russia? How do you feel about the terrorist LNR and DNR being in CONIFA?

Oh, for fuck's sake! What on earth is this about?

Before I continue with this, might you explain what this is about? Feel like you are insinuating something.

Ping. *What do you do for a living? It's about people collaborating with Russia.*

Haha, brilliant. She, him, it, is insinuating I'm a paid-up Russian collaborator.

What does that mean? I post some positive holiday tweets and that somehow makes me a spook?

Ping. *Do you hope to live in Russia? How did you afford to go to the World Cup? How did your tweets get noticed by Russian media? Does it bother you that Russia shot down MH17?*

How did you afford to go to the World Cup? haha.

I should say: none of your business, you silly cow! But instead, I write:

43 euro bus to Moscow from Latvia and 15 euro hostels. Are you being serious?

What does mh17 have to do with me being on holiday?

Ping. *Really, and World Cup tickets?*

Haha, what a complete twat.

How did I afford one ticket which actually doubles up as a free visa?

Ping. *I guess you only went there to see Iran play.*

Haha. Now I am also a closet supporter of the Iranian regime it seems by attending a football match.

Are you a real person or a spook yourself? Never had someone contact me with such strange insinuations before.

And, so it goes on… ending with me being called *a useful idiot* and XSovietNews threatening to expose me and CONIFA in a soon-to-be-published article. I click on her profile. She spends all her time spreading… well I'm not sure what word you'd use to describe it. Dozens and dozens of anti-Russian stories each and every day. If you thought the *Zimbabwean omnipresent Thing* had its tentacles into everything, then check out XSovietNews who will have you believe that Putin himself is lurking in the shadows waiting to beat you up when you are walking home alone from the pub. Yes. Moving on. I better announce her bizarre interest in me, so it is out there for everyone to judge for themselves:

Been contacted by a journalist tonight and had it insinuated that I had my trip to the #WorldCup paid for by the Russian government because I have appeared in media here 😂😂 *Apparently I am either a spook or 'a useful idiot'. Story exposing me soon to be published haha. Amazing*

On a more serious note, just before bed, I am hearing a bomb has gone off in Bulawayo, allegedly targeting President Mnangagwa. I so wish Zimbabwe could return to normality.

Saturday, June 23, 2018

I show Katya around the city then meet another two journalists: Svetlana on Bauman Street, and then the lovely Julia who is filmed interviewing me for NTV just below the Kremlin. Quite apart from the usual questions about *why I love Kazan and Tatar food* she is also asking me about my time in Zimbabwe as it turns out she grew up in Harare, when her father was working for the Russian embassy there. Today, I have apparently appeared in Sputnik News and you'd think, by the media requests that are now flooding in, that I was one of the players or managers at the World Cup rather than a nobody supporter.

Katya isn't into football. It's not a problem. I think I actually prefer it when a girlfriend doesn't like football so you can enjoy some peace with your mates down the pub. That's where I am for Sweden v Germany. What about that last-minute winner from Toni Kroos!

On the way back to the apartment, I run into CONIFA's Press boss, Kieran Pender, who is in Kazan for the night. He's not here like me on an all-expenses-paid trip on behalf of the Kremlin though. He's just covering the World Cup for the Guardian and SBS. He's rightly ripping it out of me for wearing my Matabeleland kit out in the bars of Kazan. *Haha, I am just trying to give the lads some extra publicity.*

Sunday, June 24, 2018

There's no such thing as a free lunch. Well, I tend to disagree as Katya and I munch away at our free food at Tubatay Restaurant. I have been told that I now eat here for free while I am in Kazan. England take on

Panama today, knowing that three points puts them through to the second round. Russia's premier TV channel are asking to spend a couple of hours filming with me. The Russian public apparently love the fact that an English bloke was so taken by the many delights of Kazan that he went on social media and asked for a job here and then the Kazan State Tourism people offered to discuss this with him. Russia One want to organise a job interview with the tourism department, but I tell them I want to do this when I return here from my trip down to Samara. If it is going to be a genuine interview, then I want to go in properly prepared. What they don't know is that I used to work as a tourism manager in Bristol and before that as a holiday rep in Greece back in the last century. If Kazan were actually to offer me a job here, I can think of worse ways to spend the next year or two.

But what about your football coaching? they ask me.

Well, ideally, I would work for the state tourism department and also coach for a local side. I told Alina last night.

Now she's calling me back asking to interview and film me watching the Panama match… and then she's on about taking me for a job interview with Rubin Kazan.

Sorry, did you say Rubin Kazan?

No, sorry, Dynamo Kazan.

That original tweet was meant in a tongue-in-cheek way. Or at least I thought it was. Maybe it was my subconscious typing away on my phone. Frankly, if I got a part-time job working for the tourism people and then a few hours coaching Dynamo Kazan, I'd be happier than a pig in mud.

I am back at the bar with the girls in the tight jean shorts. Not for that reason, this time, but because *Twin Peaks* has about 50 screens showing the England game live. It is absolutely rammed in here with Colombians, in the Tatar capital for tonight's encounter with Poland. I can count two English in here and, as has been the case so far in Russia, they are camouflaged, pretending to be Scots or Irish. Day 11 of this World Cup, and I am yet to see a single England shirt.

I have got chatting to a lad called Jorge, who is from Medellin, and am interviewed by Alina for Russia's leading TV channel. I explain all about the Matabeleland team and how we beat the odds to make it to London. *Sounds like a film*, she says.

Haha, actually, I am planning to write a book about it all. I'd love to get a job in Kazan and write the book here during the autumn and winter. I've emphasised that last part on purpose, knowing that the romantic Russians hearing that on TV will love it. But wait. Is that my subconscious again captaining the ship? Actually, I *would* love to live in Kazan, working for the tourism department, and coaching a decent local side while writing by candlelight in my central Kazan penthouse as the snowflakes come tumbling down outside my frosted window. There is nothing as powerful as an idea, and I have suddenly had a flash in my head, imagining all of the above. This is what I want to do next in my life!

When the ball ricochets off Kane's ankle for his hat-trick and England's sixth, I find myself giggling aloud. I came to Russia to chill out, watch some football, see some sights, and party a little bit. But, instead, this trip is taking on a life of its own, evolving every day into a slightly weirder experience. I mean, England 6 Panama 1! *It's coming home!* This is all starting to feel so unreal that I wouldn't be surprised if it does finally come home. I also suddenly remember my friend on the Vic Falls train; the lad who is the big Harry Kane and Spurs fan and who proudly showed me his picture on his phone. I know he will be celebrating somewhere in Zimbabwe right now.

Are you going to tonight's match? Alina asks me.

Oh, no. I haven't got a ticket. I am going to watch it at the fanzone with Katya and her mum's friends.

Would you like to go to the match?

Yes, of course. Wh...?

My journalist friend is back on her phone.

How many tickets would you need?

Haha. Err, two if possible.

Me and Jorge are chuckling to ourselves.

You should definitely visit Colombia, he is saying. *It is so beautiful.* There is another of those flashes in my head. Not as strong as the Tolstoy-by-candlelight one but, strong all the same.

The Mayor of Kazan, Isur Metshin, would like to host you for tonight's match. He's very grateful for all the kind things you have said about the city. After our interview at Dynamo Kazan, we will drop you at the mayor's office where you can pick up two tickets. Your friend Katya will need to go and make a fan ID if she doesn't already have one.

This is bonkers. Nice meeting you mate. Maybe see you in Colombia! Good luck tonight!

We are now parking up outside the Dynamo Kazan stadium, not far from the centre of the city. Ruslan comes out and warmly greets both Alina and I before we stroll around to the other side of the pitch for 'a job interview'. I am barely keeping it together. I feel like we are making an unscripted Russian version of the series *An Idiot Abroad*.

Ruslan asks me about my time with Matabeleland and, well, I tell him on camera about the London World Football Cup, beating a country, Grobbelaar as my goalkeeper coach, CNN making a documentary about us... he's chuckling to himself and pretty much offering me a job immediately. Alina is translating while she interviews me so, some details are getting lost. But, as I understand, his team would be happy to consider me coming in and working with them in the autumn. I would potentially get 40 Euros, twice per week, for running two coaching sessions here at the Dynamo stadium. Ironic really. This is the first club to show any interest in me since the CONIFA World Cup! I thank him for the kind offer and explain that *I cannot commit to anything right now but, if I do move to Kazan, I would like to accept his offer.* This being television, they want us to shake hands and make it appear like the job is mine now. Well, at least I think that is what is happening.

You know you have been on many television channels, Alina tells me as we drive back across the city to the Mayor's office. *Everyone in Russia loves your story.*

Inside the Kazan Mayor's office, a young official pops out and hands me an envelope with the complimentary match tickets. We pace off to Bauman Street and it takes just ten minutes before Katya has her fan ID and we are off to the stadium. Complimentary lunch, complimentary transport, complimentary match tickets. All I need now is for a brewery to sponsor me. Maybe I should tweet that out?

In the midst of all this lovely chaos, I haven't examined our tickets since I was handed them in the envelope. What would you know – we are in the Category One VIP Zone, just behind the team dugouts. Lewandowski and James soon stand there right in front of us, singing their national anthems.

I quickly nip off to buy a beer and a Russian fan points at me, gives me the thumbs up, and is only asking for a selfie with me! What is going on? Then another asks for a photo with me as I come back down the steps with my pint.

The atmosphere is electric once again inside Kazan Arena. The Colombians are here in big numbers while I think there are even fewer Poles than English in Russia. The Poles are trying to spoil the game and stop Colombia from playing football. It is really ugly. This will work for as long as Colombia don't score and when they do, through a brilliantly worked move ending with James dinking a ball onto Mina's head after 40 minutes, you know it is game over for the Polish. James is absolutely turning it on out there. It is a privilege to watch this brilliant young footballer at his best. A wonderful slide-rule pass from Quintero to Falcao. Falcao outside of the foot, 2-0! Oh, the roar of the crowd! Here we are in Katya's home country, her getting to experience this once-in-a-lifetime World Cup on home soil and with this wonderful atmosphere created by the travelling hordes of Colombians. 3-0 it finishes. What a day!

Monday, June 25, 2018

This is very real. The bus to Tolyatti appears to be falling apart at the seams. I think it's had the same net curtains since 1981. We are following the Volga south to Katya's hometown, which I am finally going to get to visit after the five years we spent together. It is a different world down here. Gone are the immaculately-dressed young ladies of Kazan, now replaced by frowning, headscarf-wearing, gold-toothed babushkas in floral dresses. It is an absolutely scorching day in the mid-30s and some of the places we are stopping off at, en route, remind me of deepest Ukraine, stuck 20 or 30 years in the *Modern Talking* past.

Katya's parents live in a typical Russian flat, in a typical Russian block, in a typical industrial Russian city. And all things being typically Russian, they are, of course, super welcoming; their apartment instantly feels like a home from home. Naturally, her father and I are on the vodka shots early doors.

I charge up my dead phone and set up the Wifi. Graham's smartphone is going bonkers again. Oh, my word, what's this? I have got Match of the Day commenting about me! NTV Russia have broadcast my interview with Julia. Kristóf from the Szekely Land FA has sent me a link to a story in the Hungarian Press! I am in Vietnam! And, I have really got to laugh, I am also on the BBC Sport webpage: *English fan asks for job in Russia – and gets offer.*

Meanwhile, @XSovietNews is back. I've resorted to being silly in response to her messages but she doesn't seem to get it and I think it is making her worse:

Sorry, got a bit distracted there watching Uruguay. Who are you again? Are you the person who was writing to me about nightclubs? Or the one who does features on fast food around the globe?

Ping. LOL, Justin, you already forgot our conversation about CONIFA and Russia ties. Doesn't matter, you can read about it in the article at @StopFakingNews.

There is so much faking out there, Sarah. Good to see someone taking a stand! Is this the cooking article?

And, so it goes on. I love how the website is called 'Stop Faking News!'

You just cannot believe some of the shite people are writing in comments on sites, such as this, about Russia. Apparently, it is only in the host cities that life is remotely bearable, and in those urban centres the population is just faking being nice for the cameras. Anywhere else in Russia is either extremely dangerous or third world. A lot of the utter bollocks on social media seems to be emanating from Americans. Out of interest, I Google Chicago, a city I know that is significantly more dangerous than any in Russia. Yep, in Chicago last weekend, 65 people were shot and 12 killed. Way to go!

Katya's Kremlin-backed father and I have almost finished off a bottle of perfectly-chilled Kremlin-backed vodka, half of an oven-baked apple pie, and a giant bowl of the sweetest most gorgeous tomatoes you have tasted in your whole life as we switch between Iran v Portugal and Spain v Morocco. I am desperately sorry for Iran not qualifying and Morocco not signing off with a win against Spain; all that madness with the VAR and some close misses. As Nordin Amrabat mouthed to the camera:

VAR, it's bullshit.

Tuesday, June 26, 2018

It is five vodka shots past ten at breakfast and 34 degrees outside. I am phoning the English FA in London to enquire about second-round tickets but the girl answering the phone says *Sorry I don't know nothing about tickets. I suggest you Google it.* Honestly.

You certainly wouldn't describe the centre of Tolyatti as one of the most attractive city centres in the world. Since its car factories that once produced *Zhigulis* for the entire Soviet Union, and *Ladas* (the foreign brand name) for the rest of the world, started to die, the city has understandably fallen into something of a decline. Much of this Russian Detroit is crumbling industry and slowly decaying infrastructure but somehow it soldiers on, certainly defying the odds. The city is located on the banks of the Volga and after a short and cheap taxi ride from the centre, you find yourself in the midst of beautiful pine forests on the attractive banks of Europe's longest and largest river. Katya's parents are treating us all to dinner. This is an amazing spot to dine and watch the sun sink in the sky. I am really enjoying being away from the World Cup and experiencing another part of Russia with not a single tourist in sight. I do love the no bullshit simplicity of Russia in certain regards.

Back at base, my phone is going mad once again. This time it is mostly because of XSovietNews who is insinuating I am a Russian asset and CONIFA General Secretary Sascha *of being in association with terrorists.* XSovietNews claims her real name is Sarah Hurst. I have my doubts. Anybody who is as bad as this person is, at doing what they do, cannot be who they say they really are. Her accusations are so absurd that I am actually wondering whether she's a Russian agent pretending to be pro-Ukrainian to make the pro-Ukrainian anti-Russian media look like they are stupid... or fake. Talking of fake, apparently, *Stop Fake* are going to expose the truth about me and the shadowy organisation known as CONIFA tomorrow. Can't wait.

She's a piece of work though because she is trying to tempt random feminists into our already absurd Twitter spat to side with her following one throwaway comment from Graham that *I think she likes you mate* and another from Robert – Lord Commander of the Pacers – who dares to call her *love*. Whoever invented Twitter has got a lot to answer for. She's even tagged a pretty famous Guardian-writing feminist in our conversations. I'm relieved said journalist isn't foolish enough to get entangled; otherwise, the feminist hate machine would be fully on my case. Mind you, she has managed to get one or two angry females involved, one of whom is the author of "A Girl's Guide to Missiles". Yeah, nothing to see here. Move along.

Katya's parents must really wonder what their daughter was doing for five years with this English bloke who is permanently on his phone, occasionally muttering to himself. If it's not the spy or the celebrity fan stuff, then it is hour after hour on the FIFA ticketing website trying to pick up tickets for the Samara game on Thursday or the possible second-round matches involving England. As if to emphasise all this, I have just discovered that there is actually a Russian-language meme of me doing the rounds in Russia.

Wednesday, June 27, 2018

I am doing a lot of trying to catch up with my rest today and make it to 4:23pm before the first vodka shot of the day. Katya and I go down to the Volga for a mini cruise, but she's cocked up the times and I am being unnecessarily angry with her for having messed up. Pretty soon my negative energy has turned everything negative and we are arguing about God knows what by the banks of the Volga to the sounds of Modern Talking's 1986 album *Ready for Romance*, which one equally ancient-looking kiosk has got playing on a loop. I have ruined the day with my histrionics, and there is nothing for it other than to go home and grab the end of the football.

Talking of negative energy, the ironically named Stop Fake have published XSovietNews, aka Sarah Hurst's exclusive scoop, about how myself and CONIFA are backed by the Kremlin. Actually, I must have really worn poor Sarah down as she barely mentions me in the article aside from the following startling revelations:

Walley's desire to live in Russia was also reported by TASS and other Russian-language outlets. Walley retweeted the articles. From Kazan (not a venue for England matches), Walley tweeted that he was heading to Tolyatti (not a World Cup host city). "I'm just here on holiday," Walley told StopFake in response to questions about his trip. "I am in Kazan because I had a ticket to Spain v Iran. And because it is an amazing city."

Walley retweeted the articles. Well, yeah, it is Twitter, that's what you tend to do. And, by, the way, XSovietNews seems to retweet absolutely everything.

I switch on the TV and discover that Joachim Löw has been playing goalkeeper Manuel Neuer as an attacking midfielder as the German gets caught 80 yards from his own goal, and the Koreans make it 2-0 to ensure Die Deutsche Fußballnationalmannschaft will be going home with them tomorrow. Yes, the reigning world champions are going home after less than two weeks here, while I feel my World Cup might only just be getting started.

Thursday, June 28, 2018

My mate Ryan messages me and asks whether I want to be on BBC World Service live from Kaliningrad. I politely decline, I am 2,000 kilometres away and en route to Samara.

Katya and I have taken the four-quid two-hour bus down here from Tolyatti, the plan being to check out the city and then find a ticket for the Colombia v Senegal game.

But Samara is huge, spread out over dozens of kilometres. This looks like a complete logistical nightmare. I have got an offer of a ticket just below face value but by the time I sort out Wifi, the bloke disappears. Colombian Jorge is also trying to organise one for me but, I am struggling.

It takes a good half hour of buses and walking just to reach Samara's impressive old town where we are soon quarrelling again, largely because of today's time pressures. This just isn't going to happen. Samara isn't a city that can be seen in a couple of hours and the stadium, meanwhile, is 20 kilometres in the opposite direction. Instead of watching the Colombia v Senegal game inside the stadium, we are actually getting on a bus headed back to Tolyatti just as the game kicks off; plans abandoned.

I have spent many wasted hours on the FIFA ticketing system over several days. Every time I 'secure' a ticket (possibly 30+ times so far), it ends up getting rejected at the 'basket stage'. Many people are having the same experience. A bit of a joke to be honest. The illusion of choice.

England v Belgium. Got a few mates at this. There's lots of chat about losing on purpose, so we go through the easier side of the draw. No one should ever pull on an England national team shirt and think of anything except trying to win. The game is predictably rather dour with both teams starting with reserve team lineups. Januzaj wins it and instead of heading off to Sochi next where, I believe, I would have had no problem picking up a ticket for the game, England are headed to Spartak Moscow… for a showdown with the Colombians!

Nikolai and I almost finish off two vodka bottles and three giant bowls of tomatoes.

Friday, June 29, 2018

Once again, Katya and I are departing from each other in tears. We had a couple of very good days and we had a couple of poor ones. I really don't know if it is the correct decision, but I have told her it is over. Waving at me from Tolyatti's crumbling bus station as her tiny, pretty figure disappears into the background, I just cannot and do not want to believe this is the last time we will ever see each other. And that makes this bearable. But, at the very least, I need a time out – to roll the dice now – and see where my own life takes me in the next few months instead of trying to formulate a plan for two people, neither of whom have jobs, and one of whom cannot live in the European Union.

Back in Kazan, I have checked into a budget Airbnb. I desperately need a couple of days of peace in my own room with no other football fans or anyone else to worry about. Wow, this is very earthy. The room is inside a *kommunalki,* with washing hanging up in the hallway and a shared kitchen that would make Zimbabwean kitchens look modern. It looks rather like the sleeping berths on a very old ferry. Thank God there is no football today. The players are not the only ones who need a rest day.

Saturday, June 30, 2018

Karima, Aigul and Aidar from the hostel are treating me to lunch in the middle of a pine forest.

There is a glistening lake nearby where bikini-clad ladies and speedo-wearing blokes with stomachs overhanging like pregnant penguins escape the searing heat to frolic in the water in an atmosphere of melodious laughter and splashing water. This is real summertime Russia: sunny days spent by the lake or in the forest, shashliks, sour cream and beers at the ready, escaping the urban for nature whenever possible.

We stop off at the Church of all Religions on our way back: a curious and absurd kaleidoscope of religious styles and influences, including Orthodox icon art and Egyptian pillars.

Then Benjamin Pavard scores that goal as France overcome Argentina 4-3 at Kazan Arena, a couple of miles up the road from a packed fanzone.

Sunday, July 1, 2018

I ended up going out last night, and sunrise in Kazan is at the rather uncivilized hour of 3am; so, yet again, I got home with the sun already beating down on the window. I haven't slept a wink all night, and used my insomnia to purchase an online train ticket for Moscow. I have got to get out of here before Kazan consumes me and all that is left is the bones, empty vodka bottles, Tubatay food wrappers, and the ticket stubs.

Opening the huge thick wooden doors to the Kazan Local Government cabinet room, I am faced by four TV cameras and more than a dozen microphoned reporters. "Our honoured guest has arrived. Please, Mister

Walley come and sit here." Surreal doesn't even start to describe all of this. I sit down with the table in front of me covered with plates of food, dictaphones, big furry microphones, and the largest pot of tea you have seen in your entire life. The room is absolutely packed full with journalists. In fact, I doubt that some of Gareth Southgate's World Cup press conferences are this well attended. It is a Sunday and I only gave them a couple of hours' notice that I was leaving today. Suddenly, the head of Tatarstan State Tourism, Sergey Ivanov, bursts into the room. *Hello Justin! Thank you for coming!*

This is a full-blown press conference. Sergey talks for a few minutes. I tell my story again. Everything is translated either from Russian to English or vice versa. There is even a five-minute video about tourism in Tatarstan. Then there is a questions and answers session.

I have got the worst sweat you can imagine on me. It is 35 outside, and I got here so early that I had to walk around the block four times. I then stupidly had a cup of tea and now the sweat is pouring out of me. Embarrassingly, my black T-shirt is dripping wet.

Thirty very surreal minutes later, "I would like to announce that Justin – if he accepts – is the new foreign brand ambassador of Tatarstan!" This feels like it is turning into *the Truman Show*. I am wearing a traditional Tatar hat as Sergey and I shake hands to the sounds of a dozen clicking cameras.

I get to the train station. Two drunk Russian lads get on the train in the compartment next to mine and offer me a vodka and cards session. I think if I drank any more vodka tonight, I'd spontaneously combust.

I was sure it was time to get out of Kazan this morning and now look what the city has thrown at me. July 1st 2018, the day I shifted seamlessly from Manager of Matabeleland to Foreign Brand Ambassador of Tatarstan.

I swerve the Russian lads in the adjacent compartment – who are already getting on it – and after quickly making my bed, crawl wearily inside its sheets, putting the soft pillow over my head. I think I am asleep in five seconds flat.

I awaken what seems like hours later to roars emanating from various parts of the train. That is strange. There are a lot of *Davais* as well. Dzyuba has just equalised for Russia against Spain. Shit! I didn't realise Russia are playing tonight.

I fiddle around with my phone and occasionally pick up Wifi. Then, finally, a decent enough signal to watch it live. I can't believe it! It has gone to penalties and the third Spanish kicker has missed. How I'd love to be in a bar in Kazan or Moscow right now. Russia have slotted away their fourth pen. If Spain miss... they have missed. Oh, my word, Russia have knocked Spain out, and are in the quarter-final. I am glad there is no one in the compartment with me because I'd scare them with all the giggling, and muttering to myself. Again, I crawl back under the sheets and again I crash out almost immediately with the pillow held firmly over my head.

Monday, July 2, 2018

We are hurtling by the endless suburbs of Moscow. It is grey outside and sleeping beauty has been out for the count for most of the 14 hours from Kazan, even hallucinating at one point that Russia beat Spain last night.

@XSovietNews has tweeted a photo of me from yesterday's Kazan press conference and written:

This is the CONIFA official who says he isn't friendly with the Kremlin, nor a useful idiot.

To be honest, I have decided to block her account. I have had enough of her bollocks now.

It is a full 20 degrees colder in Moscow than when I left Kazan, and there are drunk people everywhere as I walk from the station. Strange for a Monday morning. Ah, the penny has dropped. They are all on their way home from a night celebrating the Russia win. I am absolutely gutted I missed that. I bet there haven't been many better nights to ever be out in Russia than last night, me snoring my way through it all on a train.

Fortuitously, a very good French friend of mine lives in central Moscow and has offered to put me up *whenever and for however long I am in the Russian capital.*

Simon is one of my favourite people. He used to live in Riga where we played in the same Riga United team together, before he moved to Russia to head up a language school. He's not long going to work as I get in and, joy, I have got my own room.

Once I have caught up with more of my beauty sleep, I head off to the FIFA ticketing centre. Word is, tickets were released here yesterday. It has got to be worth a go and after one million unsuccessful attempts on their online site, this has got to be a preferable way of trying to source a ticket for tomorrow's England v Colombia match…

... If only that were true. I have been standing, crouching, tutting and sitting in this queue of 98% Colombians now for five hours. I have moved 100 metres in that time, and I am now about 30 people away from the front door. This, however, is not as positive as it sounds in respect to my chances. It has become apparent that I am only getting nearer the door as people keep giving up and leaving the queue. Nobody from FIFA has bothered to update us apart from a burly security guard who swaggers outside and shouts *No ticket!* before laughing and winking at a couple of older Colombians, suggesting, I think, that he is joking. Once you have been queuing for five hours it is very difficult to leave fearing the doors will suddenly fly open and FIFA will be welcoming everyone with open arms.

Two minutes before closing time, a young FIFA official comes out and announces:

There are no tickets today. Please try again tomorrow morning.

What complete and utter tossers! Letting us all stand outside here for 10 hours (7 hours in my case) without a single update all day, without a glass of water even. And, excuse me, but are we really supposed to believe that not a single ticket became available from the thousands of returns from departing fans (Argentina, Germany, etc.)? FIFA, well, we could write a whole book about FIFA, couldn't we?

I send out messages left, right, and centre to see if anyone can help me get tickets.

Belgium v Japan is the best match of the whole tournament for me. Absolutely epic. Simon and I are almost sucked into the TV of the bar we are watching it in, on Nikolskaya, such is the drama.

This really is a carnival. Every few yards you find a group of supporters singing and dancing: Mexicans in sombreros, Croats with their slightly scary sounding manly chanting, a gaggle of Icelanders who surely should have gone home ages ago! A mob of Argentine lads are stealing the show. They are winning the singing match and a crowd of non-Argentines is surrounding them to observe. A pretty lady smiles at me. I smile at her. Nothing unusual about that in Russia but this lady had got particularly sparkly eyes, the kind of eyes that speak to you. I pluck up the courage and approach her. Yeah, she is super smart and nice. I fumble with Graham's phone, but I am struggling to find the add contact function. *I will find you.*

But you don't know who I am.

I will find you, Justin.

Simon lives so centrally that we can simply stroll home from the bottom of Nikolskaya. Walking home in Moscow. How good is that?

I switch on my computer when I get in, in the hope of positive news about tickets. I can't believe my eyes: Tatyana has found me!

I double, then triple-take, and cannot believe my eyes: a friend is in contact with me in response to my Facebook post, saying they might be able to get me a ticket for tomorrow. He will know in the morning.

Tuesday, July 3, 2018

Get in!!!! Yesssss!!!! I have got a ticket for England v Colombia. My friend has got a spare for me. And his spare is free, *buy me a couple of beers.*

I skip into town to pick up my ticket and I am absolutely buzzing as I meet Tatjana for lunch. The company is wonderful and the food and service, amazing. The bill is 50 Euros and – wait for this – she is paying! Is this all a dream and I am going to wake up soon?

Usually, when England are away from home, you can guarantee that any city centre pub with an English-sounding name will be mobbed with English lads getting boozed up before setting off for the stadium.

I am the only Englishman in the central Moscow English pub as I get a few beers down my neck ahead of the game, overcompensating as I forget I had a couple during my lunchtime date.

It is a long trip out to the stadium. The away end turnstiles look like Rochdale away. It is absolutely deserted. 45 minutes before kickoff and I can count a grand total of eight supporters entering the stadium via one of the numerous turnstiles. I have never seen anything remotely like this at an England away game.

The Colombians have 20,000+ in the stadium. I reckon England number little more than 1,500. The atmosphere is incredible and, in many senses, I think I prefer it feeling like an away match in South America.

Former England international, and now rogue indie journalist guilty of having his own opinions, Stan Collymore is stood two rows behind me; so, I do the obvious and get a selfie with him. You can see he is passionate about England and that is why, ultimately, most of the England lads like him; more out of brotherly respect for a man who has done it and now stands with us than purely for his fame. He is very good at what he does, mind you.

Every single England fan I can see is singing his heart out as we try to compete with the noise of the Colombians. I am still necking pints in the stadium to get me doubly fired up.

The excellent Trippier delivers to the back post where Kane heads on to the roof of the net. We are huffing and puffing on the edge of their penalty area. The football gods have been super kind to us today with James Rodriguez unavailable for our opponents due to injury. And with their world-class talisman missing, instead of the delightful football (I watched them play against Poland) the Colombian players are being very, very naughty. Disgraceful in fact. Mina is riding on the back of Sterling. Cuadrado and Maguire tangle about ten yards in front of us near the corner flag. Carlos Sanchez is out of control for them. This lad is something of an enigma for me. I have seen him play at two Copa Americas where he absolutely bossed both Lionel Messi in 2011 and Neymar in 2015. On merit, he is one of my favourite no-nonsense holding-midfielders in the world. Except on days like today, when he turns the beautiful game into the ugly 1950s South American version of the game. I still love him though, because he has just fully rugby tackled Harry Kane and given England a penalty right down in front of us. How on earth can't the match officials see that the Colombian players are digging their heels into the penalty spot and trying to mess it up for the penalty taker? Kane steps up. Bang! 1-0. Goooooal England!!! Bang! Six goals and the *goalden* boot is already Kane's.

Me and the few England supporters residing in the far corner of the bottom tier of the England end are going mental, piling on top of each other and hugging. Briefly, and somewhat to my surprise, I find myself and Stan Collymore intertwined.

An England end full of Colombians. Thank you very much, Boris Johnson and the British media! It is insane that so many England lads are missing this. This atmosphere! Goosebumps all night long!

The Colombian lad next to me has got the world's dumbest and most annoying girlfriend. She has spent practically the whole match screaming *Woo! Davai! Colombia!* Over and over and over again. I even saw him frowning when she did it straight after the England opener.

England are wobbling in the final ten minutes. I think I know what is coming next.

In all my days, what a shot from Uribe from 35 yards out and what an unbelievable save from Jordan Pickford! That must be the save of the tournament... and that would have been the goal of the tournament if Pickford hadn't pulled off that almost miraculous save.

It is the 93rd minute. They have thrown everyone up for the corner, including their keeper.

Oh no! This can't be happening! In the crazy melee of a congested penalty area, Cuadrado has risen above everyone and it has somehow bounced into the net off the crossbar. 1-1. The Colombians are going completely bonkers. You can hardly blame them!

Stupid bird next to me has only gone and screamed *Woo! Davai! Colombia!* Right in my drunken face!

Oiigh mate! Please get your girlfriend out of my face!

What you say?

I said get your fucking stupid girlfriend away from me. I wouldn't be half as mad as I am had the Colombians not just scored a last-minute equalizer to take us into extra time.

Fuck you! My new friends shouts. *You in Russia!*

Well, I have worked that one out!

I am Russian. I fuck you!

Oh, haha, he's a fake Colombian fan.

I am fucking English! I will fuck you! This is the England end!

Suddenly – and fortuitously – I have got a couple of fans, one of them a very nice man I have been chatting to from the Dominican Republic, grabbing the two of us and holding us apart, so we don't actually manage to fight one another. An English girl a row in front warns me:

I'd stop if I were you; those two blokes three rows back are FSB and will throw you out of the stadium.

Oh, for God's sake love!

I am looking around for Collymore. Surely, he's got my back?!

My Dominican Republic friend has (luckily) convinced me to move forward four rows, where the English woman is still banging on about the FSB spotters. How on earth would she know such a thing? And can you imagine if I'd got arrested fighting at the FIFA World Cup after managing a team at the CONIFA World Cup? That would earn me a few more column inches.

Rose almost steals a winner for England but most of us are resigned to what is coming next and most of the England fans, truth be told, are resigned to another penalty shoot-out exit from the World Cup.

Collymore is skipping around the away end asking the England lads how they feel about penalties as he films for his live feed.

How has it come to this yet again! I think I tell him.

I heard recently that one of the reasons why England always lose on penalties is because our players take them more quickly than other teams. Another theory is that we are shit at penalties.

Colombia go first.

0-1.

1-1, Kane.

1-2.

2-2, Rashford.

2-3. Save!! Henderson has missed!! Shit, here we go!

Colombia go 4-2 up if they score here. Miss! Uribe has hit the crossbar! Still 2-3!

Trippier, 3-3!!

Sudden death.

Miss!! Pickford has saved from Bacca!! I am up off my seat jumping around!!

Pause, compose yourself. Deep breath, like I am about to take it myself.

Eric Dier .... 4-3!!!!!!! We've won!!! The players are piling on top of each other!! The England fans are piling on top of one another, bouncing off the seats and the steps and discarded pint glasses. Screeeeeeeaming *Yesssssssss!*

The players are over in front of us. The emotions are getting the better of me, and I am trying to dance on a seat.

We have been singing behind the goal now for half an hour.

Looking back to when we first met...

Southgate you're the one, you still turn me on...

Southgate comes out and applauds the fans. Total respect to this gracious man in what he has achieved with England and in how he conducts himself. No England manager has conducted himself better, in the way he talks to his players, the opposition, the press, the fans since the late great Sir. Bobby Robson. There is a lot of love behind this goal for the former England player, now forever remembered for guiding an England team to the last eight of a World Cup, rather than for a penalty miss as a player 20 years ago.

They want to lock up the stadium, but we don't want to leave. I don't know how long we've been here now. Seems like hours.

I am home at 2am; Simon gets up to give me a congratulatory French hug. Both of our teams are in the quarter-finals. This mad, mad dream, adventure, whatever you want to call it, continues.

Wednesday, July 4, 2018

After 20 nights of this brilliant madness here in Russia, I am so physically and mentally tired that I am starting to feel like I have been playing in this World Cup.

I meet Tatyana for dinner. She is such good company. We connect intellectually. And, best of all, she sees me. She gets who I am. That is such a rare thing in life.

I could travel directly from Moscow to Samara for the quarter-final, but you might not be surprised to hear that I have decided to travel there with a slight detour... via Kazan.

It is so much quieter than previously at Moscow Kazansky Vokzal. The majority of the 2.9 million foreign visitors have long since departed for home. There is no FREE RIDE for me on this train though as I don't have a ticket for Friday's quarter-final in Kazan.

Thursday, July 5, 2018

My favourite quote of the whole trip goes to the three-year-old boy, sharing my overnight train compartment with his parents, who is too young to be so funny when he declares as we cross the Volga: *Look mum! The River Vodka!!*

We left Moscow at 01.30, and I just woke up at 1pm. I feel so good for that.

Nice to see the MFC thanking every single person they can think of who helped them get to London on social media this week. A touch of class from Busani and the boys.

The CNN documentary featuring Matabeleland has been released today. It is really excellent television. Respect to Rachel, Jo, and all involved!

Matabeleland FC is now on CNN, VICE (300,000+ views), Paddy Power (100,000+ views), and in the Joel Rookwood and FC Afkicken films.

I have enjoyed a bit of banter on Twitter today with the presenter of Russia Today's World Cup 2018 coverage, Alexey Yaroshevsky, who I assume is 15 hours away in Moscow.

Imagine my shock, therefore, when I go into Kazan for dinner and bump into him 30 minutes later on Bauman Street! Imagine my embarrassment when I open my phone to take a photo of him and I only to see Alexey's profile page open on my phone like I am weirdly stalking him!!

I am so bloody embarrassed.

Friday, July 6, 2018

My old mate Tancredi Palmeri is on Russian TV as I sup my pint of Fuller's in Beer Point (one of many Kazan craft beer pubs) ahead of today's Kazan quarter-final. We played together for Riga United ten years ago in the days before he became famous as a TV commentator and Twitter celebrity. Tancredi is on Match TV, and I was on Russia One earlier. Riga United is absolutely bossing Russian television today.

France beat Uruguay, and I set off to the fanzone where I meet an Argentine called Fede, who is selling me his spare Category 3 ticket at face value. He is clearly a very decent lad and we stroll up to the stadium together, somehow getting onto the subject of Syria and then somehow getting overheard by two passing Syrians on their way to the stadium. I love that image we snap: English, Argentine, and two Syrians outside a football stadium in Russia waiting to watch Brazil v Belgium.

Belgium 1-0, bossing it with De Bruyne and Lukaku. 2-0, fantastic goal from De Bruyne right down in front of me. That boy is class. Why are Brazil playing in red?

During the halftime break, they are playing *Freed from Desire*, my summer anthem when I worked in Ayia Napa back in 1996 and now my 2018 World Cup anthem here in Russia. I have no idea why they have chosen to play this tune over and over again everywhere in Russia, but I love it.

The South Americans pull one back 15 minutes from the end, but the much better team has won, a side that could end up as world champions.

Saturday, July 7, 2018

I jump in a taxi at 6.30, passing the empty fanzone as I head across the river to the centre of the city. I think this is genuinely goodbye to Kazan for now. I really would like to return here though in the autumn and try to give it a shot living here for a while.

My mate has come up – again – with a spare ticket for the England match and, in a shared taxi, it is a five-hour drive south to Samara. Thankfully, the driver is not trying to win any races. If you like cities with wooden architecture, then Samara is the place. There are dozens of gorgeous buildings in the old section of the city, some with not too many winters left in them. The river Volga and its beach here are just as good as most European seasides, especially with a constant parade of visitors and locals up and down its atmospheric promenade all day long. This is another Russian city I'd happily base myself in for a summer. I warm up for the match with an Adjarian Khachapuri and Satsebeli vodka chaser in a Georgian restaurant just up from the river embankment. Following England seems to have gone upmarket.

The Cosmos Arena is miles and miles from the centre. And when you finally reach it, way outside the city, it seems like miles and miles again walking to the turnstiles and security checks.

You just have to laugh at how few English are here for a World Cup quarter-final.

British Press 5 England Fans 0.

Maguire, bang! 1-0!! Gooooal England!! He's deserved that. Maguire has been fantastic for England. We are, of course, jumping around like our arses are on fire. Two young England lads mate up with me as we share a few pints together and take in this fantastic experience. These lads wouldn't have been born when I went to my first tournament with England in 1992. But you look around, and so many of England are lads who've been following the team since that time and earlier; returning to each tournament in the silly hope that this time they will be there to witness England crowned as champions.

Lingard floats it to Dele Alli just in front of us. 2-0!!! Gooooal England!!! We are going double mental. That was easy! It's coming home!

Well, it certainly wouldn't be if Jordan Pickford wasn't at the top of his game today. I think he has made four brilliant saves.

This whole trip to Russia has been bonkers since almost the first minute. Now, as the Dutch referee takes the whistle to his lips, the bonkers counter has just shot up another couple of levels: England have reached the World Cup semi-final!!

1, 2, 3, 4

Woaah, England are in Russia

Woaah, drinking all the vodka

Woaah, England's going all the way

1, 2, 3, 4

Don't take me home, please don't take me home….

We have been singing non-stop behind the goal now for 45 minutes waiting for Gareth and the England lads to reappear. Surely, in their wildest dreams, they didn't believe we would reach the final four here.

Right, time to get back into town and join the Russians for their quarter-final.

There's a Swedish bloke, older than me, on the trolley bus back into town. He makes his way to the front where he gives a rousing Braveheart-type speech about our fantastic hosts and England going on to win the World Cup. It is quite something. The Russians start off a *Rossiya* chant and we all join in, jumping up and down so much that it feels like we could cause the trolleybus to lift off.

I find a basement bar to watch the epic Russia vs. Croatia quarter-final with the locals. In all my years at many tournaments, I've never seen a host nation's fans take elimination from a knock-out game in such good spirit. Within a couple of minutes, the Russians are all bouncing up and down on the street outside chanting "Well done guys!" reacting to defeat with pride and respect for their team. And instead of turning on the couple of hundred mostly drunk England fans still loudly celebrating our win – all sitting targets with their shirts and flags and marooned on one side by the Volga embankment – the Russians join us, dancing, playing drunken games of street football, joining in songs, drinking with us through the night like brothers.

Rossiya!! Rossiya!!! Engerland!! Engerland!! Absolute scenes.

I can't tell you how much I'm buzzing from it all. This is one of my best ever World Cup nights in a quarter of a century of such evenings. So many Russians keep coming up to me and wishing England good luck for the semi-final and thanking me (!) for not listening to the negative media about them and actually visiting their country. Luckily, I judge people on how they treat me, not what the mass media tells me. Russia has been an unbelievably positive experience. This whole reaction from them sums up that whole experience for me. Quite simply the best World Cup ever.

Sunday, July 8, 2018

I miss the five something o'clock FREE RIDE train by two minutes. I spent most of the latter part of the night in the park and at an outdoor club along the embankment with a red-haired Medusa. A 9.5/10 night would have been a five-star 10/10 had it not been for her jealous, arsey mate screwing things up for me at around 4am, sending me scuttling for the escape door – or should I say the park gates – and the three or four kilometre walk to the central station. Professional foul with only the goalkeeper to beat, there was no referee there to show her mate the straight red she so richly deserved; no second victory for England in Russia in the space of a few hours. No free ride.

Instead, it is back down to earth with a bang as I rest on some uncomfortable metal benches in Samara train station.

Fortuitously, I have just recalled that my Scottish mate Neil and I slept in a very decent lounge in Donetsk train station after the England Ukraine game at Euro 2012, so I have gone off to enquire if such a thing exists here.

Indeed, it does. So again a train station lounge has saved me after an England game, this time in Russia. It is good in here. It reminds me of a Japanese *onsen*. Seven quid gets me my own sofa in a small, guarded back room. There's a water cooler and a shower room. Good night! Wake me at 1pm please!

2pm I have bagged a FREE RIDE, the lovely female volunteer helping me saying: *please return to Russia!* as we part company. *You are always welcome!* How lovely have the volunteers been at this tournament?

Time for a couple of tweets on the subject: *Came to Samara by 5-hour taxi. Left my bag in a luggage room. Watched England win world cup QF. Partied with Russian girls until 4am. Slept in train station for 7 hours. Booked free FIFA train to Moscow.*

What an unbelievable night! We're in the semi-final of the world cup and I was there to witness the game and the brilliant party that followed. Thank you Samara. Thank you Russia. Samara, it's been a pleasure!

The 16-hour overnight train to Moscow has turned into one massive party. The restaurant car is mobbed with fans from all over the world, including a Mo Salah lookalike and some more very affable Colombians, whom I'm drinking with. Singing, dancing, selfies with the female train staff, sharing tales from Russia. Every time we stop at a station, 20 or 30 of us jump off and raid the station kiosks of cold beers and snacks.

This party is going to continue all night, but I am the first to bail out. I am absolutely exhausted and retire in bits to my compartment bed, hours before any of my train buddies call it a night.

Monday, July 9, 2018

My FREE RIDE bagged, that is another free night of accommodation. With me now spending my final days with my mate, French Simon, my total accommodation bill for what will eventually end up being a 34-day World Cup adventure, beginning at East Midlands Airport and ending at the Russian-Estonian border is… 122 British Pounds!! A great many football fans will have spent more than that for one night in Russia! How did I manage that? Overnighters on buses and trains, cheap hostel dormitory beds, Airbnb, friends of friends, Katya, friends, stayed out all night, train station sofa, etc.

And my total transport bill from East Midlands to that Estonian border, including a flight, two international buses and all the trains, buses, and automobiles in Russia will likely come in at around £220. Of course, I am making all of this up! This is just my cover for having stayed in Kremlin-financed five-star hotels and being flown around in private jets the whole tournament!

There's no match today, thank the football gods. Simon is at work all day, so I can stay in bed.

Tuesday, July 10, 2018

Five Live are discussing the magical experience that Russia has been, commenting, in as many words, that many of the pre-tournament scare stories now seem extremely far-fetched. One of the presenters comments that they won't so easily trust the British media again in the future. Aleluja! Question everything people! Because ultimately it is all bollocks. There is a constant war on to control our minds. Everything is about energy. By feeding us negative energy, they keep us divided; they keep us scared and prevent us doing and achieving all the things we want to do in life. Don't allow them to win!

I have spent my morning writing up an article for the Leicester Mercury to put towards my ticket budget. Fede has been in touch and agreed to let me have his one ticket for the semi-final for $500. It is much much more than I would ever wish to pay for a football match, especially with me unemployed but, this is an England World Cup semi-final in Russia. And, by the way, I haven't heard of a single England fan picking up anything 'cheaper' than that on the black market! It simply has to be done!

Frankly speaking, a great many English are spending significantly more than that on their flight tickets into Moscow today and a couple of nights' accommodation! Anyway, we need three for Michael, Josh, and me so, whatever happens tomorrow, this one is in the bag so to speak. If I can pick up something cheaper before they arrive tomorrow, then we have agreed that this ticket goes to one of the other lads.

During the past few days, I have been getting three or four media requests per day, but I just can't keep up anymore. I do manage one with Life Magazine Moscow. Sounds cool. No idea if it actually is.

It is my third date with the lovely Tatyana. Lunch is one of the best I can ever remember having, and a classy lady on the table next to us even addresses me as *Sir*. We enjoy a stroll afterwards in a nearby park, and then there is a stolen kiss behind a building, my heart going at a million miles an hour, feeling like a teenager again.

The evening is spent with Simon and a load of his French and Russian mates in a huge beer garden watching France force their way past Belgium into the final. Really, this probably should have been the final. Simon's beautiful friend Katya and her best mate are like two leading actresses out of a 1940s black and white. Smart, feminine, classy. Ladies like these two, like the girl who called me *Sir* today in the restaurant, just don't seem to exist anymore in the West. Well, barely. What happened to them? Where did they go? If Russia is allegedly such a terrible place, then why do they still exist here?

Wednesday, July 11, 2018

Michael and Josh have flown in this morning from the UK. Big up to Michael – he has been in touch with me throughout this tournament and vowed he would fly out if we reached the semi. I like people who do what they say they will do. You need a ticket before you can get a fan ID and, therefore, a free Russian visa-on-arrival. For this reason, a few thousand English are flying into Moscow today instead of tens of thousands. There is a loophole, however, which I discovered, if I recall correctly, from one of Stan Collymore's tweets: You can register for a fan ID with any World Cup ticket, and it doesn't matter how many times that ticket has been used to register an ID! Michael and Josh tried it. It works. They are in Moscow!

I meet Fede as he arrives from St Petersburg at the train station opposite Kazansky Vokzal. I have emptied my bank account at the ATM and have a grand total of $470, 30 dollars short of the sum agreed with Fede. Fortunately, my Argentine friend is good with that and hands over my ticket to the World Cup semi-final. I look at it in my hand. It seems to glisten and shine.

It's coming home! I meet Michael and Josh at *Bosco* on Red Square. It is, by far and away, Russia's most expensive pint in here at something like 8 Euros and I am obviously going without. Michael says he saw our mate Austin on the flight over from London, which stopped off in Riga en route. I first met Michael at the 2011 Rugby World Cup in New Zealand. Despite the rugby and the incredible setting, I was suffering from depression at the time after the sudden and dramatic breakup of a six-year relationship. Michael and his mate George – yes, George-Michael – pretty much dragged me out from the dark hole I was residing in at that time, took me surfing for the first time in my life on the black volcanic NZ west coast at Raglin, let me sleep in their camper van in an Auckland multistorey car park (when I briefly ran out of cash), shared some brilliant nights out and afternoons spent at the rugby, and helped enable me to recognise – once again – that life is beautiful and we must seize the day, even in our lowest moments.

I am tweeting about needing a ticket for today although, truthfully, it is a bit of a white lie as any tickets I can pick up now will be for Michael and Josh. ITV/BBC sports presenter Jacqui Oatley is suddenly in the mix. She has retweeted my message and is soon DMing me to say she might be able to sort out a ticket for me. Another surreal moment in a trip overflowing with them. The boys are understandably getting a bit nervous about not having bagged tickets with just a few hours to go. We meet a Brazilian bloke and his girlfriend who seem to have bags of spare tickets and appear to be touts rather than fans. He wants more than I'd pay but Michael and Josh drop the cash. They do have well-paid jobs after all. Jacqui is sending me the details of the person who will sell me their facevalue ticket. I'm having to politely decline, supposedly on my behalf, but actually for my mates. Three World Cup semi tickets bagged; there's time for a couple of celebratory pints before we move our bums up to the Luzhniki.

England fans banter and take photos with Central Asian street cleaners on the escalators up to the stadium tube station exit. The lads are on their backs at the sight of the attractive female horse-mounted police.

I am meeting Russia One for a brief interview next to Lenin's statue.

Are you disappoint eeresama not here?

Sorry?

Eeresama

God, this is embarrassing. Live on air. What the hell is this eeresama that he speaketh off?

Sorry, eeresama?

Yes, your prime minister eeresama?

Oh, he's actually asking me whether I am upset that Theresa May has turned down an invitation to attend today's England semi-final. Obviously, the question is politically motivated. I just point out that politicians are politicians and, frankly, I couldn't care less whether they are here or not. *The main thing is that we, the fans, are here.* I do wonder, mind you, what will happen if we reach the final. Every other leader, I am guessing, would fly out to support their team in the World Cup final. I am guessing that May won't bother, even if we make it to our first final in 52 bloody years!

Next, a Mexican TV crew has grabbed Michael, Josh, and me, and we are being interviewed live on air by a presenter who I think is literally 11-years-old and looks rather like an Hispanic Harry Potter.

What do you think the score will be today?

Oh, very confident. This will be easy. 7-1

What?

Yes, 7-1!

What a stadium the Luzhniki is; modernised but keeping its class. Worldwide, something like half a billion are tuned in for this. Back at home, 26 million are watching on their own TVs, 4 million streaming it. With public viewing, it is thought that maybe 40 million in England are awaiting the arrival on the pitch of the England team. And there are maybe 8,000 England actually here in the stadium. How privileged are we?!

It is a dream start for England. We have won a free kick on the edge of the area, and something about the goalkeeper's positioning all that way down the other end of the stadium doesn't look right to me. Or maybe it is a premonition. *We are going to score here!* I tell the Canadian lad sat next to me. Trippier's only gone and stuck it in the top corner!!!! Gooooal England!!! 1-0.

My word, it really is coming home! England haven't put a foot wrong in this first half... Kane is in... oh, no! That should have been 2-0 and game over.

I reckon that England's players have had one dodgy moment in this whole half and that is with practically the last touch of the 45 as there is a miscontrol and a moment or two of them losing their focus at the back. It has been a very comfortable half, but I really got a bad vibe there off that final 30 seconds of play.

I have managed to find the lads and move to one of the two spare seats next to them which I guess the Brazilian tout is still probably trying to sell for a fortune outside. It has become quickly apparent that this match is shifting back towards Croatia. They are bossing midfield. They have changed their game plan but England have, in no sense, adapted to the shift in tactics.

Perišić scores with England just 20 minutes away from the World Cup final. 1-1

Up here, in the general sales category threes, it is a weird, weird atmosphere. We are surrounded by hundreds of mostly Indians and Chinese, many of whom have spent the whole game on Facebook video chat to their girlfriends and half-naked uncles back home. They all wildly-celebrated the England goal... now, they are wildly celebrating the Croatia equalizer; some of them are jumping up and down wearing Shearer and Gerrard England tops! Plastic corporate fans. The future of all major sporting events.

I tell Michael *We are spent. England have dropped their heads. Croatia fancy it. We have got nothing to offer the Croats.*

Keep believing! he demands. *It's coming home!*

I think we are the only ones that are going home, mate! They are pulling us to pieces. Our central mid is non-existent. Southgate needs to change it up but I don't think he knows how to right now.

Into extra time and there are chances for both sides. They hit the post and Stones has one cleared off the line at the other end. But it is no great, great surprise when Mandžukić steals in behind a tired-looking England backline to make it 1-2 to Croatia. Kyle Walker, in particular, hasn't looked right to me since he picked up that yellow early in the second half.

The Chinese are going wild, one of them dropping her toy panda to the stadium floor.

England huff and puff but they are short on ideas. Our best players in this tournament have been at the rear with Pickford, Maguire, and Trippier. Kane will go home with the Golden Boot but nothing much is going into him, and he has looked off colour for the past couple of games. There just isn't the quality in midfield. With a Hazard or a Modrić, England could be crowned champions, but there is no one in midfield a million miles close to the quality of either of those two lads.

Croatia have won 1-2. The three of us sink to our seats and say nothing for what seems like an eternity. The England players are clapping the fans, some of the young Three Lions clearly in emotional shock that the dream was so near and in the grasp of their paws… but… now is dead. It's not coming home!

Thursday, July 12, 2018

Journalists have invited me, Michael, and Josh on a free Moscow tour in return for them filming us, but all three of us are in a million bits and pieces and just cannot face it. The creeping realisation, upon awakening, that we have failed to reach the World Cup final and perhaps it will now never happen in our collective lifetimes is all-pervading.

I keep imagining Kane finishing off that chance and us going 2-0 up in the first half. We would have reached the final then, I am sure.

Tatjana wants to take me for a pizza and a couple of pints to cheer me up. It is fine. I am gutted, but I am super-grateful for every single moment of this wonderful footballing adventure. England blew their chance. It is as simple as that. The Croats deserved to win.

The pizza and beers do go down well though. And mentally I am in a much stronger place after spending the afternoon in bed with Tatjana.

It is good to know that life can still be this much fun as I approach 50.

Friday, July 13, 2018

If you'd told me before the tournament, I'd still be here at the World Cup, 16 days after the Germans went home, I would have assumed I'd ended up in prison. I suppose there is still time.

I am reading that England will net $20 million by finishing third. It never even occurred to me that teams earn prize money at the World Cup.

There again, it's not like FIFA cannot afford it – they will end up making something like $6 billion from this tournament!

I love some of the humorous stories the World Cup conjures up: the Mexican lads who travelled to the World Cup with a cardboard cut-out of their mate after his wife didn't let him travel, the Russian pharmacist who put holes in condoms in the hope that this would *improve the gene pool* of her homeland, the German fan who drove to Russia in a tractor.

Simon and I are finally having that proper night out we've been promising ourselves. I won't go into too many details but predictably our excitement and over-keenness for said night out means that we are both absolutely hammered by the early hours, when I narrowly escape getting involved in a fight with a bloke who thinks Simon and I are trying to steal his girlfriend. The irony is that we were both completely innocent, and a third unknown individual has, in fact, stolen her behind his back and nipped off secretly with her elsewhere.

I lose Simon in the melee and God knows how I get back to his flat because I really have very little idea where I am. God bless Russia and its 24-hour corner shops. Suffering from the munchies, I have bumped into Simon who is carrying a large bag of shopping and making very little sense as he stumbles past me in the opposite direction to home.

Saturday, July 14, 2018

Simon is snoring on the kitchen floor, with his uneaten kebab and shopping bag lying beside him. Both of us are in bits, and don't leave our respective beds until just prior to the England v Belgium third-place playoff.

Belgium are much better than England and deserve to win. Not that too many people care whether we finish third or fourth. Who could have predicted before the World Cup that on July 14, five English blokes would be singing England songs outside a central Moscow pub to a crowd of Russians clapping, cheering, and taking photos of them? That is the scene outside this pub as England and its supporters take their final bow and depart from Russia 2018.

Simon and I grab dinner at an outdoor Ukrainian restaurant called Mamma Odessa which wouldn't be out of place in Provence or Tuscany. There are 27 women sat outside and, aside from us, zero men. Of the 27 women, I'd say 11 are gorgeous. I'm just being honest.

With Simon broken up for the summer from school this weekend, he is keen to get back on it tonight. But I just haven't got it in me. I feel terribly rough and tired. I am happy to just sit out here on this glorious summer evening with Simon's brilliant company, with lots of good food, surrounded by beauty. I am going to miss Simon's company, miss Moscow, miss Russia, miss all of this.

Sunday, July 15, 2018

Both of us are almost too tired to leave Simon's flat. I feel run down, exhausted, and I have now got a constant runny nose and thick cold. A month of partying has run me into the ground.

I am watching the 2018 World Cup Final in a Moscow Mexican restaurant, drinking Argentine Red with French mates drinking English beer, and their Georgian and Russian female friends drinking Czech beer, served by a Cuban waiter who speaks worse Russian than me. Oh, how I have loved all this fun and madness.

Total respect to Croatia for some of their class football in the final. The final score is a bit flattering to France, frankly. But France are the best team in this tournament, Kylian Mbappé is the standout player, along with Modrić of course. It deserved to be them or Belgium lifting the Jules Rimet trophy today.

I can't bring myself to support either team, least of all Croatia, but I do cause a few giggles when I jump up roaring with laughter after the comical second goal for Croatia, 20 minutes from the end. *See! See! The English are supporting the other team, of course!* The French declare.

The jet-black Moscow skies open and torrential rain comes pouring down, scattering us all like bowling pins to tube stations and bus stops. I briefly snooze on one of those Moscow subway escalators that seems to go on forever as Simon takes the opportunity to drape me in a French flag and snap an image of the beaten Englishman for piss-taking posterity.

It is the final night of the party – in every sense of the word – and Nikolskaya and the streets surrounding the Kremlin are absolutely mobbed. In fact, for the first time at this tournament, the security checks with metal detectors, bag checks, and body searches have completely broken down. Such is my paranoia from weeks of alcohol and a severe lack of sleep that I request we leave the excited, smiling mobs in case, some terrorist group, or government agency masquerading as one decides to blow up a load of the crowd to kingdom come; the Russia World Cup finally remembered for tragedy instead of for all the millions of happy memories, some that will last a lifetime.

A lady is casually riding a horse down one street. She seems to be taking it for an evening ride. Iranians and Americans stick their flags together and pose for the camera. The atmosphere on Nikolskaya and around Red Square has to be experienced to be believed.

The French don't seem nearly as made up about winning the World Cup as you might expect. *You have to understand what 1998 was to understand how we feel,* one Frenchman tells me. *We are overjoyed to win the World Cup but it is like a narcotic, we are searching for that feeling again we had that first time we won in France and that feeling can never be found again.*

Monday, July 16, 2018

Come and stay! Stay as long as you need and whenever you need! Simon kindly told me before the World Cup. I guess, when he made his offer, he wasn't expecting me to still be here on July 16. I bet he never thought he'd be leaving Moscow and Russia before me and would be asking me to leave the key at his school when I finally leave his apartment later tonight. Just spending the ten days I have shared with my old mate would have been reason and enjoyment enough for this Russian odyssey. *Cheers Simon! Enjoy your holiday*, I say as he leaves for the airport and, comically, I go back to bed... in his flat!

My journalist friend, Julia, is treating me to a visit of the Russia Today studios on the roof of Moscow's finest hotel, The Four Seasons. What a view up here! There are bird's eye vistas of the Kremlin, Red Square, the Bolshoi. RT are packing up and dismantling their World Cup studios. Ending my World Cup up here, proudly wearing my England shirt, with a private rooftop viewing of the finest scenes Moscow has to offer, seems like the most amazing and fitting way to end this sojourn. Julia knows that, and it's a touch of class, her organising this for me like this.

Julia also treats me to a mini-tour of Moscow showing me many terrific little areas I have never seen before. The city has really been transformed in the 20 years since I was last here. I am not a massive fan of big cities but, if I had a decent job and could afford to live centrally, I would be more than happy to give Moscow a try for a year or two.

Russia One are desperately begging me for one last interview with them, which Jim Carrey-like I agree to, despite it creating a time stress ahead of my international bus departure. The interviewer is trying to prompt me into saying things I don't want to say. Like I am definitely moving to

Russia. I am not going to go along with that. It's the same lad who did the Theresa May interview with me below Lenin. I know it's all positive propaganda. That is what this kind of 'news' always is, no matter what country the journalists come from. Anyone who has followed my Russia adventure and seen the now dozen TV interviews I have done, knows that I am a big fan of Russia, of its rich culture and its welcoming people. But I like honesty. I am not going to make shit up so that journalists can further their careers. I guess my time as a celebratory fan in Russia ends with this interview; if indeed they ever show it.

I grab my backpack from Simon's, ask Julia to give him the key when he returns from France, and we head off to the bus station where, there are more presents to add to my bag of mementos and gifts I've been given during my time here: jams, Tatar hats, a miniature World Cup ornament. Julia has also presented me with a huge bag full of snacks and drinks for the bus. I am humbled once again and hug farewell, vowing to return to this country again, sometime soon.

Tuesday, July 17, 2018

My original plan was six days in Russia visiting Kazan & Samara. And one game: Iran v Spain. Somehow six turned into 33, and one turned into six. The only World Cup I have ever stayed at from start to finish. I tweet the following not long after crossing the border back into the Baltics:

Just left Russia after 33 days. *THERE WERE NO: riots, hooligan attacks, police mistreatment, bribes, half-built stadiums, racist abuse, bad food, dilapidated transport systems, unfriendly people. Pictured are some of the gifts Russians gave me. British media - sort your shit out!*

My tweet receives 2,000 likes, 800+ retweets. A great number of those from English people who are sick and tired of our cry-wolf British media.

LATVIA

Back in Latvia, I am utterly exhausted and feel properly ill.

I plan to spend seven weeks and the remainder of the summer here (one of those weeks asleep), trying to get that tourism job in Kazan, or a coaching gig perhaps in the South Pacific. Or in Bhutan, a place I have dreamed of living in for more than 20 years. I would have hoped that my pretty successful efforts with Matabeleland would have earned me some respect out there in the coaching world but, thus far, not one single football club has approached me and asked if I am available; or offered me an interview, even in a junior role! Well, apart from Dynamo Kazan!

I need to put together some quality stuff for publishers so I can try to get a book in print about my crazy experiences of the past 10 months. I feel I want, and need, to share my story. And, indeed, I must soon begin the laborious task of typing up my endless diary notes, just in case.

And then, of course, I want to enjoy the last weeks of the summer, spending time with my many mates who live in this part of the world, switch off my phone for a few days, make sure I spend plenty of mornings enjoying Jurmala's stunning beaches… and organise my mum's 70th birthday trip to … Colombia!

I am also almost three weeks past the end of my contract with Matabeleland. They want me to decide what I am doing. I want them to decide what they are doing. The Human Rights Cup is going ahead in Johannesburg in December. I am tempted to stay on until then, travel out there, and enjoy one last hurrah with the lads, before moving on to a completely different corner of the world.

Then again…

[42] Enjoying a beer with my Colombian friend Jorge and Russia One journalist Alina as we take a break from filming during the England 6 Panama 1 match.

[43] Kazan Arena after being treated to a VIP afternoon by the Kazan mayor at the Colombia v Poland match.

[44] Becoming the Tatarstan Foreign Brand Ambassador at a packed press conference in Kazan.

[45] With former England international and now indie journalist Stan Collymore ahead of the England v Colombia match in Moscow.

[46] Party on the overnight train from Samara to Moscow.

[47] Semi-final bound! Michael (centre), Josh and I enjoy a pint after the three of us secure tickets for England's World Cup Semi-Final with Croatia.

[48] Enjoying rooftop views of the Kremlin on my final day in Russia.

Other Books from Bennion Kearny

Small Time: A Life in the Football Wilderness by Justin Bryant

In 1988, 23-year-old American goalkeeper Justin Bryant thought a glorious career in professional football awaited him. He had just saved two penalties for his American club – the Orlando Lions – against Scotland's Dunfermline Athletic, to help claim the first piece of silverware in their history. He was young, strong, healthy, and confident. But professional football, he found, is rarely easy.

Small Time is the story of a life spent mostly in the backwaters of the game. As Justin negotiated the Non-League pitches of the Vauxhall-Opel League, and the many failed professional leagues of the U.S. in the 1980s and 90s, he struggled not only with his game, but his physical and mental health. Battling stress, social anxiety, a mysterious stomach ailment, and simple bad luck, he nonetheless experienced fleeting moments of triumph that no amount of money can buy. Football, he learned, is 95% blood, sweat, and tears; but if you love it enough, the other 5% makes up for it.

OOH-AAH: The Bob Booker Story by Greville Waterman

OOH-AAH BOB BOOKAH…

And so begins one of the most iconic chants in football. A chant for a cult hero who was renowned for his hard work, tenacity, honesty, and graciousness. A chant for a player who left everything on the pitch.

This is a book that covers the challenges of dealing with fans' expectations, a long-term chronic injury that threatened to end his career, and how he dealt with the intrigue and machinations of football management.

Bob worked hard, gave his all, played wherever he was asked without complaint, wore every shirt (apart from the goalkeeper's), and was rewarded by playing or coaching in all four divisions of the Football League. Indeed, in a rollercoaster career that spanned almost five decades, Bob was a crucial part of teams – as either a player or coach – that celebrated six promotions and suffered three relegations. Perhaps most importantly, nobody who has ever met Bob has a bad word to say about him. He is still revered at all three clubs he was associated with and remains a particular hero at Sheffield United.

With contributions from former teammates, managers, and friends, the real Bob Booker is revealed in all his complexities. It is the kind, friendly, and humorous Bob that we all expected to find but also one who demonstrated grit, determination, courage, inner strength, guile and perseverance to forge such a long and successful career for himself.

Lightning Source UK Ltd.
Milton Keynes UK
UKHW022322281118
333139UK00003B/94/P